SOVEREIGNTY AND ITS DISCONTENTS

On the primacy of conflict and the structure of the political

William Rasch

Professor of Germanic Studies,
Indiana University

Birkbeck
LAW PRESS

First published in Great Britain 2004 by Birkbeck Law Press,
an Imprint of Cavendish Publishing Limited,
The Glass House, Wharton Street, London WC1X 9PX, United Kingdom
Telephone: + 44 (0)20 7278 8000   Facsimile: + 44 (0)20 7278 8080
Email: info@cavendishpublishing.com
Website: www.cavendishpublishing.com

Published in the United States by Cavendish Publishing,
c/o International Specialized Book Services,
5824 NE Hassalo Street, Portland,
Oregon 97213-3644, USA

Published in Australia by Cavendish Publishing,
45 Beach Street, Coogee, NSW 2034, Australia
Telephone: + 61 (2)9664 0909   Facsimile: +61 (2)9664 5420
Email: info@cavendishpublishing.com.au
Website: www.cavendishpublishing.com.au

British Library Cataloguing in Publication Data

Rasch, William, 1949–
Sovereignty and its discontents: on the primacy of conflict
and the structure of the political
1 Government, Resistance to 2 Opposition (Political science)
3 Political violence 4 Social conflict 5 Sovereignty
I Title
303.6'1

Library of Congress Cataloguing in Publication Data
Data available

ISBN 1-85941-984-4

1 3 5 7 9 10 8 6 4 2

Printed and bound in Great Britain by Biddles Ltd, Kings Lynn, Norfolk

In memory of my father,
William Walter Rasch (1908–1985),
who, whether he would have liked them or not,
is as responsible for these ideas as anyone

There is a war between the ones
who say there is a war
and the ones who say there isn't

Leonard Cohen

Acknowledgments

The articles collected in this volume were originally published as follows: Chapter 1 as 'Conflict as a Vocation: Carl Schmitt and the Possibility of Politics' (2000) 17.6 *Theory, Culture and Society*, pp 1–32, reprinted by permission of Sage Publications Ltd; Chapter 2 as 'A Just War, or Just a War?: Habermas, Schmitt, and the Cosmopolitan Orthodoxy' (2000) 21.5–6 *Cardozo Law Review*, pp 1665–84; Chapter 3 as 'Theories of the Partisan: *Die Maßnahme* and the Politics of Revolution' (1999) 24 *The Brecht Yearbook*, pp 330–43; Chapter 4, originally in German, as 'Schuld als Religion', in Baecker, D (ed), *Kapitalismus als Religion*, 2003, Berlin: Kulturverlag Kadmos, pp 249–64; Chapter 5 as 'A Completely New Politics, or, Excluding the Political?: Agamben's Critique of Sovereignty' (2002) 8.1 *Soziale Systeme*, pp 38–53; Chapter 7, originally in German, as 'Weltkommunikation und Weltschweigen', in Bolz, N, Kittler, F and Zons, R (eds), *Weltbürgertum und Globalisierung*, 2000, Munich: Fink, pp 109–20; and Chapter 8 as 'Human Rights as Geopolitics: Carl Schmitt and the Legal Form of American Supremacy' (2003) 54 *Cultural Critique*, pp 120–47. The Introduction and Chapter 6 were written for this volume.

I wish to thank the following people who helped in various ways in the preparation of the essays that comprise this volume: Dirk Baecker, Karlheinz Barck, Joe Bendersky, Norbert Bolz, Roger Cook, Jonathan Elmer, Andreas Kalyvas, Jan-Werner Müller, Marc Silberman, Urs Staehli, Rudolf Stichweh, Carsten Strathausen, and Marc Weiner. Costas Douzinas has been a wonderful interlocutor and most helpful in the preparation of the volume. I am especially indebted to Chantal Mouffe, for whose extraordinary generosity of spirit and intellectual exchange I am truly grateful. Above all, I value the encouragement and unselfish support shown me by my wife, Christine Farris. I hope I can repay her patience.

William Rasch
July 2004

Contents

Introduction
The primacy of the political

Based on public opinion surveys, voter apathy, and the patriotic relief with which a confused and anxious citizenry embraces seemingly perpetual war (against 'terrorism' and against states), the not surprising conclusion has been drawn that the American public is tired not only of politics, but also of 'democracy'. Weary of political debate, of having to confront more than one political issue at any one time, and of being asked to help determine solutions to problems they do not fully understand, a majority of the American people willingly and eagerly wish to leave decision making up to 'experts' or 'business leaders', and therefore wish to take such power to decide not only out of their own hands, but out of the hands of their purported political representatives. Whether what holds for the United States is an aberration or only an exaggeration of what holds for Europe and elsewhere in the world is open to interpretation. Certainly extra-parliamentary politics are alive and well in the streets of various European capitals, and elections seem still to arouse passions, but whether that indicates in kind or only in degree a fundamental difference of popular participation in political life is also an open question. What does seem clear is that, despite the casual and occasional arousal of the collected populace, what in 1941 James Burnham called the 'managerial revolution' has by and large been accepted not only as reality, but as desired *utopia* by the citizens of a modernity that has seemingly become too complex for any meaningful notion of participatory democracy.

Burnham's observation of the managerial society was, of course, but a variant of a host of similar, if philosophically more sophisticated, diagnoses from diverse political perspectives, including: (a) Weber's analyses of modern rationalization, bureaucratization, and disenchantment, that fueled (b) Carl Schmitt's critiques of liberalism's neutralization of politics and (c) Lukács' Marxist elaborations of commodity fetishism in the direction of the reification of human relations as a form of social and psychological self-alienation, until finally, (d) Adorno proselytized a near-total asceticism as a response to a modernity in which even culture becomes an industry. When linked with Heidegger's similarly sweeping negation of an expansive and all-consuming modernity, it is this last gesture, Adorno's asceticism, that leaves the greatest impression and creates the most alluring temptation. If, for the purist, in the dark night of modernity all cows are black – fascist and communist 'totalitarianism' as well as the capitalist 'society of the spectacle' – then there is no need for the political because the political, no matter how conceived, offers us no escape. Indeed, to engage with the corrupted world politically is to increase the corrosion and to implicate oneself more fully in the original sin that is modernity. Best, therefore, to hibernate and wait, if not with Heidegger for the return of the gods, then with Deleuze for the philosophers to found the new ontology.

Ironically, if inevitably, such a retreat leaves the field clear for the managers. As we take our occasional summer respite from hibernation and gaze down upon the valley below, we can see that what was once called the state is now identified with the law and thus threatens to become fully absorbed by civil society (by 'culture', Leo Strauss and his conservative followers would say) and transformed into just one bureaucratized association among many. In this way liberal rule of law and humanist pluralism minimize the importance of the state, but by no means do they thereby abolish hated state sovereignty. Rather, 'decision', that existential bugaboo of liberal theory, is taken out of the hands of the sovereign (which includes 'the people' every bit as much as the arbitrary will of the monarch) and is dispersed, distributed among the various bureaucracies, exercised by 'experts' and 'advisors', and thus rendered invisible. And this invisibilization is the cause of exhaustion and ennui. The 'managerial' society is the 'administered' society whose efficient performativity reduces the political to the routine activity of policing.

What experts in the domestic sphere see as administration has its correspondence in international relations as pacification, cooperation, legalization, and the implementation of 'human rights'.[1] Just as liberal society marginalizes politics and conditions us to be suspicious of it, the modern international order, dominated by the United States and theatricalized by worldwide media outlets, outlaws war and makes opposition to its rule something immoral. Legitimate violence is the violence that is conducted under the auspices of the United States and its vassals; illegitimate – ie terrorist – is everything else. The virtue of the American response to the events of September 2001 is to have removed, at least partially and at least at times, the rhetorical camouflage from this fundamental attitude and made it visible for all to see, even the most naive and willing believers. We no longer play with formulas like 'police actions' and 'peace keeping', but talk quite simply and directly of war, economic booty, and the installation of compliant regimes. 'Consultation' with the Allies is a gleefully open and public form of threat, extortion, bribery, and, when these do not work, punishment. And support for the United States is displayed with all the calculating opportunism of a masochistic, tail-wagging and hand-licking lapdog. But there is one element of duplicity that remains, that will always remain. Our wars are always wars of liberation, never wars of conquest. Thus the discourse that dictates the tone of both political arenas, the domestic and the foreign, is moral. Once the Good is pitted against an Evil Axis of criminal regimes, opposition, domestic and foreign, can only be illegitimate, conducted by the morally perverse and therefore the politically discredited.

Now, if the triumph of a particular species of liberal pluralism denotes the de-politicization of society, one would think that theoretical opposition to this trend would seek to rehabilitate the political. But rather than asserting the value of the political as an essential structure of social life, the post-Marxist left seems intent on hammering the final nails into the coffin. In the most celebrated works of recent years, Giorgio Agamben's *Homo Sacer* (1998) and Michael Hardt and Antonio Negri's *Empire* (2000), the political (denoted by the notion of sovereignty) is irretrievably identified with nihilism and marked for extinction. In both instances, the political is the cause of the loss of 'natural innocence' (Agamben, 1998, p 28), that flowering of human productivity that the Western metaphysical tradition has suppressed; and the logical paradox of sovereignty is to be overcome by the instantiation of a new ontology. In this way, violence, which is not thought of as part of the state of nature but is introduced into the human condition by flawed or morally perverse social institutions, is to be averted. That is, the faulty supposition of ineluctable violence that guides political theory from Hobbes to Weber is to be replaced by a Heideggerian, Deleuzean, Spinozan or Christian ontology of original harmony. In the words of John Milbank, a Christian social theorist who currently enjoys a modest following among political thinkers on the Left, there is no 'original violence', but rather an originary 'harmonic peace' which is the *sociality* of harmonious difference'. Thus violence 'is always a secondary willed intrusion upon this possible infinite order' (Milbank, 1990, p 5). This, then, is the great supposition that links the ascetic pessimism of an Adorno with the cheery Christian optimism of Milbank: the world as it is *is* as it is because of the moral perversity of (some) human agents who willfully construct flawed social institutions. To seek to remedy the perversity of the world as it is from within the flawed social and political structures as they are only increases the perversity of the world. One must, therefore, totally disengage from the world as it is before one can become truly engaged. Only a thorough, cataclysmic cleansing of the world will allow our activities to be both 'innocent' and 'productive'. Clear, though only partially acknowledged, is the fact that this cleansing, which aims at ridding the world of intrusive violence, is itself an act of fierce and ultimate violence – ultimate in its purported finality, but also, certainly, in its extreme ferocity. What remains equally clear, though *not* acknowledged, is that whoever has the power to determine the nature of this harmonious sociality is the one who can determine which acts of violence are to be judged as intrusions into the placid domain and which acts of violence are to be condoned as the necessary means of re-establishing the promise of perpetual peace. Determining the nature of this desired, nay, required originary peace is itself a sovereign act, not the abolition of such sovereignty. What our ultimate sovereign of harmonious peace will do with the willfully violent intruders can only be guessed, but it is certain that they will not be looked upon as legitimate political dissenters, and the unconditional violence that will be used to eliminate their presence will be justified by invoking the 'harmonic peace' or 'natural innocence' they have so deliberately and maliciously disturbed.

In opposition to the near universal pressure to abolish the pesky complexity of the political, the aim of this volume is to reject every resurrection of eschatological desire, and to affirm conflict as the necessary and salutary basis of political life. To this end, the work of Carl Schmitt can be of considerable help. One must be clear, however, that the term most often associated with his thought – namely political theology – is *not* a term that can be sensibly used to describe his own best work. When, in 1922, Schmitt writes that 'all significant

concepts of the modern theory of the state are secularized theological concepts'
(Schmitt, 1985b, p 36), he makes an analogous claim about the modern political
state to the one Max Weber had already made nearly two decades earlier about
the modern money economy.[2] Just as wealth, industriously achieved, serves as
a sign of grace for the Puritans in early modern Europe (and the Massachusetts
Bay Colony), so too the sovereign, as a mortal God, mimics divinity. But God
and grace soon become mere power and market value, and Schmitt's and
Weber's emphases center on the necessities of this secularization, on the
profane, not the sacred, on the political and the economic, not the theological.
Their focus is on the butterfly, so to speak, not the caterpillar. Schmitt and
Weber, each in their own way, may have recoiled from the effects of
neutralization and rationalization, even preached the occasional Jeremiad
against the vacuous sterility of the modern wasteland, but, as both recognized
and clearly stated, by at least the end of the eighteenth century neither the
monopolization of power nor the accumulation of wealth were thought to
guarantee salvation, or even hint at special dispensation when it came to God's
favors. If capitalism was born from the spirit of Protestantism, it was, for all
that, capitalist, not Calvinist. And if the concepts of the modern theory of the
state still carried the traces of their ethereal origin, they were nonetheless
political concepts, and these traces had been thoroughly profaned. In short, the
political for Schmitt was no more theological than money was for Weber. And it
made absolutely no sense to be nostalgic for an imagined other space or
fulfilled time in which the sacred and the profane were united. Indeed, it was
for the *autonomy* of the political against the prevailing political theologies, the
religions of humanity called socialism and liberalism, that Schmitt waged his
conceptual warfare. Thus, if one wants to insist on referring to Schmitt as a
political theologian, it is because he made a religion out of the political – out of
the distinction, that is, between the theological and the political – and not
because he sought either the spirit or the authority of the divine in the power
and violence that is the mundane world of politics. It behooves us, therefore, to
examine, briefly, the nature of this autonomy before we move on to the more
detailed examinations of the structure of the political in the chapters that
follow.

The political in modernity

But of course it is not as simple as all that, because Schmitt's polemic for the
autonomy of the political is contradictory. To speak of the autonomy of the
political in the way that Schmitt does is to stand squarely 'within the horizon of
liberalism', as Leo Strauss put it in his astonishingly acute analysis of *The
Concept of the Political* (see Strauss, 1976, p 105). Yet Schmitt contrarily takes his
stand in the heart of modernity not to celebrate it unconditionally, but to
bemoan its liberal neutralization of the political. To speak of the political in the
way that Schmitt does, in other words, is to remain uncomfortably enmeshed in
an unavoidable ambivalence. Schmitt accepts the order of modernity as
described by Weber as the only order currently possible, but rejects the liberal

legitimation of that order precisely because liberal semantics, as he reads it, undermines the delicate structure modernity has achieved. To speak in a more contemporary language, the political exists in a space carved out by the functional differentiation of social systems, but, Schmitt fears, in this space the political is threatened with extinction – and with it, perhaps the whole structure of modernity itself – if it cannot assert itself as something more or something fundamentally other than merely one of many such differentiated systems. We can therefore locate and identify the ambivalence that runs throughout this text by saying that Schmitt simultaneously champions the *autonomy* of the political system as well as the *primacy* of the political as something other than merely one system among many.

The trick to understanding Schmitt's endeavor is to realize that autonomy and primacy stand opposed to one another in his world much in the same way as liberalism and popular democracy do. And though Schmitt often criticized the incoherency of mixing these two political ideologies (as was done for instance in the Weimar Constitution), in *The Concept of the Political* it is precisely such a mixture or co-existence between autonomy and primacy that he somewhat unconsciously or unintentionally achieves. The liberal order is procedural and bureaucratic; it rules by law and norm and not by popular will through the quasi-spontaneous decision-making power of a person or collection of people. In the bureaucratic liberal order of autonomous systems, therefore, the political stands precariously as 'one society among some other societies', as 'one association among other associations' (Schmitt, 1976, p 44). That is, within the liberal order, the political system, like all other systems, operates in accordance with its own rules. As such, autonomy asserts the independence of the political; but this independence is realized only within a bureaucratic structure that threatens to limit the scope of its function to mere administration. Independent of other systems, but not independent of the system of systems that is called society, the political becomes enmeshed in an all-encompassing network of systems. The power of the political is thus simultaneously absolute – anything can be judged politically and thus processed by the system – and limited – the political stands in a symmetrical, not hierarchical, relationship to the other systems in the network. It is the independence of the political that Schmitt cherishes. That is, he must define the uniqueness of the political code and preserve it from contamination. Surprisingly, much like Weber before him and Luhmann after him, Schmitt insists on the incommensurable relationship of systems' codes, specifically denying the equivalence of the political and the moral, the economic, and the aesthetic. Of necessity, then, to ensure its own autonomy, the political must respect the autonomy of other systems. Therefore, though functional differentiation threatens to reduce the political to a mere managerial status, it is also functional differentiation that guarantees the independence and independent importance of the political sphere of society. It is not the 'liberal' structure of modernity that he fears as much as the liberal self-description of that structure, a description, as we shall see, that threatens the very structure it claims to represent and defend.

Now, given his hostility to what he sees as the dangers of liberal neutralization of the political, it is not surprising that Schmitt would entertain the notion of a thoroughly politicized state. And indeed, he does raise the specter of a radically democratic state in which nothing escapes political judgment. On Schmitt's reading (and here he refers to Jakob Burckhardt for support),[3] the democratic state is the total state, the insatiable state 'which no longer knows anything absolutely nonpolitical, the state which must do away with the depoliticalizations of the nineteenth century and which in particular puts an end to the principle that the apolitical economy is independent of the state and that the state is apart from the economy' (Schmitt, 1976, p 25). In *The Concept of the Political* Schmitt never fully embraces the total state, for if everything is political, then nothing is political. If all codes collapse and if therefore the political code becomes identical with the moral, the economic, the aesthetic, and all other codes, then the total politicization of the state becomes indistinguishable from the full moralization or full economization of the state, and the political loses all specificity. Political decisions in such an arena become moral if not theological decisions, power is equated with the good, the true, and the beautiful, and all semblance of the modern achievement, born of the miseries of the 16th- and 17th-century religious wars, would disappear – and Schmitt knew well how to value the modern achievement above all else. Therefore, while standing 'within the horizon of liberalism' and never fully leaving it, Schmitt articulates a necessary uniqueness of the political that demands special treatment. If the state is still to be the seat of the political – and even in Schmitt's day that was at best an uncertainty[4] – then the state has to stand over and against the differentiated modernity of which it is also inescapably a part. The political, one might say, is the sovereign social system of liberal modernity, simultaneously of and above the order that it serves. Chantal Mouffe addresses the problem nicely in her articulation of the difference between 'the political' and 'politics'. 'By "the political"', Mouffe writes,

> I refer to the dimension of antagonism that is inherent in human relations, antagonisms that can take many forms and emerge in different types of social relations. 'Politics', on the other side, indicates the ensemble of practices, discourses and institutions that seek to establish a certain order and organize human coexistence in conditions that are always potentially conflictual because they are affected by the dimension of 'the political'. (Mouffe, 2000, p 101)

The ineliminable antagonism of the political serves, then, as the condition of possibility for the limited and channeled struggles of both domestic and international politics, struggles that can never be completely pacified as long as primary antagonism remains a presupposed necessity. In terms that are less 'existential' and that reflect the pluralism of 'value spheres' famously posited by Weber and formalized as social systems by Talcott Parsons and Niklas Luhmann, we can say that the political, as the ever-present possibility of irreconcilable conflict among incommensurable social systems, serves as modernity's self-description, if not constituent power. The 'political' could therefore stand for the conflictual and non-harmonic structure of modernity's differentiated and incommensurable social systems. One might put it in the following way: The code 'friend/enemy' that guides the political system is also the code that defines the relationship among the 'warring gods' of Weber's value spheres and Luhmann's social systems. The political, therefore (and no doubt in the manner of a Weberian unintended consequence), emerges as the guardian of the differentiated society in which, as politics, it simultaneously finds its home. This I will try to explain.

Autonomy of the political system

There is no doubt that in the opening pages of *The Concept of the Political*, Schmitt takes the differentiated outline of Weber's modernity as his starting point. He uses the binary code friend/enemy to define the political in contradistinction to the other 'endeavors of human thought' such as 'the moral, aesthetic, and economic', which have their own codes: good/evil, beautiful/ugly, and profitable/unprofitable (Schmitt, 1976, pp 25–26). In language distinctly reminiscent of Weber's 'Science as a Vocation',[5] Schmitt states: 'The political enemy need not be morally evil or aesthetically ugly; he need not appear as an economic competitor.' Acknowledging that 'emotionally' one may want to treat the enemy as being 'evil' and 'ugly', that one may, in other words, wish to draw on other distinctions for 'support', he nevertheless affirms that this psychological convenience does nothing to minimize the logical autonomy of distinctions. 'Consequently', he writes:

> the reverse is also true: the morally evil, aesthetically ugly or economically damaging need not necessarily be the enemy; the morally good, aesthetically beautiful, and economically profitable need not necessarily become the friend in the specifically political sense of the word. Thereby the inherently objective nature and autonomy of the political becomes evident by virtue of its being able to treat, distinguish, and comprehend the friend-enemy antithesis independently of other antitheses. (Schmitt, 1976, p 27)

And even the intimate code of love and hate retains its autonomy. 'The enemy in the political sense need not be hated personally' (Schmitt, 1976, p 29), Schmitt writes, precisely because the friend/enemy distinction refers to a public collectivity, not to individuals, and thus not to private adversaries, but to this collectivity's 'public enemy' (Schmitt, 1976, p 28). In the final analysis – and this, for Strauss, who collapses the political and the moral, proves Schmitt's irremediable modernity – if the political defines itself autonomously by way of a primary distinction in just the same way as the other value spheres of society, then there can be no classical unity of the Good, the True, and the Beautiful to serve as the definition of a perfected political order, a right regime or just society. The non-isomorphic relationship among codes – such that the positive value of one code is placed in no necessary correspondence to the positive value of other codes – may seem counter-intuitive, at first glance, and even morally repugnant to some, but its truth – to use another such binary distinction – seems evident upon the most minimal reflection. War, to pick by way of example the ultimate political mode of being, may be ecologically disastrous or scientifically tragic in those places where natural habitats or precious archeological sites, museums, laboratories, and libraries are destroyed; but war can nonetheless be economically profitable, and aesthetically its sleek visual representations can be quite disinterestedly pleasing to the attuned eye. This disjuncture is not perverse; it is modern. And no moral or religious scruple, except ones that can be translated into explicitly political interests, can trump reasons of state.

Those familiar with the works of Niklas Luhmann may be struck by Schmitt's use of binary coding. For Luhmann, as for Schmitt, such codes define the operations of social systems, and their orthogonal relationship – as Luhmann describes it – assures their autonomy and the 'polycontexturality' of modern society. The fact that the various codes cannot be superimposed allows for the ideally horizontal and egalitarian structure of functional differentiation. The various systems – politics, law, the economy, science, the arts, and so forth – all impinge on one another and are the occasion for disturbances that are registered and processed by the codes of each system. But none gives direct guidance or instruction to the others. Much like the international relationship of states during Europe's modern history, each system is sovereign, so to speak, over its own domain, imperially wielding the weapon of its particular distinction, but none is sovereign over the whole of society. There is no 'pope' or 'emperor' among the social systems that can subordinate the codes of one system to another. 'In 1492, Columbus sailed the ocean blue' or '$E=mc^2$' may be 'true', but there is no truth of goodness, or beauty, or legality, and no 'beauty' of truth. Autonomy, then, leads to anarchic order, the type that was traditionally grasped by the image of the 'invisible hand' and more recently by metaphorical allusions to scientific notions of emergence and self-organization.

There may be no pope of social systems, but Luhmann is surely the pope of this way of describing modernity. Anarchic, self-organizing, and self-replicating order is the norm, and it is the norm that Luhmann both describes and defends – though he is loathe to use the term 'norm'. Luhmann domesticates the friend/enemy distinction to the parliamentary difference between government/opposition, one that assumes what Schmitt, writing during the crisis years of the Weimar Republic, could not, namely the explicit loyalty of both the governing and opposition parties to the constitution and thus to liberal modernity as such. Yet Luhmann also recognizes that such loyalty is not without its paradox. The old answer to the question of what 'government' distinguishes itself from is 'the governed'. This answer still holds, but added to it is a second distinction, the liberal distinction between government and opposition. Ever since this supplement was added, Luhmann states, 'the concept of government finds itself at the focal point of *two* distinctions' and thus 'it has become stable and indispensable – and paradoxical'. Yet: 'One could suspect that a problem is concealed by making the concept paradoxical. And one is likely to suspect in addition that it is the old problem of sovereignty that has been concealed in this way' (Luhmann, 1990a, p 173). Of interest to us is the way Luhmann 'solves' the insoluble problem of sovereignty, and it is worth quoting him at length here. The change of the political system's binary coding, which adds the distinction between government and opposition to the more primary distinction of government and governed, 'presupposes organizationally differentiated political parties' that are

> able to survive the change from the role of government to that of opposition and back to that of government, however painful the process may be for persons and programs. But this organizational stability that first attracted one's attention is only a part, a substrate, of the real phenomenon – like an instrument on which politics from now on must be played. Decisive is the fact that an entirely new counter concept that increasingly absorbs political attention is added to what previously had been the government vis-à-vis the governed. Ever since the establishment of this distinction, the political system has been controlled not by unity but by a difference, a top that is bifurcated. Henceforth this makes it entirely inappropriate to speak of 'domination'. (Luhmann, 1990a, pp 173–74)

This bifurcation at the top, the distinction between government and opposition, is for Luhmann the democratic element in the modern political system. It allows for sanctioned political opposition, for the possibility of opposing government policy from *within* the political system. That is, where once opposition could only be an extra-parliamentary affair of cobblestones and barricades, now opposition, however tamed and modified, can be formally located within government itself, as if the governed could somehow, if minimally, re-enter the original distinction on the side of government. The governed govern not by way of a 'general will', but by formally opposing itself. The loss of unity results in a gain of necessary contingency. However, to claim the complete disappearance of something called 'domination' because of this bifurcation where once absolute 'popular' sovereignty stood is to claim too much. 'Domination', despite the ominous overtones, need not be valued negatively, and the distinction government/opposition may *qualify* the original distinction (government/governed), pushing it in the direction of something one might traditionally want to call democracy, but that primary distinction remains, and the 'governed' are both included *and* excluded from the realm of government. That this exclusion, as necessary and inevitable as it may be, is at times felt to be oppressive makes it all the more imperative that it, the exclusion, *not* be camouflaged and *not* be denied.

Luhmann's basic schema describes normalcy. Thus, it brackets the exceptional case. 'We will not consider this post-democratic case', Luhmann explicitly states,

> nor that of an extra-parliamentary opposition to the model of government/opposition, nor the third case of rejection, viz, a political terror from below that no longer distinguishes between those who govern and those who are governed but thinks everyone is evil (except themselves). In other words, we assume that only acceptance-values are possible in reference to the admitted distinctions and that this is the sense in which democracy functions. (Luhmann, 1990a, p 176)

By taking opposition out of the streets and placing it in the parliament, one sanctions opposition within the liberal-democratic order, but not *to* it. And there lies the rub, for the seed of a dual problem lies in this 'democratic' solution of 19th-century political turmoil, and in his vast body of work, Schmitt addresses, explicitly and implicitly, both forms of this problem. If 'democracy' as Luhmann describes it is normalcy, then normalcy can become so normal, so materially and psychologically comfortable in times of relative stability, that politics is felt as an unwelcome irritant and disturbance of the peace. Governing and opposition parties become then not just formally interchangeable, but substantially interchangeable as well, as each party searches for that uncontroversial dead center of the popular political will. Here, then, we see the threat of the liberal neutralization of the political as more and more political problems are dealt with by the 'experts' precisely because the citizenry does not wish to be bothered with uncomfortable ideological debate and the disillusionment of imperfect solutions. Better, in these cases, to scapegoat than to accept responsibility. On the other hand, apathy can easily tip over into frustrated action when normalcy is experienced by those who are constitutively excluded by the liberal order – those who feel themselves represented neither by the government nor by the loyal opposition – not as welcomed neutralization, but as acute and absolute paralysis of the political. Here the smooth functioning of the autonomous political system fails to register oppositional impulses as legitimately political and can therefore actually hide the political from view. If the former articulation of the problem can be labeled neutralization by way of efficiency, the latter is neutralization by way of invisibilization.

The primacy of the political

Schmitt responds by insisting on the primacy of the political. The friend/enemy distinction – the one Luhmann translates into a government/opposition code – not only defines the political system in analogy to the other realms of liberal civil society, but also defines and delimits the entire political entity (for modern Europe: the nation-state) that *protects*, as it were, the structure that allows for these other systems. As the ability to distinguish between friends and enemies, the political asserts itself fully not only as a constituted order, but as a constituent power that reveals itself in states of emergency. If the political system is normalcy, the political is the exception that establishes the norm.

In championing the primacy of the political, however, Schmitt emphatically does not advocate the total politicization of society. His anti-liberal bias does not push him all the way in the direction of the total state. Thus, the friend/enemy distinction does not cancel or direct or attempt to control the codes that organize the other social systems. Rather, the language he uses to emphasize the primacy of the political is always the language of intensification, of 'the most intense and extreme antagonism', the 'most extreme point' (Schmitt, 1976, p 29), the 'decisive human grouping' (Schmitt, 1976, p 38). It is Hegel's language on quantity transforming itself into quality which, Schmitt writes, 'has a thoroughgoing political meaning. It is an expression of the recognition that from every domain the point of the political is reached and with it a qualitative new intensity of human groupings' (Schmitt, 1976, p 62). The political is universal, but not in a totalitarian sense. It is universal in that it can be reached, through intensification, from any starting point. All other spheres, associations and social systems remain autonomous; they are not annulled by the primacy of the political. But in extreme situations, any association, any collective, can make itself into a political body by intensifying its own binary distinction into a version of the friend/enemy one. 'Every religious, moral, economic, ethical, or other antithesis', Schmitt writes, 'transforms into a political one if it is sufficiently strong to group human beings effectively according to friend and enemy'. For example: 'A religious community which wages wars against members of other religious communities or engages in other wars is already more than a religious community; it is a political entity.' Such a religiously inspired political entity could be a theocratic state, or it could be a non-conformist sect engaged in an implicit or explicit revolution. Schmitt may not endorse such a theocratic state or disruptively subversive, political presence in modern Europe, but what he does or does not endorse plays no role in determining the nature of the political. Similarly, 'a class in the Marxian sense ceases to be something purely economic and becomes a political factor ... when Marxists approach the class struggle seriously and treat the class adversary as a real enemy and fights him either in the form of a war of state against state or in a civil war within a state' (Schmitt, 1976, p 37). To define the political as the friend/enemy distinction simply means that the political can take shape anywhere, not just in the political system of the modern liberal state.

Because of his conservative leanings, his subsequent affiliations with the Nazi regime, and the emphatic language with which he justifies the friend/enemy distinction, Schmitt has often been taken to be one who belligerently and proto-fascistically equates the political with warfare, as though he were an enthusiastic prophet of the generative qualities of violence. It is his supposed *lebensphilosophisch* existentialism in these matters, manifested by a purportedly irrational decisionism, which condemns him in some eyes.[6] Schmitt, it is said, sees in the brutal and merciless conflict that is war the substance of politics, and war, which is an existential force conducted for its own sake, needs no justification. For instance, Jürgen Habermas, who certainly has read enough Schmitt to know better, refers to a fascination with 'the First World War's "storms of steel"' and an 'aesthetics of violence', linking Schmitt explicitly with the pathos of Ernst Jünger, the writings of Georges Bataille, and the type of contemporary French way of theorizing which Habermas finds so objectionable (Habermas, 1989, pp 129, 137). In Habermas's eyes, Schmitt is part of a grand, century-long 'counter-revolutionary' and counter-enlightenment conspiracy. It is true that Schmitt claims to ground the political existentially in the act of killing. 'The friend, enemy, and combat concepts receive their real meaning precisely because they refer to the real possibility of physical killing' (Schmitt, 1976, p 33). And it is also true that in his hostility to rationalist normativity,

Schmitt can say that 'no program, no ideal, no norm, no expediency confers a right to dispose of the physical life of other human beings' (Schmitt, 1976, p 48). Thus, the ability to distinguish friend from enemy derives its 'meaning' not from rational, normative principles, but from the act itself, conceived in terms of basic self-assertion as self-defense. But when we ask *why* Schmitt makes these claims, we arrive at radically different answers from the clichés Habermas would have us uncritically accept. Opposing 'existential' to 'normative' reasons for conducting war serves aims that are light years away from any life-philosophical glorification of violence.

I believe it in order here to cite a longer passage to clarify the point. 'To demand seriously of human beings', Schmitt passionately exclaims,

that they kill others and be prepared to die themselves so that trade and industry may flourish for the survivors or that the purchasing power of grandchildren may grow is sinister and crazy. It is a manifest fraud to condemn war as homicide and then demand of men that they wage war, kill and be killed, so that there will never again be war. War, the readiness of combatants to die, the physical killing of human beings who belong on the side of the enemy – all this has no normative meaning, but an existential meaning only, particularly in a real combat situation with a real enemy. There exists no rational purpose, no norm no matter how true, no program no matter how exemplary, no social ideal no matter how beautiful, no legitimacy nor legality which could justify men in killing each other for this reason. Just as little can war be justified by ethical and juristic norms. If there really are enemies in the existential sense as meant here, then it is justified, but only politically, to repel and fight them physically. (Schmitt, 1976, pp 48–49)

I take Schmitt's claim to be both obvious and counterintuitive. We have been conditioned to believe that the anarchic order of sovereign states poses a constant threat of uncontrolled outbreaks of potentially devastating wars. During the course of the 20th century, various treaties and agreements made by assorted leagues and associations of nations attempted to limit such outbreaks by 'outlawing' war except for a series of 'justified' reasons. These reasons accord with 'values' that are said to be humane, universal, rational, or simply self-evident. Perhaps surprisingly or perhaps not so surprisingly, these attempts have not successfully prevented the outbreak of 'unjustified' wars. Nor have they prevented those who explicitly retain sovereign power and military might from conducting wars regardless of justification. Indeed, as Schmitt specifically argues, rather than limiting the occurrence of war, treaties like the Kellogg-Briand Pact of 1928 explicitly *multiply* the possible occasions for war – 'The solemn declaration of outlawing war does not abolish the friend-enemy distinction, but, on the contrary, opens new possibilities by giving an international *hostis* declaration new content and new vigor' (Schmitt, 1976, p 51) – and intensifies the ferocity of the fighting once war does break out – 'and a war as an instrument of international politics can be worse than a war as an instrument of a national policy only' (Schmitt, 1976, p 50). When a nation or body of nations who has asserted its sovereign authority by identifying which norms ought to be established in such treaties decides, for whatever reason, to wage wars, it now is able to do so in the name of an assortment of universal and international ideals (rather than traditional state interest), or simply in the name of 'humanity'. Thus, wars of territorial or economic conquest can now be justified as wars of liberation. The imposition of a particular nation's or culture's form of economic, legal, administrative, and cultural life can now be touted as the extension of human rights. The white man's burden of old is lightened when, instead of Christianity, emancipation is the outcome of the contemporary white man's efforts. So, when Schmitt grounds war 'existentially', rather than normatively, he does so to keep local control, as it were, over sovereignty. When the sovereign right to distinguish friend from enemy in a time of crisis is relinquished, when it is stripped away in the name of a universally valid norm or principle, then that political entity ceases to exist. 'For as long as a people exists in the political sphere, this people must ... determine by itself the distinction of friend and enemy. Therein resides the essence of its political existence. When it no longer possesses the capacity or the will to make this distinction, it ceases to exist politically. If it permits this decision to be made by another, then it is no longer a politically free people and is absorbed into another political system' (Schmitt, 1976, p 49). What follows, then, is the seemingly shocking conclusion: 'A world in which the possibility of war is utterly eliminated, a completely pacified globe, would be a world without the distinction of friend and enemy and hence a world without politics' (Schmitt, 1976, p 35).

It should now be clear, I believe, that for all of his talk of 'existential' grounding of the political in war, the argumentation takes place on a plane far from the actuality of death and dying, because Schmitt's focus is not on violence as such, but on establishing the *logical possibility of legitimate political opposition*. His treatment of war is a *political* treatment, and even here he makes a gesture to modernity and its differentiated structure. He does not rule out the possibility of a thoroughly pacified world, nor does he rule out the possibility that from a moral or an aesthetic or an economic perspective such a pacification could be desirable; he simply states that the 'phenomenon of the political can be understood only in the context of the ever present possibility of the friend-and-enemy grouping' (Schmitt, 1976, p 35). The emphasis is always on the *condition of possibility of conflict*, not on the conflict itself. 'War is neither the aim nor the purpose nor even the very content of politics. But as an ever present possibility it is the leading presupposition which determines in a characteristic way human action and thinking and thereby creates a specifically political behavior' (Schmitt, 1976, p 34). Specifically political behavior is thereby defined by the real possibility of opposition; and opposition could not truly be defined as political opposition, were one not able to push it to the extreme. Were, say, violence, revolution, or war *morally* precluded, vehement opposition that hinted at the threat of violence could be ruled morally unacceptable and illegitimate. Global pacification would signal the elimination of the political, not because war is politics, but because the possibility that difference could be taken to the point of violent conflict is the necessary condition for legitimate political opposition. Without it, politics, in Schmitt's eyes, would be reduced to the activities of a polite but inconsequential debating society (Schmitt, 1976, p 33).

The presupposition of evil

Here, then, is where the cry of 'nihilism' is introduced. Schmitt's notion of the political presupposes the ineluctability of violence, conventionally marked as the priority of evil; conversely, thoroughgoing critics of modernity implicitly or explicitly presuppose the ontological priority of non-violence, of peace or the goodness and natural innocence of human nature. From this latter perspective, the insistence on the friend/enemy distinction and its paradigmatic use of armed conflict is viewed as a nihilistic denial of the possibility of the good, just, or ideal society. Ironically, the most radical of such critics is John Milbank, whose neo-orthodox Christian social theory posits itself on the other side of nihilism. Indeed, it is fascinating to watch the contemporary sport of Jacobin jockeying for position among those who wish to be more utopian than thou. Although Giorgio Agamben's critique of sovereignty and the bare life it exposes, based as it is on Foucauldian analysis and a Heideggerian ontological hope, may be philologically the most sound and philosophically the most sophisticated of such analyses, Hardt and Negri, operating in a Deleuzian mode to revaluate Foucault's notion of biopower, still find it wanting, at the very least, in enthusiasm. Milbank, in turn, reads both Heidegger and Deleuze as postmodern continuers of Western nihilism and offers a cleansed and refurbished, early medieval Christianity as the only true alternative discourse able to 'overcome nihilism itself' (Milbank, 1990, p 6). It is not, therefore, too farfetched to find in Milbank the aspirations of both Agamben and Hardt and Negri carried out to their fullest in the type of logical clarity sometimes lacking in the 'postmodern'.

Milbank's thesis is simple and only novel in the erudition and scope of his historical analyses: There is an original innocence that has been obscured by a derivative evil, associated with the willful introduction of dominion, including self-possession, which is the source of all violence. Peace, in other words, enjoys both a chronological and an ontological priority over violence. Thus, to posit a City of God against which the fallen City of Man can be judged is, according to Milbank, like reading a 'concealed text of an original peaceful creation beneath the palimpsest of the negative distortion of *dominium*' (Milbank, 1990, p 417). This original text 'allows us to unthink the necessity of violence' and 'indicates that there is a way to act in a violent world which assumes the ontological priority of non-violence' (Milbank, 1990, p 411). Strictly speaking, then, the City of God is no projection into the future and no patient waiting for the blessed afterlife, but rather a recollection and recovery, a banishment of baneful intrusions upon the natural order, for which the term 'peace' stands as placeholder, as the 'transcendental attribute of Being' (Milbank, 1990, p 432). The goal, then, is to live in the world so as to fashion and participate in the coming community, a 'peaceful order' that is marked by a 'pure' and 'absolute social consensus' (Milbank, 1990, p 410), and an 'absolute harmony based on right desire' (Milbank, 1990, p 414). Participation becomes the mode of inclusion; one is a participant in a community, not the subject of a state.

What could be wrong with such a vision? Certainly it is neither verifiable nor deniable empirically, so one cannot object on that ground. Ontologies are posited, not proven; and the same goes for philosophical anthropology at this level of abstraction. What we have in Milbank, then, is an image of a primordially pacified globe, and a lovely image it is. It satisfies the demands, or so it would seem, of a non-Kantian ethics, based on expansion rather than repression of desire,[7] and a quintessentially enlightened theology that places original goodness over sin. It also sketches the outlines for an ideal, non-capitalist economics based on collective utilization of the commons, and links this sketch, much like recent radical histories,[8] to a putatively pre-fallen stage of history of the human race not yet marked by the doctrine of property and dominion. It conforms to the demand for the symmetry and 'noble simplicity' of a classical aesthetics. And its portrayal of the political, to the extent that such a portrayal exists, does offer a distinct alternative to Schmitt's friend/enemy model. But, not unexpectedly, here some difficulties arise, because the image of peaceful harmony that is found in the original text of peaceful creation is overlaid by the more violent and imperfect second text. The question becomes: How do we move from that second text back to the first one? How, in other words, do we convince those not already willing to participate in the coming community to give up their 'sinful' ways? The question is a difficult one, because if peace is the default mode of the universe and violence only 'an unnecessary intrusion' brought into the community by 'a free subject who asserts a will that is truly independent of God and of others, and thereby a will to the inhibition and distortion of reality' (Milbank, 1990, p 432), how does one combat that violence if not by violence? The exercise of a corrective violence, a 'just' violence, aimed at the sinful intrusion is, of course, a traditional Christian response.[9] It is not, however, Milbank's. Instead he offers something perhaps even more insidious. Milbank opts for 'ecclesial coercion', a form of 'non-coercive persuasion' (Milbank, 1990, p 418) that is a collective, communal pressure expressed as 'social anger' or 'calm fury'. 'When a person commits an evil act', Milbank writes, 'he cuts himself off from social peace', because 'an individual's sin is never his alone … its endurance harms us all, and therefore its cancellation is also the responsibility of all' (Milbank, 1990, pp 421, 422). Therefore, non-coercive persuasion is the collective pressure of the group that ideally leads to renewed voluntary conformity, the 'free consent of will' (Milbank, 1990, p 418), on the part of the deviant individual.

The political as Schmitt envisions it disappears completely once one presupposes the ontological priority of non-violence. But what takes its place? It may seem ironic, but once one renounces the political and embraces the community based on harmonious universal inclusion of the peaceful and absolute exclusion of 'sin', one seems to have what Schmitt refers to as 'democracy' based on homogeneity. When one excludes the political, one has to guard the borders vigilantly against those willful intruders who deviate from God's will – which also means that one need be ever vigilant within those borders as well. Such an atmosphere, it seems, lends itself well to the description, cited above, of the 'total state which no longer knows anything absolutely nonpolitical' (Schmitt, 1976, p 25), which is to say that the political loses its autonomy and becomes conflated with the moral. What then becomes of those who are not 'persuaded', who adamantly refuse to 'participate'? Is 'sin' the only category available to describe their behavior? And is there no legitimate political alternative to pure and absolute consensus? Will all dissent and all dissenters who refuse to repent be eternally damned?

We know by now what question to ask, and it is a quintessentially Schmittian question: Who decides? Who decides on what is and what is not peace, what is and what is not violence, what is and what is not sin? And we know the answer: the sovereign, here the far from non-coercive sovereignty of the collective known as the Christian community. By extension, the same question can be asked of the other proponents of the ontological priority of non-violence, that is, of Agamben and of Hardt and Negri. Does negating the presupposition of violence negate the sovereign, or is not the negation itself a sovereign act, one made by the theologian or the philosopher, or by a liberal order that claims to have solved, once and for all, the nihilistic problem of the political?

Against this background, Schmitt's claim that 'all genuine political theories presuppose man to be evil, ie, by no means an unproblematic but a dangerous and dynamic being' (Schmitt, 1976, p 61) sounds less alarming and even less traditionally conservative than at first glance. Even here, with regard to what would seem to be a basic anthropological principle, Schmitt stands firmly within the horizon of the modern, for he treats the thesis of the human's basic problematic nature as a logical presupposition, a supposition made exclusively from within the political, and neither as an anthropological fact nor a presupposition that need be made in the same way elsewhere. Rather surprisingly, he states: 'One must pay more attention to how very different the anthropological presuppositions are in the various domains of human thought.' The 'educator will consider man capable of being educated', the jurist starts with the presupposition of goodness, the theologian must start with sin and end with the possibility of redemption, and the moralist must assume freedom of choice between good and evil. But, 'because the sphere of the political is in the final analysis determined by the real possibility of enmity, political conceptions and ideas cannot very well start with an anthropological optimism. This would dissolve the possibility of enmity and, thereby, every specific political consequence' (Schmitt, 1976, p 64). Indeed, the logical chain seems to work in reverse. The presupposed nature of the political determines the anthropological ground upon which it can rest. Thus, it is not a misanthropic pessimism that guides his preference for the ontological priority of violence, but rather a logical necessity, forced by the need to justify political opposition. In all cases – the liberalism that neutralizes the political to the point of oblivion and the total democracy that creates the inescapable monism of the total community – the ontological priority of goodness and non-violence leads, paradoxically, to the *impossibility* of political life, if by political life one wishes to advance the notions of dissent, argument, and the type of pluralism that provides for the possibility of real and meaningful disagreement because such disagreement can erupt 'existentially' as violent conflict. For this type of political behavior, one must assume the human being to be a dangerous being, a risky creature (Schmitt, 1976, p 58).

It is true, of course, that within the leftist tradition, especially as represented by the eschatological strains of Marxism, the political has often been thought of in ways similar to Milbank's, as, that is, the vehicle by means of which social reality can be so altered as to match utopian expectation; and perhaps this nostalgia for infinite perfectibility accounts for the appeal of the ontological hope offered there and elsewhere in recent political philosophy. When viewed as a path to secularized salvation, the political must at least implicitly be thought of as a self-consuming artifact. Once imperfect reality and perfect expectation are 'reconciled', the purpose of this manner of imagining the political has been fulfilled and can cease to exist. On this more traditionally accepted view, then, even if the process of reconciliation is considered to be infinite and never to be completed, the political must be seen as a constitutively non-essential and negative feature of social life, a feature that reflects undesired imperfection. Thus, at the imagined fulfillment of reconciliation, politics, along with the other sins of the world, simply vanishes. In a world that sees perfection as its goal, the end of politics is the end of politics.

Given the experiences of the 20th century – both the totalitarian abolition of the political and the more recent liberal legalization and moralization of politics – the non-Heideggerian and non-Deleuzian Left ought to be more than a little leery of the eschatological promise of a 'completely new politics' (Agamben, 1998, p 11). Dreams of a truer, more authentic ontology, of a more natural expression of human desire, a more spontaneous efflorescence of human productivity and re-productivity, feed rather than oppose the contemporary compulsive lurch toward universal pacification and total management of global economic and political life. Rather than dream those dreams, we should return to more sober insights about the ineluctability of conflict that not only calls the political into being but also structures it as a contingent, resilient, and necessary form of perpetual disagreement (Rancière, 1999). To claim the primacy of 'guilt' over 'innocence' or disharmony over harmony does not imply a glorification of violence for its own sake. It merely registers a pragmatic insight, namely, that assuming incommensurable conflict as an ineradicable feature of social life leads to more benign human institutions than the impossible attempt to instantiate the shimmering City of God on the rocky hills and sodden valleys that form the environment of the various cities of men and women on this very real and insurmountable terrestrial plain. The political does not exist to usher in the good life by eliminating social antagonism; rather, it exists to serve as the medium for an acceptably limited and therefore productive conflict in the inevitable absence of any final, universally accepted vision of the good life. The political, therefore, can only be defined by a structure that allows for the perpetual production as well as contingent resolution of dissent and opposition. If conflict is *its* vocation, then maintaining the possibility of conflict and thus the possibility of opposition ought to be *our* vocation, especially in an age when the managers of our lives carry out their actions in the name of democracy, while the majority of their weary subjects no longer even register what those actions are.

Notes

1   'Political action finds itself today trapped in a pincer movement between state managerial police and the world police of humanitarianism' (Rancière, 1999, p 136).

2   Reference is to Weber, 1958.

3   'Democracy must do away with all the typical distinctions and depoliticalizations characteristic of the liberal nineteenth century. ... The more profound thinkers of the nineteenth century soon recognized this. In Jakob Burckhardt's *Weltgeschicht-liche Betrachtungen* (of the period around 1870) the following sentences are found on "democracy, ie a doctrine nourished by a thousand springs, and varying greatly with the social status of its adherents. Only in one respect was it consistent, namely, in the insatiability of its demand for state control of the individual. Thus it blurs the boundaries between state and society and looks to the state for the things that society will most likely refuse to do, while maintaining a permanent condition of argument and change and ultimately vindicating the right to work and subsistence for certain castes"' (Schmitt, 1976, p 23).

4   See for instance the opening section of Schmitt, 1976.

5   See Weber, 1946, pp 147–48.

6   See especially Wolin, 1992, pp 83–104, for an example of this view.

7   See the discussion of Hardt and Negri, 2000, below, Chapter 6.

8   See for instance Linebaugh and Rediker, 2000.

9   See for instance Stevenson, 1987, and the discussion below, Chapter 8.

PART I
POLITICS AS CONFLICT

Chapter 1
Conflict as a vocation:
Schmitt, Lyotard, Luhmann

Do we define ourselves by the enemies we make? Carl Schmitt thought so, and those who disagreed made an enemy of him. So maybe he was right. Maybe our ability to distinguish with a fine temporal and spatial sense between friend and enemy is the mark of our political existence, and thus we can say: Conflict is our vocation. There is, nonetheless, a caveat. The antagonism that determines the political is not the antagonism of the war of all against all in the state of nature. That war and that state, Derrida would say, is discourse itself, 'the emergence of speech and appearing'. He would also say that no 'messianic triumph' could abolish this originary violence that is our condition except by way of a greater and fiercer violence, a total violence (Derrida, 1978, pp 116–17, 129–30, 141). But, as Kant's joke ought to have told us all along, the war to end all wars can lead to perpetual peace only if it is the peace of the graveyard.[1] So, which conflict is the conflict that is politics? It *is* war, but it is not the war of nature, nor is it the violent suppression of the war of nature. On the contrary, politics is the refinement of war; it is war's double, a force that matches, but channels and gives particular form to, the violence of nature. That form preserves difference, but not indifferently. It takes shape as the differentiation of autonomous unities that serve as the carriers of difference. Operating as a logic of autonomy and differentiation – or, if you prefer, a dialectic of homogeneity and heterogeneity – politics preserves the ability to initiate and the ability to put a halt to conflict, the ability to recognize and determine the difference between conflict and peace. Political antagonism, in the final analysis, is a discrete and fragile structure that limits conflict by legitimizing it. Such bounded discretion, according to Carl Schmitt, is the apogee of civilization.

If political conflict is disciplined conflict and not the war of all against all, we have to ask: How is conflict possible? We defer an answer by asking a second question: How is difference possible? As Zeno's paradox shows, difference is infinite and, as such, invisible. Further distinctions can always be made, making the task of perceiving difference paradoxical, because difference is all we have. If a structure of difference is to be made visible, difference must be suspended and bundled into unities. Conflict is possible as a structure of difference, and such a structure is only possible as a differentiation of unities, a differentiation, that is, of bundled differences. Thus, the specific nature of politics is determined by the specific constitution of opposed unities, making the origin of politics already political, already a battle about what constitutes a politically legitimate unity. We can now phrase our original question in a somewhat more paradoxical form: If politics is conflict, at what level is politics (conflict) suspended in order to make politics (conflict) possible? Since we have already eliminated the pre-political anarchy of the state of nature and the post-political universal stillness of the world state, we are left with two historically viable alternatives: the archaic but nevertheless lingering memory of the sovereign nation-state, and the quite modern and quite liberal concept of autonomous associations, social groups, or social systems. It is the latter pluralism of functionally differentiated social systems that seems to have carried the day, thus it is against this species of pluralism that Schmitt wages his political war – not because he opposes pluralism, but because the pluralism of associations, in his view, is sham pluralism. Simply and succinctly put, Schmitt sees in early 20th-century, Anglo-American, liberal pluralism an underlying universal monism, an extremely dangerous ideology of 'humanity' that leaves both the dissenting group and the dissenting individual dehumanized and defenceless. His solution is to rehabilitate the monism of state sovereignty in order to guarantee a greater pluralism, an international pluralism of autonomous unities that refuse to be subsumed under the legal or economic supremacy of a particular instance (the United States, say) that has authorized itself to be the privileged carrier of the omnipotent and universal moral principle. The sovereignty of the state, as the carrier of difference, enables the arena of this larger pluralism in which the political is to be found.

In this chapter, then, we will investigate Schmitt's notion of sovereignty, since for him the sovereignty of the state, and not the autonomy of the social system, is the site of political legitimacy. We will next need to examine Schmitt's critique of liberal pluralism, because this form of pluralism threatens, in his view, not only the sovereignty of the state, but also the very existence of a viable concept of politics. Finally, since the pluralism of autonomous social systems has superseded, in large measure, the sovereignty of state action, as Schmitt conceived it, we will have to ask whether the structure of conflict that he defines as 'the political' remains a possibility if the political unities in question are associations and not states.

Sovereignty and sufficient reason

All of Schmitt's most famous Weimar-era arguments against liberalism center on its deliberate attempt to disintegrate the authority of the sovereign state, disabling the state's ability to act as an autonomous 'moral subject' on the international stage. Schmitt's polemic against Hans Kelsen in *Political Theology* (Schmitt, 1985b), for instance, is motivated by what he sees as the latter's attempt to negate sovereignty and replace it with the rule of law. But legality, Schmitt counters, is both impotent, unable to protect itself from its enemies, as Hitler's 'legal' revolution was subsequently to demonstrate, and deceptive, camouflaging its violent uses of force under the fig leaves of rule and norm. In a similar vein, his analyses of the contemporary situation of parliamentary democracy are aimed at exposing the empty formality of discussion as an epistemological and political procedure. What is theorized as an open and free ('uncoerced') exchange of ideas in the pursuit of truth is, in actuality, a clash of (predominantly economic) interests (Schmitt, 1985a, pp 1–18, 48–50). Perhaps most telling, however, are Schmitt's critiques of Gierke's 19th-century analysis of associations as they are updated in GDH Cole's and Harold Laski's pluralism (Schmitt, 1976, pp 40–45; Schmitt, 1988b, pp 152–53). Here the issue of conflicting loyalties arises. If the relationship of the individual to the state is defined as one of obedience and protection – as Schmitt, following Hobbes, believes – then the pluralist undermining of the legitimacy and sovereignty of the state, coupled with its recommendation that we transfer our loyalties from the state to social groups, leaves us all dangerously exposed. The group cannot defend us, Schmitt insists, only the state can. For most (if not all) liberals, who have traditionally seen the state as the supreme enemy, this line of reasoning appears monstrously counterintuitive. It is not in the state, according to liberal belief, but in the pluralist limitation of state power that political freedom finds it home. In Schmitt's view, however, this neutralization of the state does leads not to political freedom, but to the total domination of civil society and thus the elimination of politics in the name of morality, legality, and the economy.

In his writings of the 1920s and 1930s, Schmitt traces a fairly conventional history of the modern state from its origins in absolutism to the rise of 18th- and 19th-century liberalism. The 19th-century state is marked by a 'dualism', a tension between the state and a rapidly 'self-organizing' civil society (Schmitt, 1988b, pp 172, 176). By the 20th century, we see the outlines of a total victory of civil society, one in which the state (as the self-description of the political system) no longer stands in opposition to society, but becomes just one more association among many. What Schmitt observes in state-theoretical terms is the modernization process. In pluralist theories of the state, he notes, 'the state simply transforms itself into an association which competes with other associations; it becomes a society among some other societies [eg religion, art, the economy, etc] which exist within or outside the state' (Schmitt, 1976, p 44). The autonomy of the state as the unity of the difference of society is replaced by the autonomy of the social system, which guarantees the differentiation, not the unity, of society. Like many critics of the modernization process, Schmitt bemoans the loss of the political. If the political becomes just one association among many, then it reduces to the technology of administration. The full emancipation of society from the state that Schmitt abhors is but a variation on the theme of the ethos of efficiency (Lyotard) that is the administered society (Adorno). It is not only that the pluralism of party politics serves as a cover for the machinations of dominant economic interests, but also that political decisions are openly and publicly justified simply on economic terms. In this way, the modern state threatens to become, if it has not already done so, a total *Wirtschaftsstaat* (Schmitt, 1988b, pp 173–75).

To rescue the political, Schmitt reaches back to an older, Hobbesian version of the state, in which the state ensures a structure that allows for the possibility of politics. The 'achievement of the state', he writes in 1930, consists of its ability to 'determine the concrete situation in which moral and legal norms can be valid'. Since norms are neither divinely revealed nor rationally reconstructed (as Rickert would like us to believe), they must be determined by their context.

'Every norm presupposes a normal situation', Schmitt writes, deliberately emphasizing, by word play, the conventionalism involved (Schmitt, 1988b, p 155). Thus, states neither arise nor are legitimized by way of a logical deduction from universal norms; rather, norms presuppose the legitimacy of states. One can then say that the articulation of a concrete norm is not the result of a derivation, but the effect of a performative. Declarations such as 'We, the people' do not describe, they constitute the 'we' and the 'people' in their very utterance. They may presuppose such an entity – 'people' – and they may presuppose that the speaker is a duly qualified representative of that entity, a legitimate enunciator of the 'we', but that which is presupposed only actually comes into being in the act of articulating the declaration. What is needed for such an emergence is a space (logical or physical) within which the language can be heard. It is the situation, the condition, the 'state', which structures this enabling space. 'No norm is valid in the void' ('*Keine Norm gilt im Leeren*') (Schmitt, 1988b, p 155).

Sovereignty is the name Schmitt gives to this condition and this space. His famous definition reads: 'Sovereign is he who decides on the exception' (Schmitt, 1985b, p 5). But before we can begin to explore what this might mean, we need to examine the description he rejects. The classical definition, traceable back to Jean Bodin and always repeated, has a more rational, a more logical ring: 'Sovereignty is the highest, legally independent, underived power' (Schmitt, 1985b, p 17). Schmitt, however, finds this definition useless, unreal. 'It utilizes', he says,

> the superlative, 'the highest power', to characterize a true quantity, even though from the standpoint of reality, which is governed by the law of causality, no single factor can be picked out and accorded such a superlative. In political reality there is no irresistible highest or greatest power that operates according to the certainty of natural law. (Schmitt, 1985b, p 17)

Schmitt's dismissal of the traditional definition is not casual and not merely strategic. It rehearses, *in nuce*, a long-standing critique of Western rationalism that Schmitt uses to undermine the self-understanding of the liberal rule of law. Central to this critique is the recognition of the paradoxical limits of the law of causality. The law states that for every effect there must be a cause, for every Y there must be an X – and this chain of reasons for reasons necessarily goes on to infinity. Within the immanent chain of cause and effect there can be no originary cause. If we imagine the law of causality as an infinite series in which every cause of an effect is itself an effect of a prior cause, then there would be no ultimate, no sufficient reason, no point or origin that could serve as explanatory ground, no reason for things that itself has no reason. Leibniz saw this clearly and thus suggested a meta-level solution. 'We cannot find in any of the individual things, or even in the entire collection and series of things, a sufficient reason for why they exist', he writes, because no matter how 'far back we might go into previous states, we will never find in those states a complete explanation [*ratio*] for why, indeed, there is any world at all, and why it is the way it is' (Leibniz, 1989, p 149). Consequently, Leibniz is necessarily led to conclude:

> Therefore, the reasons for the world lie hidden in something extramundane, different from the chain of states, or from the series of things, the collection of which constitutes the world. And so we must pass from the physical or hypothetical necessity, which determines the later things in the world from the earlier, to something which is of absolute or metaphysical necessity, something for which a reason cannot be given. (Leibniz, 1989, p 150)

Leibniz, of course, calls this 'something for which a reason cannot be given' God, thereby, he thought, establishing His necessity, and thus, His existence. As 18th-century critics of reason soon pointed out, what Leibniz in fact established was not the rationality of the world created by a God who serves as its sufficient reason, but rather the irrationality of reason itself, which, like all other systems of belief that seek foundations in origins, requires a leap of faith. Leibniz must posit a level above the immanent level of causality to provide a sufficient reason for this lower-level chain of cause and effect; and this meta-level reason – this God – must itself remain without reason, must remain rationally unexplainable, for to posit a yet higher level explanation for the meta-level explanation for the immanent chain of reasons would be to replicate the infinity one sought to put a halt to. If God does not represent an arbitrary stopping point, then the horizontal infinity of cause and effect that one hopes to avoid would be displaced into a vertical infinity of meta-levels – turtles standing on the backs of turtles, as one Hindu creation myth has it. But to posit God as the groundless ground of causality is to posit the irrationality of reason. Thus, the logical pattern that Leibniz provides becomes the pattern that fierce defenders of the superior irrationality of religion like Jacobi and Kierkegaard use to prove the limits of reason and therefore the inability of reason to come to terms with the real meaning of the world, a meaning that can only be subjectively discerned and existentially enacted by way of a non-rational leap of faith.

Max Weber translates this collapse of the self-justification of reason into a vision of modernity. He acknowledges the fact that scientific rationality cannot be scientifically or rationally justified, and that meaning is a matter of choice that precedes the utilization of reason; but he does not opt for the glorification of irrationality which he sees motivating his contemporaries, especially in the immediate context of World War I and its revolutionary aftermath. If reason no longer reigns supreme as some ersatz deity, then the divine throne should simply remain empty. He accepts the limit that Kant imposed on theoretical reason, a limit that prohibits it from providing definitive and obligatory answers to the practical question of how one should live. Accordingly, Weber, like Kant, is confronted with both a *fait accompli* (the limit of reason) and a challenge (the necessity of championing it nonetheless). Reason is impotent when confronted with the determination of ends, yet reason is extolled as an ethos, as a means by which human dignity and human sociability can be preserved. Weber comes to this conclusion by way of a history of science (*Wissenschaft*, both natural and human), a history that is presented as a progressive substitution of justifications until virtually no justification at all is left. Whereas Platonic reason could once present itself as the search for truth by way of logic and the philosophical concept, in order to determine how one should act (could present itself, that is, as the unity of theory and practice, as the unity of the True and the Good); and whereas early modern science could once present itself as the search for the truth of nature, accessible by way of experiment; and whereas theological reason could once present itself (as we have seen) as the search for the truth of the transcendent ground of all being (God); now all that the rationality of science can do is present itself as the distinction between means and ends (Weber, 1946, pp 140–43, 150–52). Forced to acknowledge its impotence when confronted with questions regarding ends, eg regarding the form and conduct of the good life, modern rationality is restricted to offering advice on the use of the best, the most proper and the most efficient means in the pursuit of goals which themselves cannot be rationally justified. And even this facility – science's claim to optimal efficiency – cannot be scientifically established, for reason can no more rationally justify its own reasonableness than medicine can justify the desire to prolong life, aesthetics the desire to create beauty, or law the legality of law (Weber, 1946, pp 143–46). We are confronted, then, with a vast, 'flat' landscape of relentlessly expanding, technically efficient spheres that are unable to articulate a definitive reason for their own existence and thus are unable to offer any 'meaning' for ours. No value sphere or system has a rationally justified reference point external to itself by means of which its own distinctions could be judged, and the self-application of its own distinction to itself ends in paradox and undecidability. Thus, Weber's analysis of modernity is the classic problem of the self-justification of reason – its inability to ground rationally its own rational activity – extended to all spheres of society. As a result, neither reason nor revelation nor any other form of communication linked to a specific value sphere can serve as the representative voice of society as a whole. The beautiful unity of the true and good no longer holds, for, as Weber says, evoking the authority of Baudelaire and Nietzsche, we all know that 'something can be sacred not only in spite of its not being beautiful, but rather because and in so far as it is not beautiful', and that 'something can be beautiful, not only in spite of the aspect in which it is not good, but rather in that very aspect', and finally that 'something may be true although it is not beautiful and not holy and not good' (Weber, 1946, pp 147–48). The result of this differentiation of values, along with spheres or systems in which, and only in which, these values hold sway, is a 'polytheism' of warring gods in which no one god emerges victorious, because all the gods exert equally powerful (equally legitimate) forces. 'So long as life remains immanent and is interpreted in its own terms', Weber concludes, 'it knows only of an unceasing struggle of these gods with one another ... The ultimately possible attitudes toward life are irreconcilable, and hence their struggle can never be brought to a final conclusion. Thus it is necessary to make a decisive choice' (Weber, 1946, p 152).

In his rejection of the classical definition of sovereignty, Schmitt presupposes this collapse of Leibnizian sufficient reason and thus presupposes the Weberian image of modernity.[2] Despite his famous Catholicism, he does not call for a return to an ancient, medieval, or early modern version of natural law. Carl Schmitt, in other words, is no Leo Strauss.[3] He does not attempt to save philosophy from the mathematical ravages of modern rationality by positing a classical unity of reason and nature, or of the True and the Good; rather, he accepts the demise of natural law and ponders the limits of legality in a positivist age. His starting point is Weber's observation that 'the axioms of natural law have lost all capacity to provide the fundamental basis of a legal system', a fact which has 'destroyed all possibility of providing the law with a metaphysical dignity by virtue of its immanent qualities' (Weber, 1978, pp 874–75). All norms are thus ineluctably relativized. Without the meta-level self-sufficiency of a God-like natural law to provide positive law its groundless ground, all immanent norms must themselves be derived from previous norms, producing the nightmare of a never-ending quest for ultimate normativity. Schmitt therefore concludes that the rule of law is a mere, free-floating fiction, 'for no norm ... interprets and administers, protects and guards itself; no normative validity validates itself; and there is ... no hierarchy of norms, only a hierarchy of concrete people and instances' (Schmitt, 1993a, p 53).

This negation of a hierarchy of norms, coupled with the affirmation of a hierarchy of concrete instances, brings us back to the definition of sovereignty favoured by Schmitt: 'Sovereign is he who decides on the exception.' Three notions – sovereignty, decision, and the exception – come together here to form a constellation that can do justice, Schmitt feels, to the particularity of social reality, a particularity rendered invisible by the self-mystifications of the liberal rule of law. The sovereign is figured as an autonomous entity, an agent, or at least agency, which has the authority to make decisions. That agent may be a monarch, a dictator, a ruling body, or any of a variety of other decision-making mechanisms. What is crucial, however, is that the power and executive authority to make decisions is lodged somewhere in times of extreme emergency, in times of the exception. 'It is precisely the exception', Schmitt writes, 'that makes relevant the subject of sovereignty' (Schmitt, 1985b, p 6). The exception makes itself known as the failure of subsumption – as the impossibility, one might say, of determinate judgment. 'The exception is that which cannot be subsumed; it defies general codification, but it simultaneously reveals a specifically juristic element – the decision in absolute purity' (Schmitt, 1985b, p 13). The exception presents itself as the ineluctable necessity of choice precisely at the moment when none of the normal criteria is available to guide selection. From the perspective of the rule of law, the exception can be seen, when it is seen at all, only as a 'disturbance' (Schmitt, 1985b, p 12) that must be made invisible again. The 'unity' and 'purity' of the system 'are easily attained when the basic difficulty is emphatically ignored and when, for formal reasons, everything that contradicts the system is excluded as impure' (Schmitt, 1985b, p 21).

Accordingly, the reality of the concrete instance or the exception – whatever it may be – is opposed to the validity of norms, and the groundless rule of law is attacked on simple logical grounds. Referring to political philosophers like

Hans Kelsen, Schmitt notes that liberal theory defines the legal order as a 'system of ascriptions to a last point of ascription and to a last basic norm', and identifies this legal order with the state. The liberal state (the *Gesetzgebungsstaat*) therefore becomes 'the terminal point of ascription' (Schmitt, 1985b, p 19), not because it is autonomous from, or situated above, the legal order, but rather because it is coterminous with it. However, as we have seen, if the state does not stand outside of the legal system either as its 'creator' or 'source' (Schmitt, 1985b, p 19), then it cannot logically claim to be the highest or terminal point of ascription or the ultimate norm, for within the infinite chain of ascriptions that define the immanent rule of law, no such point exists. To equate the state with the rule of law, therefore, would be to equate it with the 'system' that cannot account for the exception and thus leave it vulnerable to the exception's eruptive force. The state, in fact, would disappear and sovereignty – or whatever term one would now wish to use as a replacement for that disagreeable concept – would simply reside in the 'unity of the system of norms', a unity often identified with a constitution. Thus, the rule of law not only dispenses with the notion of sovereignty, but also attempts to do without the existence of the state altogether.[4]

But, Schmitt argues, raising legality to the level of sovereignty fails to acknowledge the crucial and empirical distinction between 'actual power' and the 'legally highest power' (Schmitt, 1985b, p 18). With this distinction, Schmitt introduces a bifurcation of his notion of sovereignty that is of political and not just logical interest. When considered as the 'highest legal power', the problem of sovereignty can be defined as a problem of judgment. The rule of law ignores this problem by identifying all judgment with determinate judgment, assuming, as it were, that decisions become superfluous because logical judgments simply 'make themselves'. In his pre-1918 (which is to say, pre-crisis) critique of legal positivism, Schmitt had already shown that the legitimacy of legal decisions within the legal system was the result of what we, leaning on Kant, could call 'reflective', not determinate, judgment. 'A judicial (*richterliche*) decision', he writes in *Gesetz und Urteil*, 'is correct (*richtig*) today when it can be assumed that another judge would have decided in the same way' (Schmitt, 1912, p 71). There is an attribution of universality in this statement that is neither logical nor empirical, but rather 'aesthetic', echoing Kant's claim that the judgment of taste is a subjective judgment that can never be demonstrated according to rules, but yet is one that 'demands' (*sinnet an*) 'agreement' (*Beistimmung*) (Kant, 1974, B64, paragraph 19). It is this performative attribution of system-wide applicability that serves as its legitimacy.[5] The problem of sovereignty, then, involves the generalization and extension of the domain of reflective judgment beyond the system (aesthetic) in which it first found its theoretical articulation. A political judgment – a *decision* – is called for precisely at the moment where 'knowledge' fails.[6] However, if sovereignty as the 'highest legal power' sees itself as the need to exercise reflective judgment, then sovereignty as 'actual power' is concerned with survival and must be defined as the paradoxical self-preservation of the law by extra-legal means, or rather, by the legal suspension of the law. Indeed, Schmitt's critique of the rule of law during the Weimar years centers on its impotence and inability to protect itself from usurpation. Not only does it collapse because of its own logical insufficiency, but it lays itself open to the legal takeover of the state by forces expressly committed to destroying the existing legal order. As has often been noted (eg Bendersky, 1983), Schmitt, in his writings of the late 1920s and early 1930s (eg Schmitt, 1993a; Schmitt, 1996), was extremely troubled by the possible legal takeover and thus the legal negation of the Weimar Republic by parties, like the KPD and NSDAP, that explicitly advocated its abolition. Without a distinction between legality and legitimacy – which is to say – without a distinction between the legal order and a sovereign entity that was empowered to suspend the legal order, when necessary, in order to preserve it, the legal state was perpetually threatened with liquidation (Schmitt, 1993a, p 29). In this regard, then, sovereignty entails the political decision to save politics by (temporarily) suspending normal political activity. Sovereignty here emerges as a 'supplement', one might say, that attaches itself to the system as if from the outside to serve as a kind of communal bodyguard. Schmitt called this supplement the state, and the modern, neutral state, he stressed, could not be neutral toward its own continued existence (Schmitt, 1993a, p 28). Therefore, the issue of sovereignty, which the liberal rule of law thought to have settled once and for all, was as relevant as ever.

The structure of pluralism

It is not difficult to see that the polemical elevation of sovereignty over the rule of law replicates a lively historical opposition, one that can be perhaps best evoked by that happy pair, Hobbes and Locke. Within the liberal tradition, the rule of law invokes reason and calculability in its battles against the arbitrary and potentially despotic whim of an unrestrained sovereign. The legitimacy of the sovereign is thus replaced by a legality that claims to provide its own immanent and unforced legitimacy. Predictable and universally accessible reason – the normative validity of an 'uncoerced consensus', to use the words of a prominent modern exponent – gently usurps, so it is claimed, the place that would otherwise be occupied by a cynical, pragmatic utilitarianism and the tyranny of a dark, incalculable will.[7] The rule of law brings all the comforts of an uncontroversial, rule-based, normative security, as if legality proceeded by way of simple logical derivation, abolishing, above all, the necessity of decisions. Schmitt clearly will have none of this and in his various writings attempts to expose what he considers to be the two-fold fallacy of the liberal position. As we have seen, if taken at its word, legality, or the rule of law, is seen by Schmitt to be impotent; it can neither legitimize nor effectively defend itself against determined enemies in times of crisis. Were law truly the opposite of force, it would cease to exist. But this self-description is deceptive, for if judged by its deeds, the same liberal regime that enunciates the self-evident validity of universal norms strives to enact a universal consensus that is, indeed, far from uncoerced. The rule of law inevitably reveals itself, precisely during moments of crisis, as the force of law, perhaps not every bit as violent and 'irrational' as the arbitrary tyrant, but nonetheless compelling and irresistible – indeed, necessarily so![8] Thus, Schmitt would argue, the distinction between 'decision', 'force' and 'sovereignty', on the one hand, and the 'rule of law', on the other, is based on a blithe and simple illusion.[9] What agitates Schmitt is not the force, but the deception. More precisely, what agitates Schmitt is what he perceives to be the elimination of politics in the name of a higher legal or moral order. In its claim to a universal, normative, rule-bound validity, the liberal sleight-of-hand reveals itself to be not the opposite of force, but a force that outlaws opposition. In resurrecting the notion of sovereignty, therefore, Schmitt sees himself as one who rescues a legitimate notion of politics.

Of course, this rescue attempt is itself political, a battle over the correct definition of politics. That is, we are not merely dealing with a logical problem, and not merely dealing with a desire to provide constitutional mechanisms that would prevent the self-dissolution of the constitution. Rather, we are dealing with a contest between a particularist notion of politics, in which individual conflicts can be resolved, but in which antagonism as a structure and reservoir of possible future conflicts is never destroyed, versus politics as the historical unfolding and pacific expansion of a universal morality. To evoke the long shadows of an ongoing contemporary debate, we are dealing with the difference between a politics of dissent and a politics of consensus. The latter ideology entails an explicit or implicit belief in a 'highest good' that can be rationally discerned and achieved, a 'right regime', to use Leo Strauss's term, or the 'just society' that hopes to actualize aspects of the City of God here on earth; whereas the former stresses the necessity of determining a workable order where no single order bears the mantle of necessity, in fact, where all order is contingent, hence imperfect, and thus seeks to make the best of an inherently contradictory world by erecting structures that minimize self-inflicted damage.[10] In Schmitt's eyes, the elements of such a structure must be the manifold of sovereign states. The liberal says there can only be one worldwide sovereign, the sovereignty of a universal moral and legal order. Schmitt counters with a plurality of equal sovereigns, for only in this way, he believes, can the economic and moral extinction of politics be prevented. Politics, on this view, is not the means by which the universally acknowledged Good is actualized, but the mechanism that negotiates and limits disputes in the absence of any universally acknowledged Good. Politics exists, in other words, because the just society does not.

Schmitt, then, is a pluralist and a particularist, but his pluralism is not the one that we have all grown to love. His is the pluralism of neither social associations nor autonomous individuals. If politics as conflict is to survive, he warns, then the carrier of political difference must remain the state. 'It is', he bitterly complains, 'an intellectual (geistesgeschichtlich) misunderstanding of a most astonishing kind, to wish to dissolve these plural political unities [the

European nation-states as they emerged in the 16th and 17th centuries] by referring to universal and monistic concepts, and then represent this attempt as pluralism' (Schmitt, 1988b, p 161). This astonishing 'misunderstanding' is committed by, among others, Laski and Cole, whose differing versions of liberal (or quasi-socialist) pluralism are advanced in the name of the emancipation of the individual who is to be freed from state fetters. It is a 'misconception' that all of us who have grown quite comfortable in liberal societies share (and, thus, ones we would be quite loathe, and reasonably so, to give up). According to the type of liberal pluralism that Schmitt opposes, we have come to think of ourselves as autonomous individuals (even when we view our 'selves' as socially constructed), in charge of our own choices with regard to religion, occupation, trade union membership, political parties and the like, by virtue of the state's gradual neutralization. As a result of the 16th- and 17th-century civil wars, the state traded, so to speak, freedom of conscience for obedience. But this initial and necessary trade has finally led to a more or less complete switch in loyalties, from the state to associations, or, more generally, from the state to civil society. With this switch has come greater freedom, as a matter of course, for liberal freedom is defined precisely in terms of greater choice, something that the state, apparently, must always restrict. Pluralism, then, is simply the modern condition of universal and unrestricted participation in the differentiation of a vast variety of social systems. In theory, because of a common humanity, criteria of class, race, gender, religion, political affiliation, or any other category cannot be used to deny full and free access to the various spheres of social activity.

But is this freedom of full participation in civil society *political* freedom? We say yes, for this is how we have come to define politics, but Schmitt says no. At times, Schmitt is quite careful to grant the autonomy of social systems. Indeed, as Leo Strauss already recognized (and bemoaned), Schmitt's entire political theory depends on the autonomy of politics from, say, morality and religion, and thus depends on the Weberian differentiation of value spheres (Strauss, 1976, pp 103–05). In his famous attempt to locate the essence of the political in the friend/enemy distinction, Schmitt is careful to note that the various distinctions used by the other realms of human endeavour – especially the moral, aesthetic and economic spheres – are not homologous. 'The political enemy need not be morally evil or aesthetically ugly; he need not appear as an economic competitor' (Schmitt, 1976, p 27). But he is equally adamant that not only is there an overarching unity of these differences, but that that unity must be the state. Though politics identifies itself by way of operative distinctions, like the other associations of society, it cannot for that reason be regarded as just another social sphere; it is not just the administrative arm of civil society, according to Schmitt, but something that stands outside of and opposed to it. The primacy of the state preserves the primacy of the political by replicating difference as a plurality of sovereign states on an international scale. On this greater stage, no higher unity, no world state or ultimate sovereign, can exist.

In Schmitt's view, then, the sovereignty of the state as the unity of the difference of civil society serves a higher pluralism, the pluralism of an international order of autonomous states. He starts, in other words, with a unity of difference in order to attain a difference of unities. Liberal pluralism, on the other hand, is misnamed, he believes, because it works in the opposite direction. It too seeks the unity of the difference of associations, but the unity it finds is singular and 'sovereign'. There is no resultant difference of unities, no true pluralism, according to Schmitt, because liberal unity is represented by the ultimate 'monism' of 'humanity'. Whereas the sovereignty of the state is local and plural, and therefore gives rise to legitimate, political contest among sovereign equals, the sovereignty of the ethos of humanity is absolute and incontestable. In the name of individual autonomy and emancipation, liberal pluralism annihilates the space of the political. The 'political world is a pluriverse', Schmitt emphasizes, and if a single world state 'embracing all of humanity' were to appear, foreclosing both conflict and civil war, then what would remain would be 'neither politics nor state' (Schmitt, 1976, p 53), but rather a violence far worse than the structured conflict of politics. What would remain would be the concept of humanity as an 'ideological instrument of imperialist expansion' (Schmitt, 1976, p 54). Used politically, in other words, the term 'humanity' takes the form of a particularly brutal weapon. When one works with distinctions such as those between friend and enemy, good and bad, economic partner and competitor, educated and uneducated, employer and employee, and so on, 'humanity' remains an inconspicuous and unsurpassable horizon within which such distinctions can be drawn. Indeed, 'humanity' as horizon guarantees that both friends and enemies are human, even the good and the bad, the partner and the competitor, the employer and employee. When, however, the term is itself manipulated as one side of a distinction, when, for instance, bourgeois society is contrasted with a future, 'truly human' society, or the purported characteristics of one racial group are stylized as 'ideal types', as it were, then 'humanity' needs a counterpart – it needs the dehumanized and inhuman enemy, the subhuman. Once it is displaced from its position as the horizon of possibility and wielded as a weapon, 'humanity' has to be opposed by its other, and, quite simply, that other cannot be human. As Reinhart Koselleck, building on Schmitt's insights, states:

> The dualistic criteria of distribution between Greek and Barbarian, and between Christian and Heathen [two distinctions he examines], were always related, whether implicitly or explicitly, to *Menschheit* as a totality. To this extent, *Menschheit, genus humanum*, was a presupposition of all dualities that organized *Menschheit* physically, spatially, spiritually, theologically, or temporally. It will now appear that *Menschheit*, up to this point a condition immanent in all dualities, assumes a different quality as soon as it enters into argument as a political reference. The semantic function of distributional concepts alters as soon as a totalising concept – for this is what is involved with *Menschheit* – is brought into political language, which, in spite of its totalising claim, generates polarities. (Koselleck, 1985, p 186)

And so, as Schmitt had already observed, those who fight in the name of humanity are free to deny 'the enemy the quality of being human and declaring him to be an outlaw of humanity; and a war can thereby be driven to the most extreme inhumanity' (Schmitt, 1976, p 54).[11]

The background to Schmitt's complaints is not difficult to reconstruct. His polemic against the 'confiscation' of the word humanity is all part of his critique of the new, post-World War I world order, a critique that only intensifies during the 1930s and after the second war as well. His specific definitions of sovereignty and politics are aimed not just at liberalism in general, but at the particular 20th-century carriers of liberal values, specifically the Anglo-American world led by the United States. Targets of his critique are, for instance, the war guilt clause in the Versailles Treaty, the rehabilitation of the 'just war' doctrine and the Kellogg-Briand Pact of 1928, and the presuppositions behind the creation of both the League of Nations and the United Nations. To put it mildly, revisionist, nationalist, and eventually fascist interests were served by his analyses. Within the political and intellectual framework of the day, to argue against the new international order was clearly perceived to be illiberal, could only be carried out by a critic not afraid of being tarred with the illiberal brush, and could only give aid and comfort to illiberal forces. Furthermore, though the left in the 1930s was illiberal too, anti-internationalist and anti-universalist sentiment could only survive on the right – or, at any rate, could only be exploited on the right. For many present-day critics, then, Schmitt's notorious 'conversion' to the Nazi cause in the spring of 1933 serves to confirm the general trajectory of his thought. Fascist to the core, so the argument goes, Schmitt's notion of the political is to be avoided at all costs. That it has not been avoided, that even leftist, post-Marxist, and poststructuralist theorists, ranging from Kojève to Mouffe to Derrida, have found Schmitt to be of interest, produces an ironic anxiety, one that calls itself Enlightenment, yet one that fears untutored *Mündigkeit*. Accordingly, political philosophers and cultural critics like Jürgen Habermas and Richard Wolin feel compelled to erect a moral prophylaxis around the body of Schmitt's work, encapsulating it in a political isolation ward labeled 'fascism'. To have unprotected intellectual intercourse with this body would, it is feared, irremediably contaminate one, causing, at the very least, an acute onset of neo-conservatism.[12]

That Schmitt's most zealous apologists, on both the right and the left, may fairly be accused of minimizing his most egregious and shameful failings – eg his anti-Semitism and his open attempts to legitimize Hitler's regime in the mid-1930s – is not to be denied. A defensiveness about Schmitt, born of a frustration with inept or deliberate misreadings, can easily turn into polemical aggression. Nevertheless, as tainted as Schmitt's arguments may be, tainted by interest and tainted by affiliation, neither their structure nor their continued relevance can be so simply dismissed. The point, or points, he makes against progressive, universalist doctrines have been made, in various registers, by conservative and leftist critics alike, most recently by French thinkers like Jean-François Lyotard. Schmitt's quarrel with America's post-1917 role as 'arbiter of the world' [*Schiedsrichter der Erde*] (Schmitt, 1988b, p 196) centers on the presumptuous and deceptive nature inherent in any particular instance that designates itself to be the carrier of the universal principle. In Lyotard's view, the particular application of the universal, the particular enunciation of the rights of man, say, or the universal proletariat, always carries with it the potential for terror. Noting the 'aporia of authorization' in the fact that a particular people – his example: the French in 1789 – assumed the position of declaring a universal right, Lyotard asks:

> Why would the affirmation of a universal normative instance have universal value if a singular instance makes the declaration? How can one tell, afterward, whether the wars conducted by the singular instance in the name of the universal instance are wars of liberation or wars of conquest? (Lyotard, 1993, p 52)

Schmitt would recognize these as the right questions to ask; would recognize them, in fact, as his own questions.[13] They go to the heart of the nature and possibility of conflict (which is to say – of politics), for wars conducted in the name of the universal normative instance are wars fought to end all wars, conflicts conducted in the name of the self-transcendence of all conflict. But what if, afterward, we find out that the heaven of consensus and reconciliation turns out to be a realm in which conflict has been outlawed in the name of the Good, the Efficient, the Comfortable? In a world where conflict has been outlawed, how is opposition to be staged? As uncoerced agreement?

It is precisely against this type of outlawry of opposition in the service of the status quo – more accurately, in the service of the unfolding and global expansion of a new type of moral and economic imperialism – that Schmitt launches his counterattack. Since, to his mind, the non-decomposable sovereignty of the autonomous state is the only form of resistance available in the fight against this seemingly relentless expansion, it is to the philosopher of state sovereignty par excellence, Hobbes, that he is drawn. Schmitt's '*Kampf mit Weimar-Genf-Versailles*'[14] is quite explicitly an updated version of an older '*Kampf mit Rom*'. In an interesting and clever move, Schmitt notices that Cole's guild-socialism, Laski's liberalism, and French syndicalism all share arguments and perspectives with the social philosophers of Roman Catholicism as well as those of other churches and sects, arguments that are aimed at relativizing the power of the state (Schmitt, 1988b, pp 153–54). Both the call to follow the dictates of conscience and the more explicit appeal to a higher morality as embodied in international structures (like the League or international revolutionary movements) are political weapons. The battle between 'internationalism' and 'nationalism', then, is fought not simply between the forces of freedom and oppression, but rather between the authority of one type of sovereign power and another. But, Schmitt warns:

> The Roman Catholic Church is no pluralist entity, and in its [the church's] battle against the state, pluralism, at least since the 16th century, is on the side of the national states. A pluralist social theory contradicts itself if it wishes to remain pluralist and still play off the monism and universalism of the Roman Catholic Church, as secularised in the Second or Third International, against the state. (Schmitt, 1988b, p 156)

To repeat: the battle, as he sees it, is between a sham and a true pluralism, between a pluralism in the service of a universal morality (accompanied, not so coincidentally, by a universal economy) and a pluralism in which no contestant can claim the moral high ground. It is the latter, morally neutral pluralism, based on autonomous entities, that best represents the structures and possibilities of a Schmittian form of politics.

We can re-figure this debate in even more classical terms. What Schmitt argues for is a politics commensurable with the conditions found in the Earthly City, and what he argues against is the 'fanaticism' of judging this terrestrial domain with standards only applicable in the City of God. Though his choice of Hobbes and the notion of state sovereignty may be deemed unfortunate and can be contested, his aim is to reconstruct a space of legitimate conflict as a space of secular politics. This space must remain immune to moral and theological infections; the Earthly City must retain a legitimacy that is autonomous from the moral but otherworldly claims of the City of God, claims that can only be redeemed at the end of history – which is to say, not on this earth. Accordingly, his critique of the 'humanism' of modern liberalism is akin to an older critique of religious fanaticism. Despite his Catholicism, Schmitt is much like the Luther who supported the princes, even though he recognized their greed and cruelty, against the prophetic iconoclasts and the Armageddon of the peasant uprisings.[15] The eschatology of religious or secular revolutions are precisely anti-political. They advocate change to outlaw change. They oppose the order of the world in order to welcome the Messiah. Once His arrival is imminent (no matter how long imminence lasts), opposition to the order of the world becomes sin. They wage wars, repeatedly, to end war. They wage wars, but not just any wars; they wage *just* wars. 'They', the particular instance, wage wars in the name of the universal principle, in the name of humanity, outlawing all opposition: as, for example, was attempted in the war guilt clause of the Versailles Treaty, which turned a war of competing national interests into a just war against an unjust enemy; and as was attempted in the Kellogg-Briand Pact of 1928, turning wars in the national interest into crimes, and wars in the interest of the universal principle into crusades. 'Imperialism does not conduct national wars', Schmitt ironically observes, referring to what he sees as the particularly modern, ie legal (*völkerrechtlich*) and economic, form of imperialism conducted by the Anglo-American world; 'at most it conducts wars that serve international politics; it conducts no unjust, only just wars' (Schmitt, 1988b, p 200); or, as Wyndham Lewis was to put it a few years after the Second World War: 'But what war that was ever fought was an "unjust" war, except of course that waged by the enemy?' (Lewis, 1984, p 45).[16]

Sour grapes? To be sure! The great irony of Schmitt's life may very well be that if Germany had won the First World War, he might never have risen above the level of a mediocre apologist for the status quo; for if the more despicable aspects of his thought are fueled by his resentments, so are the most brilliant. As with a whole host of other modern, politically compromised artists, intellectuals, and theorists – Wagner, Pound and Celine come immediately to mind – with Schmitt one cannot cleanly separate the origin of the 'good' from the 'bad'. And even if one were able to, the question regarding the legitimacy of a particular instance wielding the universal principle in an attempt to distinguish unjust from just wars remains. In a sober and interesting examination of this problem, *The Nomos of the Earth* of 1950 (Schmitt 1988a; Schmitt 2003 [English translation]), Schmitt suggestively nudges the issue in the direction of normativity and the highest instance. Just wars, after all, must pit good against evil and thus transcend squalid self-interest. They must be fought in the name of a higher moral order, in other words, and if some national interests (economic or other) happen to coincide with that higher moral purpose, it must be looked upon as mere coincidence – or as a divine reward. Such self-assured self-transcendence may have been possible during the Middle Ages, when absolute standards seemed accessible – at least for saints. But even then, Schmitt remarks, two of the most saintly of medieval saints, St Augustine and St Thomas Aquinas, had their difficulties (Schmitt, 2003, pp 154–55). And now, with the growing agnosticism, scepticism and decisionism of the post-medieval age, attempts to determine just causes become even more arbitrary (Schmitt, 2003, pp 155–56). Just as the 'loss' of transcendence meant the loss of sufficient reason with regard to the determination of the legal and political order within a state, so the 'decisionism' of modernity has affected the international scene as well. Schmitt's notion of sovereignty, then, serves as the focal point for both 'crises', though in diametrically opposed ways. Whereas on the domestic scene the sovereign is the last instance and has no rival, in the international arena there is no such highest or last instance. No sovereign ranks as final arbiter or meta-sovereign over the others. The question on both levels, then, is the same: Who decides? The answer in both instances also remains the same: The sovereign. But the consequences differ. Within the state as between states, the sovereign (ie the decision-making individual or governing body) serves as exclusive and authoritative agent, but in international relations, where a plurality of sovereigns represents a plurality of interests, there is no highest and last instance that stands over two contending parties. Here the fundamental principle of equality among sovereigns rules: '*Par in parem non habet jurisdictionem* [Equals have no jurisdiction over each other]' (Schmitt, 2003, p 157). As no objective, transcendent norm exists to guide judgment, here, as on the domestic scene, only a decisionist answer can be given; but unlike the decision made within the state, on the international scene the conflict caused by a plurality of decisions cannot be resolved by a reigning sovereign. If a conflict arises between two sovereign entities, others line up as friends or enemies. Whoever remains neutral becomes the excluded middle, not the impartial judge, for neutrality does not bring with it the power to ascend to a higher, 'objective' or 'non-partisan' level. If one judges, one participates; and if one participates, one is no longer neutral. On the international scene, no 'Russellian' logical or legal solution to the 'paradox' of the conflict exists (Schmitt, 2003, pp 157–58).

We see that the notion of sovereignty – of ultimate, if 'decisionist', authority – is the linchpin that holds together both the 'top-down' homogeneity of the state and the heterogeneity of a structured plurality of states that guarantees the space of legitimate politics. This self-organizing, pluralist structure depends, however, not just on a logic of autonomy and differentiation, but also on a specific reading of European history that reconstructs an idyllic interlude between two competing universalist doctrines, an interlude that is characterized by the equilibrium of autonomous European nation-states and a limitation of warfare achieved not by moralistic legislation, but by a normalization of conflict. The European civil war of the 16th and 17th centuries signaled, in Schmitt's view, a transfer of power from one universalist doctrine to another. The English war against Spain was a world war between northern and southern Europe, between Calvinist Protestantism and Jesuit Catholicism. Perhaps even more importantly, the conflict of the time was one between two 'world pictures', one continental and land-based, and the other a global vision, based on control of the seas. What eventually emerges from this battle is a form of Anglo-American economic imperialism that is conducted under the banner of civilization, humanity, progress, and pacifism (Schmitt, 1988b, pp 271–72).[17] Though the conquest begins in the 16th century, the new world order only fully emerges in the 20th, in the aftermath of the First World War. During the hiatus or transition period from universal Catholicism to universal (secularized) Protestantism – and Schmitt dates this period precisely, from 1713 to 1914 – a legal and diplomatic system develops which normalizes war, thereby limiting it, and normalizes the friend/enemy distinction, calibrating clearly defined friends and clearly defined enemies with clearly defined states of war and peace.

The actual history or the accuracy of the historiography is not as important to us here as the architectonics of the system described.[18] Expressed in terminology borrowed from Kant, Schmitt argues for a domestic, democratic despotism based on the indivisibility of sovereignty in order to construct an international republican order, one that is to remain immune from the temptation of terror because of its conflictual separation of powers.[19] The immunity against terror lies precisely in this regularization of conflict. In Schmitt's reconstructed history of the 18th and 19th centuries, there is no last instance in the international sphere of action because no sovereign has authority over any other sovereign and no Pope, no international tribunal or organization, is charged with adjudicating disputes. Thus, since no third party or meta-sovereign exists to settle disputes, conflict becomes the *functional equivalent* of sovereignty, the mechanism by which decisions are made in the extreme or exceptional case. However, this vision of the 'sovereignty' of conflict, as chilling as it may seem, is quite the opposite of a Sorelian glorification of violence. Such a regularization of conflict is thought of by Schmitt as a sophisticated means of limiting the effects of conflict. It is viewed as a supreme European achievement, a stage of complex order, briefly reached, then lost again. The following passage, again from *The Nomos of the Earth*, should give an indication of what Schmitt is after:

The essence of European international law was the limitation of war.[20] The essence of such wars was a regulated contest of forces gauged by witnesses in a bracketed space. Such wars are the opposite of disorder. They represent the highest form of order within the scope of human power. They are the only protection against a circle of increasing reprisals, ie, against nihilistic hatreds and reactions whose meaningless goal lies in mutual destruction. The removal and avoidance of wars of destruction is possible only when a form for the gauging of forces is found. This is possible only when the opponent is recognized as a enemy on equal grounds – as a *justus hostis*. This is the given foundation for a limitation of war. (Schmitt, 2003, p 187)[21]

The picture painted here is quixotic at best, wholly unimaginable with regard to contemporary international relations. Not only has the issue of national sovereignty become more or less moot – it only ever held for a minority of European states – but the nature of 20th-century warfare deviates irrevocably from the limits Schmitt desires, not least of all, as Schmitt himself recognized, because of the development of technologically overwhelming means of destruction (Schmitt, 2003, pp 309–22). And finally, the types of quasi-legal, collective, international organizations Schmitt railed against have become the norm. Whether they have been the bane of human civilization as Schmitt contended is certainly open to debate. However, one thing is clear. They have not succeeded in outlawing or banishing war, nor, as recent history amply shows, have their moral exhortations managed to limit the violence exercised on civilian populations. Religious civil wars, wars of 'ethnic cleansing', 'terrorism', and the 'surgical strikes' that inevitably cut away healthy tissue, so to speak, with the diseased seem to have carried the day. Indeed, even those states that blithely see themselves as the carriers of the universal principle have certainly not been innocent of the types of violence they habitually condemn. Perhaps the structure that Schmitt favoured is irretrievable, but this does not necessarily mean that what has replaced it is inevitably superior.[22]

Conflict as a vocation

The value of Schmitt today lies more with the structure of conflict that he outlines than with any attempt to rehabilitate his particular carriers of that structure. We saw that for Schmitt, sovereignty is the linchpin that holds this structure in place. The unity of the state, which is guaranteed by a supra-legal and personified notion of sovereignty, enables the plurality of the world, and thus enables politics. The irony is not lost on us. If politics is marked by the friend/enemy distinction, then *within* the state, politics is not possible. Internal conflict can only be seen as civil war, that is, war designed to undermine sovereignty and thus designed to undermine the structure of politics that the 'pillar' of the state supports. Schmitt's logic starts with a simple presupposition: what is to be avoided is the hegemony of a single system. As he puts it, 'As long as a state exists, there will thus always be in the world more than just one state. A world state which embraces the entire globe and all of humanity cannot exist' (Schmitt, 1976, p 53). 'World', then, must be the horizon that enables a plurality of systems, not the unity of that plurality. 'World' is not 'world-system'. But his state is no microcosm of the world; there is no self-similarity, no internal replication of the differentiation required on the international scene. From a perspective that represents itself as liberal and democratic, this homogenization and pacification of the state is the great flaw of Schmitt's grand design. He postulates the necessity of two levels, one 'domestic' (or internal to the state) and the other 'foreign' (or between states), and assumes that politics can only exist on the higher level, that a uniformity and suppression of politics must exist within the state for politics to exist anywhere at all. Schmitt could not see a structure of differentiation carried by a unity that itself was structured by differentiation. This, then, becomes our challenge. If we accept conflict as the basic definition of politics, and if we take seriously the claim that the old European system of delimited warfare represents 'the highest form of order of which humans are capable' – if, in other words, emergent order trumps planning – then it becomes necessary to extend his 'logic' of conflict, to 're-enter' his friend/enemy distinction within the state, *without* thereby collapsing the grander structure he outlines.

But beyond merely replicating the order of differentiation, there is a second complication. We no longer deal with the historical reality (or fantasy) of nation-states. The battle between the plurality of sovereign states and the plurality of associations has been won by the latter. States still exist, of course, but the modernization process rarely yields to their border guards. Systemic boundaries cut through spatial and political ones, and we watch the world sub-divide into autonomous and equal social systems: economics, religion, science, education, morality, art, even politics. Thus, the structure we face is parallel to, but not the same as, the structure of state and international relations as described by Schmitt. Indeed, what we are looking at is the structure of modernity as the differentiation of social systems, and so we ask how these systems are to be ordered. Is there, or should there be, a single system – economics, say, or morality – that stands in a meta-sovereign relation to the rest? Is there, or should there be, a 'league' of systems – the allied systems of economics, morality, and religion? – that can assume the role of impartial yet adjudicatory neutrality? If one says no, or wishes to say no, then one asks what ordering principle can be used. To order them by reason would be to assume that the traditional role of philosophy or the scientific system rules all others; would, in fact, betray a naive belief that reason orders rather than divides.[23] To order them by norms would be to assume that morality or law or perhaps religion rules. In such cases, the horizontal ordering that one starts with reverts to an implicit or explicit hierarchy. But if we assume that equilibrial difference can only be achieved as a difference of unities, a heterogeneity based on homogeneity, then the continuous intellectual challenge becomes one of re-entering difference within unity, of opening our operational black boxes to reveal the existence of further, lower level black boxes. Thus, if we are to assume the same field of pluralist anarchy within the state that Schmitt wished to reconstruct on a global scale, then we must envision political and social structures that freely acknowledge the ordering and civilizing power of antagonism. It remains an intriguing task to think of society's channeled political and cultural battles not as disturbances to be excluded, but as an organizational achievement of the highest order.

Such a structure of discrete, precise and insurmountable disagreement has been traced in a succinct and quasi-logical form by Lyotard, for, as we know, Lyotard's vision of modernity is based on the necessity of difference, and thus on the necessity of conflict. In the face of the irremediable differentiation of modern society into incommensurable value spheres, language games, or social systems, Lyotard does not ask how a functional equivalent for unity can be achieved in order to proceed politically – as Habermas does – but rather, how to proceed politically in the face of the impossibility, even undesirability, of any re-established harmony. In his Preface to *The Differend*, Lyotard presupposes two features of our present predicament: '(1) the impossibility of avoiding conflicts (the impossibility of indifference) and (2) the absence of a universal genre of discourse to regulate them (or, if you prefer, the inevitable partiality of the judge)' (Lyotard, 1988, p xii). Lyotard's juridical definition of a differend follows from these presuppositions. 'A case of differend between two parties', he writes, 'takes place when the "regulation" of the conflict that opposes them is done in the idiom of one of the parties while the wrong suffered by the other is not signified in that idiom' (Lyotard, 1988, p 9). Not all conflicts result in a differend, but conflicts between incommensurable idioms – between competing values, between operationally closed or autonomous social systems – necessarily exclude the conciliatory third term, the reconciliation of opposites magnanimously offered by the superior neutrality of a universal discourse. 'The idea', according to Lyotard,

> that a supreme genre encompassing everything that's at stake could supply a supreme answer to the key-questions of the various genres founders upon Russell's aporia. Either this genre is part of the set of genres, and what is at stake in it is but one among others, and therefore its answer is not supreme. Or else, it is not part of the set of genres, and it does not therefore encompass all that is at stake, since it excepts what is at stake in itself. ... The principle of an absolute victory of one genre over the others has no sense. (Lyotard, 1988, p 138)

Thus, consciousness of a differend necessitates the view that the third term merely becomes the first term of a new conflict, a new opposition or irreconcilable difference. It cannot remain immune from antagonism under the pretense of a meta-level and thereby superior neutrality. Whether desirable or not, conflict is inevitable, and resolution of conflict is a matter of decision, not a matter of sublation. All adjudications of disputes are simultaneously declarations of a new war.

Decisions are not thereby rendered arbitrary, but once the ineluctability of decision is acknowledged, the question of what regulates decision in the absence of logical necessity becomes pre-eminently political, contestable, and arguable. For Lyotard, the type of indeterminate judgment that is called for by the Kantian Idea guides decision, thus political judgments are of a different order than cognitive ones. A political decision always entails 'a reflective use of judgment, that is, a maximization of concepts outside of any knowledge of reality. So, the alternative is not a choice between a rational politics and a politics of opinion' (Lyotard and Thébaud, 1985, p 75). Rather, the alternative is between a politics that denies its own political character – a politics that, once in power, denies its own constitution, so to speak, by claiming to *know* the qualities of a just society – and a politics that sees itself as a field of battle in which contending parties are never fully consumed by victories and defeats, and thus are never fully reconciled. Indeed, Lyotard explicitly identifies this condition of un-reconciled plurality as the space of the political. 'Politics', he writes, 'is the threat of the differend'. It is not a 'genre', but rather:

> the multiplicity of genres, the diversity of ends, and par excellence the question of linkage. ... It is, if you will, the state of language, but it is not a language. Politics consists in the fact that language is not a language, but phrases, or that Being is not Being, but There is's. (Lyotard, 1988, p 138)

Accordingly, politics cannot compensate for the lack of unity, but rather, by being its effect, *guarantees* this lack. It does not repress violence in the name of the good life; it structures and limits it. As Richard Beardsworth has emphasized in his examination of *Derrida and the Political*, politics does not avoid, in the name of law or consensus, the forcible exclusions that come with all choice, but rather recognizes the necessity as well as the necessarily violent nature of decision. Indeed, the recognition of the necessity of decision forces a decision about decision. '[G]iven this irreducibility of a decision', Beardsworth writes, 'there are different kinds of decisions – those that recognize their legislative and executive force and those which hide it under some claim to naturality *qua* "theory" or "objective science"' (Beardsworth, 1996, p 12). The violence of a decision, then, can be acknowledged and reflected, or it can remain unthought. Decisions can recognize that they agonistically constitute a field within a contingent universe (since it is contingency that necessitates choice among competing possibilities),[24] or decisions can represent themselves as passive reflections of a pre-constituted reality, as if knowledge of a given order, a Straussian state of nature or the destiny of world history, preceded and thus dictated our observation of it. Decisions, in other words, can reflexively affirm their status as decisions, or they can silently deny their contingency and assume the gesture of logical subsumption. For Derrida and Lyotard, as for Schmitt, it is the unthought violence of this latter possibility that poses the greater danger, the violence that camouflages itself as innocent neutrality or universal reconciliation. It is a violence that masks itself as peace and hence criminalizes opposition.

This brief exposé of 'postmodernism' (a postmodernism, by the way, that turns out to be an apology for the modernization process)[25] also reviews some of the essentials of Schmitt's position, even if the sovereignty of the state never makes an appearance. Lyotard's language games or genres translate almost effortlessly into a variety of other pluralities, from Cole's and Laski's associations to Weber's value spheres and Parsons' and Luhmann's social systems. But unlike Cole and Laski (or unlike Schmitt's reading of them, at least), and like Weber and Luhmann (or like *my* reading of them), there is no 'humanity', no 'language' or comprehensive meta-system that serves as the unity of the plurality of 'There is's'. The 'postmodernism' of a Lyotard, the 'ultra-modernism' of a Luhmann, and the 'anti-modernism' of a Schmitt all find themselves on common ground, for, as Albrecht Wellmer has observed, 'the critique of the modern, inasmuch as it knows its own parameters, can only aim at expanding the interior space of modernity, not at surpassing it' (Wellmer, 1991, p vii). The configuration of this ever-expanding 'interior space' is relentlessly reproduced as the differentiation of autonomous and antagonistic unities, now best described *not* as sovereign states, but as operationally closed function systems. The differentiation of systems that is modernity dictates that the description of differentiation must also paradoxically become a political imperative.

Luhmann's theory of modernity is a celebration, as it were, of the victory of associations and therefore, at first glance, should be diametrically opposed to Schmitt's attempts to save modernity from itself. Since, for Luhmann, the notion of the state simply serves as the self-description of the political system,[26] and since that system is placed in a non-hierarchical order with all the others, the state can neither stand opposed to civil society, nor function as the unity of its difference. Thus, as Schmitt feared, the state participates in civil society; or, since the notion of civil society loses its oppositional and, therefore, political meaning, the state participates in functional differentiation. Similarly, though the rule of law is as logically impossible as ever, it is so firmly ensconced as the only viable principle of government in liberal democracy, that the problem of derivation, even of definition, can be cavalierly avoided. The rule of law rules performatively, it enacts its own sovereignty, such that it is not even mentioned, as Luhmann points out, as the principle on which the state is founded in the constitution of the Federal Republic of Germany. To so include 'an additional conceptual determination of the state as one founded on law would be superfluous and confusing' – superfluous, because the very fact of a constitution signals such a foundation; and confusing, because it would needlessly raise the logically thorny issue of tautology and self-reference (Luhmann, 1990a, p 187). The self-organization of society (Schmitt's as well as Luhmann's term) sovereignly replaces state sovereignty, with the effect that we have an autonomous legal system and an autonomous political system, along with the economy, religion, science, pedagogy and the like; and these systems stand in an independent relationship to each other. By way of operational closure they develop such high levels of internal complexity that they sensitize themselves to 'perturbations' and 'irritations' coming from the outside, coming from the other systems of society, for instance (Luhmann, 1990a, p 197). But despite these mutual irritations – or perhaps because of them – they do not stand in any sort of dominant or subordinate relationship to each other. Like Weber's value spheres, they stand under the injunction to legitimate themselves, even if self-legitimation must take the form of an 'originary' paradox.[27] They do not receive their legitimation from 'above' or 'outside'.

Here, then, is where the political (or 'meta-political') conflict begins and ends. On the level of 'associations' we have the structure that Schmitt sketched out as the clash of sovereign states. Just as there is for Schmitt no overarching, 'meta-sovereign' or third term to adjudicate disputes among nations, so for Luhmann there can be no system nor 'league' of systems that can dictate the 'domestic' or 'foreign policy' of any of the other systems.

Again, as with Schmitt, the linchpin is autonomy. Recall that for Schmitt, the sovereign state served a dual purpose, guaranteeing unity on the one hand in order to guarantee difference on the other. For Luhmann, the autonomy or operational closure of social systems serves a similar purpose, for functional differentiation can only be the differentiation of autonomous entities. However, the 'unity' or identity of the system, unlike the Schmittian state, cannot be imposed from above. On the contrary, the system – including the 'state' as political system – reproduces itself by way of difference. As Luhmann's bird's-eye view of the historical progression has it, in the Middle Ages the sovereign (the 'lord') was seen as part of the natural order (the 'logical' order, one might say). The European civil wars disturbed this natural order, requiring the Hobbesian solution, ie, the absolute sovereign as the arbitrary (no longer logically determined) origin of legality. In both instances, unity (sovereignty) reigned at the top, for the operative distinction was simply the protection-for-obedience contract between the (undivided) government and the governed. Modernity, on the other hand, can only be characterized by a bifurcation, a difference, where the sovereign once reigned. The 'sovereign', ie government, is now divided, in that a government/opposition distinction operates within government, a binary code that legitimizes politics within, not just between, states. It is this 'bifurcation at the top' that determines the identity of the modern political system (Luhmann, 1990a, pp 169–71).[28] 'Every code', Luhmann writes,

> has a positive value that symbolizes the system's capacity to continue. ... It also has a negative, counter value that symbolizes that things could also have been different. This upholds the contingency of the system in spite of its constant reduction by continuous operations. It is not difficult to see that this is true even in the case of the distinction of government/opposition. Only the government can continue to act officially within the political system. Only the government has legitimately applicable political power at its disposal. Only the government is a component of the distinction of those who govern/those who are governed. On the other side, only the opposition guarantees continual reflection and the constant presence of a mirror in which one can see that things could also be otherwise or had possibly been otherwise. (Luhmann, 1990a, p 177)

What marks modern, parliamentary democracies, then, are the institutional and organizational carriers of opposition – political parties, for instance – that can act alternately as placeholders of stability and placeholders of contingency (Luhmann, 1990a, p 173). 'Ever since the establishment of this distinction [government/opposition], the political system has not been controlled by unity but by a difference, a top that is bifurcated' (Luhmann, 1990a, p 174).

Thus, we have the autonomy of the political system, continually reproduced 'politically', that is, by way of the difference or conflict between government and opposition. This 'autonomy of difference', then, serves as the carrier of a higher-order 'difference of autonomies', namely, the differentiation of autonomous social systems. The lower-order unity required to carry this latter, higher-order difference is itself also carried by a difference of unities. Conflict, in other words, is grounded in conflict – all the way down and all the way up. How, then, is this highly improbable and fragile order to be preserved? This, too, is a political question – not one posed within the political system, but a question concerning 'the political'. What Luhmann describes as the distinction between government and opposition may seem banal, certainly seems boring, a thoroughly unexciting domestication of the friend/enemy distinction. What he describes are the daily operations of liberal democracies, the manoeuvrings of 'government' and the manoeuvrings of 'opposition' who would like to be 'government', manoeuvrings, by the way, that result in the 'binding decisions' that are the outcomes of the political system and, thus, the perturbations that irritate other systems. All of this is 'politics' in an administrative sense. But what makes politics possible, and what politics makes possible, is functional differentiation as the organizing principle of modernity. 'As long as society as a whole was ordered hierarchically according to the principle of stratificatory differentiation', Luhmann writes, as if responding directly to Schmitt,

> such a bifurcation of the top was inconceivable or had been associated with experiences like schisms and civil wars, ie disorder and calamity. Only if society is structured so that, as society, it no longer needs a top but is arranged non-hierarchically into function systems is it possible for politics to operate with a top that is bifurcated. (Luhmann, 1990a, p 233)

The 'political' (or 'meta-political') imperative par excellence, therefore, becomes the difficult preservation of difference by way of observation. The task is paradoxical at best. No 'sovereign' position can oversee differentiation in order to preserve it, without, by the very fact of its existence, collapsing the structure it is charged with protecting. There is no all-encompassing unity of society that enables its difference – no 'Being', only 'There is's'. The 'world' remains a horizon, not a vantage point, and 'the highest form of order of which humans are capable' remains precarious.

As Luhmann carefully acknowledges, this order is protected both by and from distinctions. Distinctions can always be observed by yet further distinctions. Always present is the ability to judge the established code morally, to accept or reject it. So too with the political code, though this has its consequences. 'If the binary code of government/opposition is accepted as "democracy", then all attempts at a transition to an additional distinction in terms of acceptance/rejection of the primary distinctions are "undemocratic".' This second, superimposed distinction, then, 'becomes sovereign and can be practiced in all directions – thus as a rejection of the distinction of governed/opposition by the government that still continues to govern' (Luhmann, 1990a, p 175). In simpler terms, this super-distinction defines a *coup*, precisely the kind Schmitt hopes to ward off with his notion of sovereignty, but also precisely the kind that would inevitably result from an application of his notion of sovereignty. Thus, Luhmann presupposes a liberal-democratic order.[29] His analysis does not apply to the 'post-democratic case', nor to 'a political terror from below that no longer distinguishes between those who govern and those who are governed but thinks everyone is evil (except themselves)' (Luhmann, 1990a, p 176) – an extreme case, to be sure, and a hyperbolic barb aimed at the '68-generation, but a case that nevertheless resembles the 'fanaticism' of civil wars that so scared both Hobbes and Schmitt. What prevents 'fanaticism' in the modern world, however, is not the undivided sovereign, but the sovereignty of division. There are no coronations here, for this modern form of 'sovereignty' cannot be represented; it can only be reproduced as a distinction, as the 'threat of the differend', inasmuch as each system reproduces its own autonomy. The old 'illusion' of 'reconciliation' that Lyotard identifies with 'terror' reveals itself to be the very real threat of de-differentiation. To combat this threat, Luhmann targets 'politicians with Mosaic pretensions' (Luhmann, 1990a, p 233) and those 'drunk with morality' (Luhmann, 1990a, p 237), precisely because they wish to collapse the political friend/enemy distinction, one that assigns equally legitimate roles to government and opposition, and replace it with a moral friend/enemy distinction that can only envision the total destruction of the 'evil' enemy and thus the system that allows this enemy to have a voice. To collapse the moral and the political codes is to subordinate the political to the moral. Once one has done that, the whole structure of differentiation is in jeopardy. Not only is the conflict within the system outlawed, but also that among the systems, for universal morality always results in 'reconciliation', whether one wants it or not. Such 'outlawry' never operates neutrally; such 'reconciliation' always camouflages a differend and masquerades as peace.

*

Though the terrain of Luhmann's modernity is different from the *nomos* Schmitt commemorates, and the battle is over the autonomy of systems and not the sovereignty of states, the enemies are the same. What for Hobbes and Schmitt were the threats of universalism (whether represented by the Roman Catholic Church and the Protestant conscience, or by the Anglo-American maritime 'church' and the humanist ethos) is for Lyotard the terror of reconciliation and for Luhmann the threat of de-differentiation. Contrary to most political theories of the past century or two, which have argued precisely *for* de-differentiation, all of our contestants – Schmitt, Lyotard, Luhmann – recognize that the political depends on preserving a structure of difference. Oddly, their appreciation of differentiation goes against some well-ingrained impulses. Our collective reflex seems still to dictate that we should despise alienation, reification, rationalization, the division of labour. We habitually seem still to long for consensus and community, *Versöhnung*, a civic religion – if not, in fact, for a genuinely transcendent, or at least secular and revolutionary, salvation religion. And we still seem to dream of the total pacification of the globe, to dream of the day when the lion will lie down with the lamb, despite the persistent howling of wolves. Perhaps some day we will get our wish, though God's or History's instrument may be more economic than moral. Differentiation may not be as resilient or inevitable as its pessimistic critics sometimes make it out to be. There is – there can be – no sovereign to watch over and protect differentiation, only the multiple battles for autonomy. Description is our only prescription. One wonders, though: If the order that sustains these conflicts is lost, devoured by efficiency and *Gesinnung*, will we eventually come to remember it as fondly as Schmitt once remembered the *jus publicum Europaeum*?

Notes

1   The joke is actually that of a 'Dutch innkeeper'. See Kant, 1970, p 93.

2   The most thorough treatment of Schmitt's relation to Weber is, of course, Ulmen, 1991. See also McCormick, 1998, and Colliot-Thélène, 1999.

3   Given Strauss's famous distinction between exoteric and esoteric teachings, however, the possibility always exists that Leo Strauss is no Leo Strauss either. For a provocative, but unconvincing, attempt to construct Schmitt and Strauss as matching bookends (political theology/political philosophy; Jerusalem/Athens), see Meier, 1995. On Schmitt's gradual estrangement from the Catholic Centre Party and from the Catholic intellectuals associated with the journal *Hochland*, including some of his most devoted followers (eg Waldemar Gurian), see Bendersky, 1983, pp 178–79, 185–86, 189, 224–26, 229.

4   'Kelsen solved the problem of the concept of sovereignty by negating it. ... That is in fact the old liberal negation of the state vis-à-vis law and the disregard of the independent problem of the realization of law' (Schmitt, 1985b, p 21).

5   For a more detailed analysis of *Gesetz und Urteil* along these lines, see Balke, 1996, and Rasch, 2000a.

6   We are, of course, approaching territory that Hannah Arendt explored late in her life. See especially the second lecture in Arendt, 1982, pp 10–16.

7   Schmitt gives a characterization of the liberal argument in Schmitt, 1993a, p 15. See also Scheuerman, 1994, pp 102–04.

8   On the 'force' and 'violence' of law, see Derrida, 1992, pp 6, 13–16; see also Luhmann 1990a, pp 193–96.

9   That 'rationalization' and 'democratization' (ie 'modernization') increases and distributes rather than eliminates decisions is a point made by Luhmann, 1981, pp 344–47.

10 On the medieval distinction between 'intellectualism' and 'voluntarism', from which the above analysis is drawn, and its afterlife in early-modern moral and political theory, see Schneewind, 1998, pp 17–36, as well as the chapters on Grotius, Hobbes and Pufendorf.

11 Again, Koselleck, 1985, p 193: 'The totalizing concept of *Menschheit*, once applied politically, gave rise to totalitarian consequences.' Ironically, Schmitt's use of the term 'inhumanity' indicates that once the concept is deployed politically, no critique can bring us back to a state of innocence.

12 For Habermas's tendency to regard all critiques of universalist morality as neoconservative, see his 'Neoconservative Cultural Criticism in the United States and West Germany' in Habermas, 1989, pp 22–47, esp pp 41–42, and Habermas,

1981. For examples of his battle against any reconsideration of Schmitt's thought, see 'The Horrors of Autonomy: Carl Schmitt in English', in Habermas, 1989, pp 128–39, and 'Carl Schmitt in the Political Intellectual History of the Federal Republic', in Habermas, 1997a, pp 107–17. Richard Wolin's critique centers on Schmitt's purported decisionism, for Wolin is eager to read neo-Nietzschean and *lebensphilosophische* overtones in the word. From there, the step to Heideggerian *Existenzphilosophie* and the proto-fascism of the conservative revolutionaries (Jünger, Spengler, Moeller van den Brock) is almost automatic. See his 'Carl Schmitt, Political Existentialism, and the Total State' in Wolin, 1992, pp 83–104, and 'Carl Schmitt: The Conservative Revolution and the Aesthetics of Horror' in Wolin, 1995, pp 103–22. See also Löwith, 1995, in the volume of Löwith's essays edited by Wolin. Schmitt's affiliation with the conservative revolutionaries is disputed by Bendersky, 1983, pp 57–58, and Bendersky, 1987; and his supposed 'decisionism' is discussed by Hirst, 1987. In the US, a leftist reception of Schmitt has been energetically promoted in the journal *Telos*. See, for example, the special issues #72 (Summer 1987) and #109 (Fall 1996), but reference to Schmitt abounds in many other volumes as well. For examples of a 'poststructuralist' reception of Schmitt, see Derrida, 1997, Mouffe, 1993, Mouffe, 1999, and Agamben, 1998. Finally, for dispassionate, intellectual biographies of Schmitt that, among other virtues, attempt to trace Schmitt's turn to the Nazi party in the spring of 1993 without resorting to wholesale condemnation or apology, see Noack, 1996, and Bendersky, 1983. The former places greater faith in a conversion narrative to explain Schmitt's turn to the Nazis in 1933 while the latter attributes Schmitt's shift of loyalties to the Nazi state to a combination of arrogance, fear and opportunism.

13 In a sense, they both re-open Lessing's speculations about the relationship between contingent, historical truths and universal, rational ones by translating his theological question into a political one. Needless to say, neither Lyotard's nor Schmitt's answer is Lessing's. See Lessing, 1957, p 53.

14 Part of the title of Schmitt, 1988b.

15 In addition to Schneewind, 1998, see Colas, 1997. Her discussions of Luther are found in chapters 3 and 4; her (mis)characterization of Schmitt (pp 324, 344), however, seems to be based more on hearsay than on an actual reading of the relevant texts.

16 See also Davidson, 1998, pp 271–98, and Davidson, 1997, p 590, in which he writes: 'In major conflicts, it is obviously true that to be successfully indicted as aggressor or a war criminal one must first lose the war. No victor is likely to call himself by such names or to submit to an international court (nor does one exist) where he would be answerable to such charges – the aggressors must be members of the defeated nation. This holds true for the commission of war crimes and crimes against humanity; such crimes can only be committed by members of the losing side.' Since 'just wars' and the hunt for 'war criminals' are breaking out all over the post-Cold War world, a renewed discussion of the issue may well be in order. Walzer, 1992, offers us a handy field guide for spotting unjust wars, but since the issue of power (ie winners and losers) is never addressed, we are left in the dark about what we are to do when we see such a creature in the wild. For a Schmittian perspective, see Quaritsch's 'Nachwort' to Schmitt, 1994b.

17 The basic distinction between land-based and maritime powers is outlined in popular fashion in Schmitt, 1993b, which can, in fact, be read as a political counterpart to Heidegger's famous *Weltbild* essay.

18 For a recent survey of warfare and its social effects in the 17th and 18th centuries, see Anderson, 1998.

19 Here again, the 'postmodern' form to this claim is provided by Lyotard, 1993, pp 15–16, who admonishes us not to 'expect the slightest reconciliation between "language games". Kant, in naming them the faculties, knew that they are separated by an abyss and that only a transcendental illusion (Hegel's) can hope to totalize them into a real unity. But he also knew that the price of this illusion is terror'.

20 Translation modified. The German phrase *'Hegung des Krieges'* (Schmitt, 1988a, p 158) is translated in Schmitt, 2003, as 'bracketing of war'. With this phrase Schmitt refers to the 'containment' or 'limitation' of war. That is, Schmitt has the distinction between a 'limited' and a 'total' war in mind, a much-discussed issue between the two World Wars. (See, for instance, Nickerson, 1934.) I prefer, therefore, to translate the phrase as 'limitation of war'.

21 Mid-century British military historians made similar claims. See, for instance, Liddell Hart, 1946, p 45: 'The improvement made during the eighteenth century in the customs of war, and in reducing its evils, forms one of the great achievements of civilization.' See also Fuller, 1968, pp 15–41. One must remind oneself, however, that such claims count only for warfare among European states and not warfare between Europeans and the non-European world. See below, Chapter 8.

22 Though Jürgen Habermas clearly thinks so. See his explicit critique of Schmitt's views in Habermas, 1997b, and the discussion of Habermas below, Chapter 2.

23 See, for instance, Larmore, 1996, p 12: '... on matters of supreme importance, reason is not likely to bring us together, but tends rather to drive us apart.'

24 On decision-making and contingency, see Luhmann, 1995, pp 294–98, and Luhmann, 1981, pp 337–39, 344–46.

25 The conservative, German philosopher, Odo Marquard, sums up the relationship between postmodernity and modernity as follows: 'What comes after the postmodern? In my opinion, the modern. The formula "postmodernity" is either an anti-modernist or a pluralist slogan. As an anti-modernist slogan, it is a dangerous illusion, for doing away with the modern world is in no way desirable. As a pluralist slogan, it affirms an old and respectable modernist motif. The modern world is and always has been rationalization and pluralization' (Marquard, 1989, p 7). See also Keane, 1992, p 91: '[P]ostmodernism of the type defended by Lyotard does not constitute a radical (or even mediated) break with the modernization process, but instead a dialectical intensification of its democratic impulses.'

26 'The state, then, is not a subsystem of the political system. It is not the public bureaucracy. It is not only the legal fiction of a collective person to which decisions are attributed. It is the political system reintroduced into the political system as a point of reference for political action' (Luhmann, 1990b, p 166).

27 The reference is to Weber's discussion of the necessarily ungrounded presuppositions of science, medicine, law, etc in Weber, 1946, pp 143–46.

28 For a more extensive treatment, see Luhmann, 1989.

29 Conservative Schmittians, then, would have to see Luhmann, like Habermas, as a product of the Americanization of Germany. What distinguishes him from Habermas, however – that is, besides his theory design – is his renunciation of reason and rational or moral normative grounding. For an irate, near hysterical (if entertaining) critique of Habermas as the most radical representative of 're-education' culture, see Maschke, 1987, pp 115–64.

Chapter 2
A just war? Or just a war?
Schmitt vs Habermas

Germany: A Winter's Tale I

I like to think of Jürgen Habermas as the Rhine River – not *in* the Rhine, nor *on* it, but *as* the Rhine. More precisely, I see him as the muttering and sighing Father Rhine of Heinrich Heine's *Deutschland. Ein Wintermärchen* [*Germany: A Winter's Tale*]. In 1843, after 13 years' exile in France, Heine returns home to Germany, to Cologne, among other cities, and engages in conversation with his beloved river. Father Rhine complains about the turn of political events, specifically about the nationalist appropriations of his image by hack poets, and worries that they may compromise him politically if the French were ever to return – a return, by the way, that he longs and prays for.

Ich habe sie immer so lieb gehabt,	[I was always so fond of them,
Die lieben kleinen Französchen –	Those lovable little French –]

he tells Heine, and then asks:

Singen und springen sie noch wie sonst?	[Do they sing and dance like they used to,
Tragen noch weiße Höschen?	Still wear little white pants?]

Heine can reassure him – though this reassurance must surely sting – that politically he has nothing to fear, for the new French, well:

Sie sind die alten Franzosen nicht mehr,	[They are not the same old French any more,
Auch tragen sie andere Hosen	And they wear different pants]

Worse still:

Sie philosophieren und sprechen jetzt	[They philosophize and talk now
Von Kant, von Fischte und Hegel,	Of Kant, of Fishte and Hegel,
Sie rauchen Tabak, sie trinken Bier,	They smoke tobacco, they drink beer,
Und manche schieben auch Kegel.	And some even go bowling.]

(Heine, 1997, pp 588, 589 [Caput V, v 41–44, 59–60, 65–68])[1]

I see Habermas as Father Rhine because he too is nostalgic for the old, clear-eyed, eloquent, and simply enlightened French in their optimistic and spotless white pants. Furthermore, as the quasi-official, philosophical spokesperson for the postwar Federal Republic of Germany, symbolized by the Rhenish town of Bonn, Habermas sees himself as one of the mechanisms by which this re-educated and republican Germany has been integrated into the order of the West. Such integration, in Habermas's view, necessitates a transfer of loyalties from the particular traditions and histories of the nation-state to the rational and universally valid truths of natural law and morality. The exceptionality of local history, particularly the notorious *Sonderweg* of German history, is held up as the negative example that potentially results from all critiques of the universalist ethos and the rights of man. Consequently, one is enjoined to renounce one's affiliation and identification with the specifically German (or, for that matter, the specifically French) and become, instead, a cosmopolitan citizen of the world. However, much like Father Rhine before him, Habermas, over the past few decades, has had to watch not only the Germans, but also the French, become more German again, though the talk now on the left bank is of Nietzsche and Heidegger. Thus, Habermas is engaged in a two-front war against what he calls neo-conservatism in Germany and (following Manfred Frank) neo-structuralism in France. Armed, like Father Rhine, with wistful memories of an older France, Habermas stands poised to beat back the twin devils besieging him from both the right and the left.

Needless to say, others see the situation otherwise. In their introduction to a volume of essays entitled *Terror and Consensus: Vicissitudes of French Thought*, Jean-Joseph Goux and Philip R Wood declare war on a decade-old '"normalization" of French society' that is 'characterized by the "consensus" that has emerged around the fundamental values of "the West" – democracy, liberal capitalism, and human rights. This process', they go on to say, 'has included the attenuation of the avant-garde in the arts, the decline of the kind of intellectual figure exemplified by Sartre, and a systematic assault on the last representatives of the philosophical avant-garde', by which they mean Derrida, Foucault, Lyotard *et al* (Goux and Wood, 1998, p 1). In a separate essay included in the volume, Wood sees the 'assault on post-structuralism' and the attempt to 'normalize' French thought 'as simply one more instance of that complex, ongoing struggle over the progressive alignment of France with the transnational capitalist order of the European Union and the broader global system the latter represents' (Goux and Wood, 1998, p 78). To ears accustomed to the polemical terminology of contemporary German debates, Goux and Wood's use of the term 'normalization' sounds odd. If, in their view, the neo-liberal Habermas stands as the philosophical representative par excellence of universalist and capitalist normalization, in Habermas's vocabulary, normalization stands for the attempt of neoconservative critics to make German history acceptable again – for instance, by denying the uniqueness of the Holocaust – and therefore making German history worthy of national, if not nationalist, identification. Paradoxically, then, the particular uniqueness of the Holocaust, and, thus, the exceptionality of German guilt, must be preserved as the rationale for Habermas's universal, normative standard, a standard which, at the same time, must relativize, must 'normalize', what Goux and Wood call the 'French exception' (Goux and Wood, 1998, pp 1, 78). The necessary relationship of the German exception to the type of neo-liberal normalization that is represented not only by the European Union, but by the order of the entire postwar 'West', is implicitly recognized by Wood when he explicitly denies the uniqueness of the Holocaust (Goux and Wood, 1998, p 102) and asserts that, 'for Heidegger and Derrida, both Nazi and communist totalitarianism were merely variations of a larger cultural space that constituted the West as a whole in a continuity with the Greeks and the Christian tradition' (Goux and Wood, 1998, p 103). With these odd convergences and crossings – the French exception denying the German exception, the German exception upholding the exception of the West, which, in turn, presents itself not as an exception, but as the universal norm that must deny the French exception – is it any wonder that clear distinctions between left and right seem to be increasingly difficult to draw? Is it any wonder, in other words, that Carl Schmitt finds himself increasingly at home on both sides of the Rhine?

Ah, but thank God, one can almost hear Habermas say, thank God for the Atlantic! What Habermas has, that neither Father Rhine nor Heine had, is the United States. What Habermas has, in other words, is the moral and, not so incidentally, economic universalism, backed by military coercion, that characterizes the American presence in world politics since the time of Woodrow Wilson. 'It is difficult to think of Carl Schmitt', Habermas wrote in 1986, 'in the context of Anglo-Saxon discussions', adding: 'I do not think that Carl Schmitt will have a similar power of contagion in the Anglo-Saxon world' (Habermas, 1989, pp 128, 135). Habermas miscalculated. As is by now well known, the New World has not remained immune, despite the efforts of some of our most enlightened spiritual physicians, and we have become at least somewhat infected – so much so, in fact, that some critics have treated the journal *Telos* like an open, running sore (eg Holub, 1997). But Habermas is right in looking to what Goux and Wood call 'the West', that is, the Anglo-Saxon norm, in his opposition to the exception of the rest. His confidence that his philosophical interests are in harmony with the interests of a universalist *Weltgeist* and a United Nations based on that *Geist* is reminiscent of our own self-confident, post-World War II celebrations of the 'American century'. It is thus appropriate that Habermas's most detailed *Auseinandersetzung* with Schmitt revolves around notions of perpetual peace, just wars, and an international order that is designed to ensure the former by conducting the latter. It is this debate that I wish to examine here.

The world state

Jürgen Habermas's essay, 'Kant's Idea of Perpetual Peace, with the Benefit of Two Hundred Years' Hindsight', was written for a conference held in Frankfurt in 1995 to commemorate the 200th anniversary of the publication of Kant's 'Perpetual Peace: A Philosophical Sketch' (Kant, 1970, pp 93–130), as well as the 50th anniversary of the end of World War II and the founding of the United Nations, two events that are seen by the conferees as steps toward the fulfillment of Kant's dream. The debate that unfolds among the various German, American and English participants does not center on whether 'perpetual peace' is a worthy goal, or even whether Kant's 'cosmopolitan ideal' is the correct means by which that goal could be achieved. Rather, the discussants assume the validity of both the utopian end and the liberal means to that end, and only differ on the way the cosmopolitan law can best be implemented. The terms of the debate are Kant's. In his earlier 'Theory/Practice' essay (Kant, 1970, pp 61–92), Kant had argued for the eventual necessity of a 'world state' in order to tame the lawless state of nature that exists among rival nations. Eventually, however, he came to fear the potential of a 'soulless despotism' arising from such a single global government and therefore advocated, in 'Perpetual Peace', a confederation of sovereign states with republican constitutions, 'each of which respects the basic rights of its citizens and establishes a public sphere in which people can regard themselves and others as free and equal "citizens of the world"' (Bohman and Lutz-Bachmann, 1997, p 3). Habermas, however, is fearless. Opting for the former, stronger version of cosmopolitanism, he uses his essay to nullify the sovereignty of independent nation-states and promote a single world government with executive powers to punish any and all agencies or individuals who violate the cosmopolitan law, a law that is deemed universally valid for all humans in all places at all times. Accordingly, the task he sets himself is to demonstrate, in explicit opposition to Carl Schmitt's criticisms, that such a world state does not represent a moral or political despotism.

Woodrow Wilson and the creation of the League of Nations laid the foundations for the new world order envisioned by Habermas, he reminds us. This initial work was furthered by the 'institutions, declarations, and policies' of subsequent transnational organizations, including, most importantly, the 'outlawing of war' that was articulated in the Kellogg-Briand Pact of 1928 and in the war-crimes tribunals of Nuremberg and Tokyo following World War II. These tribunals, Habermas claims, made it possible to prosecute war itself as a crime and to hold private individuals responsible for crimes against humanity. 'With these two innovations', he writes, 'governmental subjects of international law lost their general presumption of innocence in a supposed state of nature' (Habermas, 1997b, p 126). Taking these various events and initiatives at face value, never once asking about whose interests (*Erkenntnis* – or other) are being served, and only expressing marginal concern about structural inequities in the organization of these transnational institutions (eg the Security Council of the United Nations), Habermas assumes that since 'the World Spirit, as Hegel would have put it, has jerked unsteadily forward' thus far, it will continue to do so in the future (Habermas, 1997b, p 126). Thus, what interests him is the eventual possibility of abrogating the sovereignty of the nation-state and replacing it with the sovereignty of a code of law based on rationally and universally valid human rights. Habermas's revocation of the assumption of innocence in a supposed state of nature, in which autonomous and sovereign states confront each other as moral equals, signals his whole-hearted acceptance of what Schmitt referred to as the turn to a discriminatory concept of war (Schmitt, 1988c). That is, for Habermas, combatants can always be distinguished by a simple binary code of aggressor/victim. Accordingly, when conflicts break out, they should be viewed as illegal breaches of the peace subject to adjudication, with a verdict of relative guilt and innocence the outcome. More specifically, when a world-citizen's human rights are violated by a local entity (presumably a national, regional or religious-based agency), that citizen is to be protected by the single sovereign power of the cosmopolitan law. This, then, is how the World Spirit has progressed: In the original state of nature, individuals confronted each other in a war of all against all. For purposes of self-preservation, they banded together into larger units, trading obedience to a sovereign for protection from others. As a result, there emerged a second-order state of nature in which nation-states as 'moral (ie autonomous) subjects' found themselves in a war of all states against all other states. Now, this higher-level state of nature is to be done away with in the same manner as the first. As individuals, we are to abandon allegiance to the nation-state and trade our obedience to the universal moral and legal order in return for a guarantee of perpetual peace. Therefore, Habermas believes, we now stand at an existential crossroads. We can either view the current age as a 'period of transition from international to cosmopolitan law' and continue traveling down the avenue of opportunities opened up in 1945, or we can regard the symbolic year of 1989 as signaling a 'regression to nationalism' with all its bloody consequences (Habermas, 1997b, p 130). The choice is between pacific cosmopolitanism and regressive, belligerent loyalty to one's tribe.

Clearly, Habermas chooses the spirit of '45 over the harsh realities of the post-1989 world. Specifically, he insists on the symbolic primacy of 1945 over any attempt to re-orient one's thinking in accordance with the events of 1989 and after (Habermas, 1997a, pp 161–81). The true break with the past, he insists, must remain the liberation of Europe and Germany from a criminal and inhuman regime and not, as recent historiography would have it, the purported end of a near century-long civil war played out, in part, between bolshevism and fascism (eg Nolte, 1997). Thus, both the poststructuralist and neo-conservative resurrection of Carl Schmitt as an ideological 'player' in the high stakes game of determining the ideological contours of the new, post-Rhenish Berlin Republic is simply anathema to Habermas, for it treats 1989, not 1945, as its main point of departure. At best, Habermas would say, 1989 is a stage – an important and necessary stage – on the way to the completion of the promise of 1945, but not a break, not a rupture with the past as was the case with the end of the 'German wars'. Thus, this long-time champion of discussion and deliberative democracy seems oddly threatened by the post-1989 proliferation of a variety of possible political attitudes and models, including not only the resuscitation of Schmitt, but also the re-emergence of Hannah Arendt on the German scene (Müller, 1997). The alternative that Habermas presents – ie that between a transition from the good present to the better future vs a regression to the bad, old past – leaves no room for other possibilities. Anything that might deviate from the expansion of the internationalist spirit is simply declared a reversion to the type of gratuitous, tribal bellicosity associated with the first half of the 20th century. The road, therefore, becomes clear and our goal simple, namely, consolidation of the gains of '45 and the full political – which is to say legal – actualization of the cosmopolitan ideal.

What is this ideal? As Habermas sees it, it is the absolute autonomy of the individual as subject of a universally valid code of law. 'The point of cosmopolitan law', he declares, 'is ... that it goes over the heads of the collective subjects of international law to give legal status to the individual subjects and justifies their unmediated membership in the association of free and equal world citizens' (Habermas, 1997b, p 128). The key term here is 'unmediated'. In promoting the absolute sovereignty of the cosmopolitan law, Habermas wishes to avoid the dilemma, diagnosed by Schmitt, that would attend the dual sovereignty inherent in any confederation of independent republican states that sought to implement the cosmopolitan ideal. If, as a totality or unified 'moral subject', a confederation of such states (or all states) promulgates a cosmopolitan law that is to be binding on all individuals, yet continues to grant internal sovereignty to those states (as, say, was the case with the League of Nations and still is, more or less, with the United Nations), then any given individual who is subjected simultaneously to particular state laws as well as to the cosmopolitan law regarding universal human rights may find herself in an inextricable double-bind, because the dual obligations may stand in conflict with one another. Obeying the dictates of one law may very well mean necessarily disobeying the other. The recent case of former East German border guards may be taken as an example. Having failed to sacrifice their liberty and quite possibly their lives by refusing orders to shoot East German citizens attempting to flee the country, they now find themselves deprived of their liberty thirty-some years later for having committed crimes against a higher law, one that they may or may not have known they were subject to. The problem becomes even more difficult when private citizens, not members of a state bureaucracy or the armed forces, are at issue. To what extent are such private individuals responsible for governmental actions? Are, for instance, citizens of a state who are employed by industries that engage in weapons research and production to be held morally and legally liable for crimes committed with such weapons during times of war? In a legal brief, prepared in 1945, Schmitt explicitly addresses the existential dilemma facing German industrialists who were threatened with prosecution for having conspired to conduct an aggressive – and thus an unjust – war. Citing an American Supreme Court decision of 1931[2] which denied the right of an individual citizen to determine whether, in any particular instance, the United States was conducting a just or unjust war, Schmitt concludes that 'the individual citizen has within the state [*innerstaatlich*] no legal possibility of asserting [*durchzusetzen*] his judgment against his own state concerning the unjustness of a war'. Furthermore: 'In international law ... he can find no form of authority [*geordnete Instanz*] or institution to which he can turn.' With this second observation, Schmitt emphasizes that the obedience to the cosmopolitan law required of the individual is not reciprocated with protection. The individual remains a subject of the state and thus exposed to state retaliation. As Schmitt goes on to point out, if it is, therefore, impossible in a liberal society, that is founded on human rights, for a citizen to act based on his or her own individual judgment regarding the justness or unjustness of a nation's course of action, the situation can only be worse in a totalitarian, one-party state, where any act of resistance is regarded as treason and sabotage. He wonders, then, about the legitimacy of compelling individuals to observe the dictates of international law that purportedly override positive, state law. 'If one obliges [*Verpflichtet man*] an individual citizen subjected to such a totalitarian system to resist, this means nothing else but legally requiring a futile attempt at civil war or legally requiring martyrdom' (Schmitt, 1994b, p 78). It is precisely for this reason, which forces individuals to 'choose' to become martyrs, that Schmitt upholds the accepted restrictions on subjecting individuals to international law.

Habermas, however, celebrates the post-World War II scrapping of such discretion. 'The most important consequence', he writes, 'of a form of law that is able to puncture the sovereignty of states is the arrest of individual persons for crimes committed in the service of a state and its military' (Habermas, 1997b, p 129). The ability to 'puncture' the integrity and autonomy of the state implies, of course, the abrogation of internal state sovereignty. Habermas is quite clear on this necessity. 'The rights of the world citizen', he emphasizes,

> must be institutionalized in such a way that it actually binds individual governments. The community of peoples must at least be able to hold its members to legally appropriate behavior through the threat of sanctions. Only then will the unstable system of states asserting their sovereignty through mutual threat be transformed into a federation whose common institutions take over state functions; it will legally regulate the relations among its members and monitor their compliance with its rules. (Habermas, 1997b, p 127)

The United Nations of the World, in other words, ought to be cast in the image of the United States of America. In this way, dual sovereignty – and the painful dilemma that Schmitt identified as its consequence – disappears. There will be no discrepancy between state and cosmopolitan law because state law will simply be cosmopolitan law realized at the local level. The 'community of peoples' will not be hindered by the internal sovereignty of nation states and therefore will be able to exact 'compliance with its rules', presumably by use of military might. The triumph of this strong version of the cosmopolitan ideal not only necessitates the obsolescence of historical nation-states, reducing them to 'provinces' of a larger, all-encompassing federation; it also requires the global establishment of liberal constitutions, guaranteeing (as yet unspecified) human rights and the dismantling of regimes that are deemed illiberal, traditionally authoritarian, or theocratic. Not only will there be one world government, there will be one world religion, a secular religion of the rights of man.

Habermas is not totally oblivious to charges that what he advocates might seem capricious. Acknowledging the existence, but not the validity, of Schmitt's objections regarding the moral and political deployment of 'humanity' (Habermas, 1997b, pp 135–36), Habermas emphasizes that 'the conception of human rights does not have its origins in morality', but rather is 'distinctly juridical in nature' (Habermas, 1997b, p 137). With this caveat, he wishes to emphasize that extending human rights does not simply entail the imposition of an arbitrarily favored philosophical or moral vision of the good life, which

Schmitt would accuse him of, but rather entails the expansion of a particular, if universally valid, legal tradition – universally valid, not because these rights are derived from moral norms, but because their 'form of validity ... points beyond the legal order of the nation state' (Habermas, 1997b, p 137). Habermas makes a fine discrimination here, reminiscent of the neo-Kantian distinction between the absolutist metaphysics of natural law, from which positive law is to be simply derived, and the objectivity of values that are themselves not part of the real, empirical world, but which are held to be universally valid (see Lask, 1905, for instance). 'As a component of a democratic legal order', Habermas states, human rights 'share with all other legal norms a dual sense of "validity": not only are they valid de facto and implemented by the sanctioning power of state violence; they can also claim normative legitimacy (that is, they are capable of being rationally justified)'. Legal norms are *linked* to moral norms, but are not simply concretizations or manifestations of them. Key here is the mode of their justification. Basic human rights are addressed to citizens of a particular state not in their roles as citizens, but 'in their properties as "human beings"'. As such, they share a structure with moral norms, even if they do not logically or prescriptively arise out of these norms. Law, in other words, is not derived from morality, but rather both law and morality, to the extent that they claim universal status, are derived from a structure of validity that logically precedes the distinction between law and morality. Habermas calls this structure of validity a fundamental discourse principle, which reads as follows: 'Just those action norms are valid to which all possibly affected persons could agree as participants in rational discourses' (Habermas, 1996a, p 107). Thus, when Habermas claims that 'basic rights are equipped with such universal validity claims precisely because they can be justified *exclusively* from the moral point of view' (Habermas, 1997b, p 138), this exclusive moral justification can only be possible by virtue of a common origin, namely, the same form of validity which, to follow the neo-Kantian reasoning a bit further, is itself not a social fact, but the 'blind spot' outside the empirical realm that conditions our evaluation of reality. Whereas Kant's categorical imperative served somewhat modestly as the origin of the universal moral law alone, Habermas's exists as the fount of both moral and legal universalism.

A critic might intervene at this point, however, and note that once this imperative is uttered as a principle, it is difficult to see how the principle can continue to serve its function. Collectively binding values are only valid, Niklas Luhmann claims, by virtue of implied attribution. They work only as implied horizon, not as specified theme. Therefore, once the putatively universal form of validity is made a theme, once the gaze is directed at it and makes it a topic of rational investigation, it loses its universally binding character, because like all themes or 'social facts', it can now be discussed and thus be subject to acceptance or rejection (Luhmann, 1993, p 18). What, for example, is 'rational discourse'? What are its rules and whom and what does it exclude? And if such discourse does exclude things and people, in what way can it be the basis for universally valid norms? These questions become inevitable and unavoidable –

unless, of course, they are preemptively outlawed. Nevertheless, Habermas's faith – one is tempted to say, his unreasonable faith – in the consensual, rather than diremptive, powers of reason obviates that apparent difficulty. His intersubjectivity operates with a monological vigor. Consequently, he can start with a historically specific constitution, on the one hand, and a rational structure of universal validity claims, on the other. In this particular constitution there exist positive laws addressed to citizens of the state in their capacity as human beings. These laws have a positive legal validity, but also, by virtue of the fact that they can be rationally justified on the basis of validity claims shared with universal moral principles, they enjoy universal, not just positive, validity. Thus, any extension of these rights beyond the borders of their origin is seen as the extension of an essentially human birthright to all individuals the world over.

Sadly, Habermas is forced to report, this expansion is not complete. The World Spirit is stalled. Indeed, we still inhabit a disturbingly divided planet, distinguished by three worlds, though these worlds are no longer limited to geographically homogenous regions. The post-1989 Third World consists, according to Habermas, of 'those territories where the state infrastructure and monopoly of the means of violence are so weakly developed (Somalia) or so decayed (Yugoslavia) ... that indirect violence of a Mafia or fundamentalist variety disrupts internal order'. Members of the Second World, largely comprising the decolonized regions of an older Third World, duplicate the power politics of their former European masters and therefore 'obstinately insist on sovereignty and non-intervention from the outside'. Only in the First World – and it should not be difficult to discern where that world is located – have states been able to bring their 'national interests into harmony with the normative claims established by the United Nations, an organization that has come at least part of the way toward achieving the cosmopolitan ideal'. For this reason, the First World 'constitutes the temporal meridian of the present' against which the rest is to be measured (Habermas, 1997b, pp 131–32). But it is not only that the Second and Third Worlds are to be measured against the achievements of the First, they are fated or destined to join their more temporally advantaged cousins, even if they need some coaxing, or, as Habermas puts it, even if they need the 'gentle compulsion'[3] that is required by the 'undistorted perception of current global dangers' (Habermas, 1997b, p 133).

As a description of the current state of affairs, the picture that Habermas develops is as accurate as any. The First World is not only the economic engine that drives the rest, but also the source of virtually all current political ideologies; the nations of the Second World do obstinately insist on independence, sometimes in ways that irk their former superiors and cause them, with heavy hearts, to engage in punitive measures; and the Third World is beset by what at best could be called chronic civil war. Although in our post-Marxist age good old-fashioned critique of ideology appears at least as naive and ideological as that which it attacks, nevertheless, Habermas's matter-of-fact equation of the First World with the universal spirit, his unreflected belief that the particular instance of the West can be the unproblematic carrier of the universal principle, cries out for some form of critical scrutiny – especially now that the United States, in a fit of uncharacteristic honesty, has torn off the veil of legality once provided by the United Nations. When Habermas converts this hierarchical description into a teleological prescription for a new cosmopolitan orthodoxy, when he, in effect, identifies the *telos* of the West with 'what is essential to humanity as such, its *entelechy*' (Husserl, 1970, p 15), does he not offer us another version of the type of salvation religion that we have, with good reason, learned to mistrust? Do we not have all the required elements for a comfortable, reassuring, quasi-religious and ultimately uncritical certitude? The Bethlehem of this new incarnation of the universal principle is to be found in the Virginian wilderness, Philadelphia and Paris; the new gospels are the Virginia Bill of Rights, the American Declaration of Independence, and the French Declaration of the Rights of Man (Habermas, 1997b, p 137). The Holy Spirit is Reason. From this particular and humble beginning arises a force destined to encircle the globe. To resist is to be obstinate and *unzeitgemäß*, to be out of step with the times and to suffer from a distorted perception of reality – or, as Kierkegaard would simply say, to live in error. To resist means to block, unreasonably, the spread of universal justice, and thus means to be unjust and illegal. Therefore, to suppress this unreasonable resistance is 'gently' to 'compel' sinners to alter their evil ways.

Now, as far as I am concerned, it would certainly be no tragedy were illiberal and theocratic states to disappear and be replaced by constitutional republics – but then I am an atheist who lives in a liberal, constitutional republic. What would be tragic, however, would be to watch that which presents itself as the most liberal of all possible worlds actualize itself precisely as the most *il*liberal of all possible liberalisms. Tragic would be to watch the global conquest of a political philosophy that effectively prohibited political activity by translating politics into 'the police actions of a democratically legitimate world organization' (Habermas, 1997b, p 140). Even if one accepts that Habermas successfully differentiates morality from legality – and I remain unconvinced of this – one still fails to see where he locates political conflict, the compromise and stubborn refusal to compromise that is located outside the realms of the True, the Good, and the Beautiful. Of Schmitt's friend/enemy distinction, Habermas complains that it is more like the 'nature of the strategic' (Habermas, 1989, p 128) than it is the nature of the political, without recognizing that perhaps the strategic *is* the political. Can we not say that the marshaling of reason is every bit as strategic as identifying enemies? Indeed, is not identifying – and silencing – enemies, those who would question the truth of reason, one of the things that reason does? Habermas's advocacy of the universal structure of communicative reason has led him to specify and condemn reason's enemies in chilling ways – not as *actual* enemies, to use Schmitt's terminology, but as *absolute* ones, traitors to the one, true cause (Schmitt, 1963, pp 87–96). In excusing Kant for his apparently naive belief in the power of rational persuasion, Habermas notes that 'historical skepticism about reason belongs more to the nineteenth century, and it was not until the twentieth century that intellectuals engaged in the gravest betrayals' (Habermas, 1997b, p 124). We know who these *clercs*[4] are and what they have done. In the wake of Nietzsche and Heidegger, and confronted with the dead end offered by Adorno, they have, in Habermas's eyes, reduced reason to myth, rational debate to manipulation of interest, and politics to existentialist decision. 'Thus', he concludes, 'in the expressionistic style of his time, Carl Schmitt constructs a dramatic concept of the political in the light of which everything normally understood by the word must seem banal' (Habermas, 1989, p 129). But could we not rather say of Habermas that in his reduction of the political to the legal, everything normally understood by the word simply disappears? It seems ironic that in Habermas's attempt to banish Schmitt from the Anglo-Saxon mind, he complains, and rightly so, that Schmitt's insistence on domestic homogeneity relegates politics exclusively to the realm of 'foreign affairs' (Habermas, 1989, p 129). It seems ironic, because by extinguishing the nation-state and reducing politics to the legal (and military) implementation of human rights, by replacing conflict with consensus, thus making the entire world a pacified domestic sphere, Habermas abolishes politics altogether.

It is at this point that Schmitt's well-known objection to liberal pluralism gains a measure of credibility. Throughout most of his career, Schmitt accused liberal theorists like Harold Laski and GDH Cole of committing 'an intellectual misunderstanding of a most astonishing kind' in their desire 'to dissolve these plural political unities [the European nation-states] by referring to universal and monistic concepts, and then represent this attempt as pluralism' (Schmitt, 1988b, p 161). As you will of course recall, the 'universal and monistic' concept par excellence is 'humanity', a notion Schmitt famously dissects in *The Concept of the Political*. The 'political world is a pluriverse', he maintained, and if a single world state 'embracing all of humanity' were to appear, foreclosing both conflict and civil war, then what would remain would be 'neither politics nor state' (Schmitt, 1976, p 53), but rather the concept of humanity as an 'ideological instrument of imperialist expansion' (Schmitt, 1976, p 54). The context of his remarks – the fact that he eventually aligned himself with a regime and an ideology that used the concept of 'race' in a way far more brutal than he could ever have imagined – certainly puts Schmitt's intellectual integrity in doubt, but not necessarily his logic. Habermas's emphasis on human rights is an integral aspect of liberal pluralism as Schmitt describes it. It 'punctures' state sovereignty to give billions of individuals 'sovereign' rights, as it were. Yet, as a result, each of these 'sovereign' individuals is thoroughly subjugated to the one and only, universal, cosmopolitan law – The Law – against which no other law is allowed to stand. The pluralism of rights not only reduces the pluralism of customs and traditions to a monism of the Law, but also subsumes the pluralism of states under the hegemony of the singular but exemplary nature of the First World.

Schmitt's critique of the just war doctrine follows from these reflections, a fact that Habermas understands well. 'According to Schmitt', Habermas writes, 'the morality of humanity falsely abstracts from the natural order of the political' by replacing the categories good and evil with friend and enemy. Therefore, Habermas continues, still paraphrasing Schmitt, 'because the discriminating concept of war derives from the universalism of human rights, it is ultimately the infection of international law with morality that explains why the inhumanity of modern war and civil war occurs "in the name of humanity"' (Habermas, 1997b, p 146). Schmitt contends, in other words, that the just war doctrine does as much, if not more, to cause the crimes it seeks to avoid as to prevent them. On this view, modern total wars, in which, for instance, the distinction between combatants and non-combatants is no longer made, are precipitated by the theory of war that presumes both the ability and moral necessity to discriminate between aggressive and defensive wars, and therefore between the guilt of unjust causes and the innocence of just ones. What results, according to Schmitt, is both a moral fundamentalism and a legal criminalization of the enemy that ultimately sanctions all measures taken by the 'just' belligerent (that is, the future winner) of the armed conflict. Indeed, Schmitt trumps the drafters of the Treaty of Versailles. Where they merely saddled Germany with the sole responsibility for the outbreak of World War I, Schmitt, in effect, says that the incipient cosmopolitanism of a Habermasian hero like Woodrow Wilson in the early part of the 20th century could be held responsible for what Habermas's more fully matured version attempts to combat. The fact that a 'war to end all war' fails to provide the promised 'perpetual peace' has as much to do with the structure of that vision of war, Schmitt claims, as it does with the perfidy of individual nation-states who 'obstinately' cling to the notion of sovereignty.

When one links what Schmitt says about the political deployment of the term 'humanity' with the simultaneous emergence of the United States as a world power and the re-emergence of the just war doctrine at the beginning of the 20th century, one has the ingredients of a critique of ideology that is not linked to an eschatology or utopian *telos*, but rather takes aim at the 'imperialism' of moral universalism. Habermas notes that Schmitt's complaint resembles both Hegel's and Horkheimer's criticisms 'directed against the false and transfiguring abstraction of a Platonic general concept with which we often only cover up the dark side of the civilization of the victors', yet rejects the complaint in a typically Habermasian move, by noting the performative paradox involved. Such a critique requires, Habermas notes, 'a kind of egalitarian respect and universal compassion validated by the very moral universalism Schmitt so vehemently rejects' (Habermas, 1997b, pp 145–46); and, indeed, the critique of the term 'humanity' that locates its 'inhuman' effects can, paradoxically, only take place within the space marked by that term's deployment. Nevertheless, Habermas acknowledges the problem of moral fundamentalism and even admits that the 'true thesis at the core of [Schmitt's] argument consists in the fact that an *unmediated* moralization of law and politics would in fact serve to break down those protected spheres that we as legal persons have good moral reasons to want to secure' (Habermas, 1997b, p 146). It is for this reason, as noted above, that he feels it necessary to distinguish constitutionally guaranteed, legal human rights from 'free-floating' moral rights, though they share the same, universal validity claims. Though Habermas concedes the importance of Schmitt's observations, he finds that the latter ignores the 'decisive moment' of the cosmopolitan ideal, namely, 'the legal presupposition of an authority that judges impartially and fulfills the conditions of neutral criminal punishment' (Habermas, 1997b, p 147). Habermas maintains, in other words, that if the legal order can remain differentiated from the moral sphere, even though certain basic rights may share the same form of validity as moral imperatives, then the realm of the political can safely be conflated with the emancipatory expansion of the neutral and universal rule of law. With this fine differentiation between moral fundamentalism and legal constitutionalism, therefore, the police actions undertaken by a world government which has institutionalized, on a global basis, rights that were first discovered and enunciated by English colonists in an ethnically cleansed Virginia wilderness can be positively contrasted with repressive moral or cultural crusades that might otherwise emanate from the First World.

Regardless of whether we have faith in such a distinction or not, we may still wish to pause here and remind ourselves of Lyotard's question about the 'aporia of authorization' concerning declarations of universal rights. 'Why', he asks (Lyotard, 1993, p 52), 'would the affirmation of a universal normative instance have universal value if a singular instance makes the declaration? How can one tell, afterward, whether the wars conducted by the singular instance in the name of the universal instance are wars of liberation or wars of conquest?' This question need not lead to indecision. We in fact do make distinctions. We do decide that *this* war was fought for the right reasons, and *that* one for the wrong ones; that *this* ideal is worth fighting and dying for, while *that* one is not. We do decide, for example, that abortion is morally wrong and a crime against humanity or, conversely, that access to abortion is a basic human right, but we do not really *know* whether we are correct or not. Barring revelation, which remains incommunicable, we have no ultimate or transcendental assurance that our decisions are valid for all times and all places. We make them without the assurance that their structure, that their 'form of validity', absolves us from all responsibility of their having been made. These decisions we make are political decisions; and what Schmitt fears most of all, one might say, is the loss of our ability to make political decisions once their contingency is masked by a façade of necessity. Thus, Habermas is certainly right about Schmitt in one crucial area, though he does not know how right he is. '[I]t is not at all certain', Habermas writes, 'that [Schmitt] truly saw the total delimiting of war and hence the inhuman character of the conduct of war as the real evil, or whether it is much more the case that he mostly feared the discrediting of war as such' (Habermas, 1997b, p 143). Schmitt, I would say, legitimately feared both and saw them as linked; for if, as Habermas claims, Schmitt relegated politics to the realm of international relations, then, in his writings, war becomes the preeminent figure of legitimate political conflict. Its possibility, in fact, becomes the condition of possibility for all political activity. Consequently, if the totalization of war that comes with the re-introduction of the just war doctrine ultimately delegitimizes war, we also have to recognize, Schmitt clearly warns, that the moralization or universal reduction of political conflict to legal procedures may similarly lead to the total elimination of the realm of the political in which decisions are both made and contested. Despite the attractive rhetoric of perpetual peace and the seemingly inescapable logic and desirability of universal rights, the question that Schmitt forces us to confront is whether reducing the foreign to the domestic and the domestic to the legal, as Habermas would have us do, still preserves a place for political conflict that escapes moral supervision. Is a world that outlaws war, Schmitt asks us today, also a world that outlaws opposition in general, consigning the political to the illegal realm of the terrorist? If so, can we afford the pacification that we have been promised?

Germany: A Winter's Tale II

While in Cologne, and shortly before engaging in conversation with the river Rhine, Heine visited its famed Cathedral, at that time still an unfinished relic of the 'gothic' middle ages. Heine, an inveterate foe of both medieval Catholicism and romantic medievalism, considers the 'incompletion' (*Nichtvollendung*) of this 'Bastille of the Spirit' (*Geistes Bastille*) a 'monument of Germany's strength' (*Denkmal von Deutschlands Kraft*), because its aborted shape represents the triumph of 'German reason' (*deutsche Vernunft*) over Catholic superstition (Heine, 1997, Caput IV, v 41, 44, 50, 51). Call it dialectic of enlightenment, if you like, or just perverse irony, but the resurrected spirit of that old 'Catholic', Carl Schmitt, is certainly one of the Heines of the present who fight the completion of our contemporary *Geistes Bastille*, the monolithic cosmopolitan law envisioned by Habermas. Originally constructed as a subversive counter to the tyrannies of positive law, the universal structure of cosmopolitan law, once completed, would neither embody opposition nor even allow it. Certainly the classic figures of 'left' and 'right', progressive and conservative, can do little to escape the paradoxes of the moment. On the one hand, in the name of perpetual peace, Habermas advocates the perpetual war of 'gentle compulsion' and continuous police actions; on the other hand, in the name of a belligerent, homogenous particularity, Schmitt urges on us the universal value and possibility of politics as both affirmation *and* opposition. Thus Schmitt the nationalist might also be Schmitt the international multiculturalist, who offers those who 'obstinately' wish to resist the 'West' a theoretical foothold. And Habermas the internationalist is also Habermas the touching patriot, who not only sees his spiritual home, the First World, as the temporal meridian of the planet, but would, no doubt, also love to see German self-effacement and German self-immolation in a vast sea of universal interest be the temporal meridian of the First World. Whereas German conservatives may deny German exceptionality in order to make Germans as acceptable as everyone else, Habermas fights to preserve the memory of Germany's exceptionally evil past so that contemporary Germans may deny their Germanness and bask in the glow of an exemplary universalist present. If the rest of us remain somewhat confused, maybe it is because not even a modern Heine can make sense out of Germany's, or the world's, 'Zukunftsduft' (Heine, 1997, p 640; Caput XXVI, v 57).[5]

Notes

1 Reference is first to page number, then to Caput and verse. The misspelling of Fichte by Heine is a deliberate pun, which I reproduce.

2 See United States v MacIntosh, 283 US 605 (1931).

3 This essay, translated anew, is included in Habermas, 1998, pp 165–201. There (p 186), the 'sanfte Nötigung' of the original German (Habermas, 1996b, 217) is tempered to a less threatening 'gentle pressure'. The term Nötigung, however, especially when used in legal language, denotes force, intimidation or compulsion. To give the flavor of both translations, in subsequent chapters, when quoting from this article, I will do so from Habermas, 1998.

4 The reference to 'clercs' is, of course, a reference to Benda, 1927.

5 'Zukunftsduft' is 'aroma of the future' and refers to a scene in which the narrator is invited to stick his head under the seat of Charlemagne's nighttime 'throne' in order to get a glimpse of Germany's future.

The Measures Taken represents one of the most compact and economical disquisitions on revolutionary politics to come out of the turbulent decade and a half following the Russian Revolution.[1] It not only depicts a concrete situation in which the ability to decide on right action is repeatedly required, but it also aims at modeling the types of behavior – for and with an audience – that such decision and such action demands. Because of its clear and precise presentation of Marxist-Leninist principles in action and because of its relatively pathos-free invitation to reflect on the efficacy of these principles – indeed, according to Steinweg,[2] its theoretical 'participatory' sublation of the audience/actor distinction – it has been said to be the epitome of political theater. One is not merely aroused by revolutionary sentiment, but offered the chance, at least virtually, to accustom oneself to the necessities of revolutionary behavior. However, the seemingly counterintuitive question I wish to raise here is whether what is depicted and what is modeled in *The Measures Taken* has anything to do with politics at all. Let me be clear. My aim is not to question Brecht's commitment to Marxism nor to 'rescue' or make him 'safe' for a post-Marxist age by rhetorically removing all embarrassing traces of political concerns from his writing. Rather, the notion of revolution itself and its presentation in the play is at the center of my investigation. Thus, I ask whether revolutionary politics is really political, or whether revolution merely forms the prelude to the end of politics. Does not the successful revolution, in other words, also represent the successful elimination of politics? This question presupposes a particular definition of the political, a definition I will elaborate below with the help of Carl Schmitt. By way of his famous friend/enemy distinction, Schmitt identifies conflict as the essential and indispensable ingredient of political action. The question I pose, then, has to do with the role conflict plays in Brecht's staging of revolution. There is no shortage of conflict in this parable about oppressors, oppressed and liberators; but what I wish to investigate is whether the 'lesson' that the *Lehrstück* (teaching play) invites us to learn is a political lesson, or whether participation in the revolutionary process is meant to be training for life in a post-political state.

*

There is no question about the revolutionary agitators' self-understanding of their mission in *The Measures Taken*. In their view, it is preeminently political. As the Control Chorus tells us at the outset, whoever fights for the communist revolution knows that there is a time for telling the truth and a time for lying, a time for keeping and a time for breaking promises, a time for facing and a time for avoiding danger. Of all the virtues, only one remains absolute: 'He who fights for Communism/ Has of all virtues only one:/ That he fights for Communism' (Brecht, 2001, p 13). These words unambiguously subordinate one's ethical convictions to one's political commitments. The immediate reason for doing so is strategic. As you may know, this play's plot finds one of its centers in the character of the Young Comrade whose heart beats for the revolution because he believes in humanity, whose suffering he has seen with his own eyes. Whereas 'teachings of the Classics' and 'the ABC of Communism' motivate the remaining agitators (Brecht, 2001, p 11), this new recruit proudly proclaims that 'The sight of injustice compelled me to become a fighter' (Brecht, 2001, p 10). On one level, then, we have in this young pilgrim's progress to eventual *Einverständnis* (agreement) a parable about liberal humanism, the faults of which are displayed with every mistaken and disastrous decision he makes. Each misstep is triggered by a common virtue – sympathy, for instance, or the nobility of an outraged sense of honor. Each displays that the Young Comrade's vision is restricted by these virtues, which are focussed too narrowly on the immediate case at hand. It is a common Brechtian theme. To be fought is not the evil that men do, but the system that makes this evil inevitable, no matter the man or the woman involved. The agitators sum up the situation in the following way: 'We had no bread for the hungry, but only knowledge for the ignorant; therefore we spoke of the primal causes of misery, not of the eliminations of misery, but of the elimination of the primal causes' (Brecht, 2001, p 14). The object of the agitators is to spread knowledge, raise class consciousness, and give voice to the experience of a successful revolution (Brecht, 2001, p 11). Consequently, by acting compassionately and honorably, by attempting to intervene immediately in order to alleviate individual suffering, without educating or organizing the workers to make their own demands, the Young Comrade acted too *'gefühlsmäßig'* (emotionally) and therefore became a liability.[3] Conventional virtues must be subordinated to the pragmatic program of promoting and executing a successful revolution. Thus, it is not so much that the heart should beat, but that the head should learn and think, should plot and strategize for the revolution.

But beyond its tactical value, the relativization of virtue also evokes a substantive Marxist critique of liberal, bourgeois morality, a critique that links ethical order with social – and that means property – relations. As Max Horkheimer, writing in 1933, states: 'The moral conception of the bourgeoisie found its purest expression in Kant's formulation of the categorical imperative' (Horkheimer, 1993, p 18). This imperative, which pits duty against inclination, formalizes, indeed eternalizes, the division of general and individual interest. Horkheimer objects to the naturalization of the conflict of interests, for in his view, this conflict is, in actuality, a product of history. The chasm that separates individual interest from the general will is not to be located in a tragic metaphysics of human nature; rather, the split represents, Horkheimer believes (echoing both Hegel and Marx), a fixable distortion that results from unequal property relations. These relations, and the moral reasoning which supports them, are reproduced and further naturalized with every tragic triumph of duty over inclination. For Horkheimer, then, the logical antinomy is grounded in social reality, thus the resolution of the antinomy must also be social. 'If people want to act', Horkheimer notes, 'in such a way that their maxims are fit to become universal law, they must bring about an order in which this intention … can really be carried out according to criteria. Society must then be constructed in a manner that establishes its own interests and those of all its members in a rational fashion' (Horkheimer, 1993, p 25). In such a future transformed society, 'productive property is administered in the general interest not just out of "good intentions" but with rational necessity' (Horkheimer, 1993, p 28). The image here of a post-revolutionary, rational social order is one in which conflict of interests – the antinomy of theory and practice as well as the antinomy of duty and inclination – have been successfully resolved on a material, not just spiritual or logical, level.[4]

Horkheimer, of course, understands this critique of bourgeois morality to be a critique motivated by political interests – which is to say, by emancipatory interests. On this view, concordance of ends can never be realized in the present social order, but a society can be imagined in which such a concordance is not only possible, but necessary. Given this *theoretical* reality, political activity must have as its goal the *practical* and material establishment of a just and rational society. Since those who benefit from present property relations will not voluntarily see them altered, political activity is, of necessity, revolutionary action. Thus, revolutionary politics, which advocates the violent overthrow of the present order, entails conflict, to be sure, but conflict in the service of a pacific ideal. Just like Wilson in April 1917, so Lenin in October becomes the prophet of a war to end all war. The new order to be established transforms the social bases that cause the conflict of interests; therefore the nature of politics is transformed as well. In the rational and just society of the future, politics can no longer be defined in terms of an antagonism (for opposition can only be reactionary aggression), but in terms of consensus, a form of *Einverständnis* (agreement) achieved through political education.[5]

Our belief in the possibility of a rationally ordered, just society, in which individual and collective interests necessarily coincide, and our conviction that such a society can be brought about by political action, presents us, however, with a paradox. The belief in complete political emancipation is just that – belief. Horkheimer stresses that 'morality cannot be proven, … not a single value admits of a purely theoretical grounding' (Horkheimer, 1993, p 45). The same can be said of the value of revolution. The critique of bourgeois morality in the name of revolutionary politics itself requires a moral leap of faith. To put it in the terms of Brecht's agitators, the teachings of the Marxist-Leninist classics and the ABCs of communism may indeed be derived from the conditions of reality, but our knowledge of these conditions hinges on our acceptance of the teachings of the classics. Before we can recognize the reality that the classics make present for us, we must be raised by the teachings of the classics to class consciousness and be exposed to the experience of the revolution. If reality were self-evident, *The Measures Taken* would be redundant. Reality must be construed theoretically before it can be practically effective, but this theoretical construal must also emerge practically for it to be accurate. There is a circularity here that may or may not be vicious, it may very well be hermeneutical, indeed, dialectical; but our entrance into this circle is not the result of logical deduction or material necessity. It is as 'absurd', to evoke the inevitable Kierkegaard, as any other decision based on faith.

Georg Lukács identified this problem clearly in his earliest post-revolutionary reflections of 1918. The dilemma he faced as a democratic socialist who found himself confronted with the choice of joining or rejecting the Leninist vanguard party (the Bolsheviks) was the dilemma he resolved by way of a necessary ethics/tactics distinction. In his essay 'Bolshevism as a Moral Problem', Lukács recognized the inherent, contradictory tension within Marxism, namely, that it weds the inescapable reality of class conflict, which 'has always been the moving force behind every existing social order', with the *'ethical objective'* of socialism, a 'utopian postulate of the Marxian philosophy of history' that dictates the *resolution* of class conflict in a future society marked by harmony and absolute justice (Lukács, 1977, p 420). Thus he realized that the demands made by the revolutionary party are based not only on empirical analyses of class conflict, but also on an ungrounded yet necessarily presupposed belief in the latter, ethical and utopian goal. In other words, sociological analysis confirms the necessity and inevitability of social conflict (of interests, of class, etc), but political messianism insists on an immanent and historically conditioned transcendence of present, imperfect reality, a transfiguration and self-transcendence of all conflict. If one believes in the utopian goal but rejects democratic reformism because of its 'risk of infinite delay' (the goal may never be reached by peaceful means), then one must navigate the ethically challenging waters of revolutionary politics and accept 'dictatorship, terror, and the class oppression that goes with it ... in the hope that this last and therefore most open and cruel of all class oppressions [the dictatorship of the proletariat] will finally destroy itself and in so doing will put an end to class oppression forever' (Lukács, 1977, p 422). The dilemma one faces, therefore, is posed by Lukács in terms quite similar to those of the Young Comrade's. If we believe in a future social order in which class (or any other) conflict will no longer exist, then we must advocate the dictatorship of the proletariat here and now. Put the other way around: We can only justify the use of terror and the repression of democracy and standard moral behavior in the present if we believe that by such means the better, more perfect world will be brought about. The realism of Marxist sociology – that 'history consists of a continuous sequence of class struggles between oppressors and oppressed', a 'law' that 'the struggle of the proletariat cannot escape' – must be trumped by the secular salvation religion of Marxist philosophy of history. 'We have to accept', Lukács says of those who successfully make the leap,

> the wrong as wrong, oppression as oppression, and class oppression as oppression. We have to believe – this being the true *credo quia absurdum est* – that no new class struggle will emerge out of this class struggle (resulting in the quest for a new oppression), which would provide continuance to the old sequence of meaningless and aimless

struggles – but that oppression will effect the elements of its own destruction. (Lukács, 1977, pp 423–24)

It is as if the proletariat class, in the moment of its emancipation, becomes the 'agent of the social salvation of mankind' by intensifying and bearing responsibility for the accumulated sins of the ages. It is not for nothing that Lukács refers to it as 'the messianic class of world history' (Lukács, 1977, p 421).

Of interest here are the two definitions of politics that emerge in this discussion: one derived from Marxist sociology, which identifies conflict as the essential and unavoidable feature of social reality; and the other derived from its messianic philosophy of history, which promotes the vision of future harmony, free from all strife. If one adopts the former view, politics becomes the continual negotiation of conflicting interests, never their final resolution; whereas the latter view insists that politics be the means by which a new social order can be realized in the imminent future. In other words, if one accepts as untranscendable a society marked by the intellectual and social antinomies identified by Horkheimer, then politics becomes an end in itself, an autonomous or 'operationally closed' system that finds itself in a field of equally autonomous systems.[6] Such a society organizes itself around the differences of these systems as the differences among political, economic, cultural, scientific, and other interests. If, on the other hand, one cannot accept the existence of these 'reifications' and modes of 'alienation', if the differentiation of social systems can only be seen as the consequence of differential property rights, then politics must subordinate itself to a vision of the good life and become the mechanism by which a flawed society can be transformed into a just one. Serving the ideal of a just society, politics becomes both total (all is justified) and transitory. Operationally, politics reduces to a tactical activity, a self-consuming artifact that uses itself up in its own success.

We can elaborate this basic insight and apply it to the notion of partisan and/or revolutionary warfare with the help of Carl Schmitt. In his *Theorie des Partisanen* (Theory of the Partisan), published in 1963, Schmitt uses an anecdote about the trial of Joan of Arc to clarify the meaning of his much disputed definition of politics as the friend/enemy distinction. Asked, during her trial, by an ecclesiastical judge, whether she believes that God hates the English, our heroine is reported by Schmitt to have replied: 'I do not know whether God loves or hates the English; I only know that they must be driven out of France.' Schmitt comments: 'A fundamental limitation of the notion of enmity is given with such a basic defense. The actual enemy is not made into the absolute enemy and therefore not into the ultimate enemy of humanity' (Schmitt, 1963, pp 93–94). With this second distinction – the one between an actual and an absolute enemy – Schmitt wishes to differentiate between the partisan who defends her homeland from foreign invaders and the revolutionary who is guided by a universalist ideology and therefore not bound to the land. But this difference between the 'telluric' (or territorial) partisan, whose goal is limited, and the professional revolutionary, who seeks a total and global solution, replicates the two diametrically opposed types of political conflict discussed above. On the one hand, as ideologically driven revolutionaries, we must regard our opponents as absolute enemies; our war against them is total. If God hates the English, so to speak, then we, as God's servants, must execute His will – by executing His enemies. On this view, politics must be described as the attempt to effect a radical transformation of society, a destruction of one social framework and the establishment of another. It must, in Lukács's words, be 'directed towards the emergence of a social order which differs from that of every previous society in that it no longer knows either oppressors or oppressed' (Lukács, 1972, p 5). True conflict, *legitimate* conflict, must then be seen as revolutionary practice with the aim of establishing the Kingdom of Heaven on earth. The political enemy becomes the absolute enemy, and, as such, the ultimate enemy of humankind. He, after all, opposes the pacific concord of the just society out of particular self-interest, and must therefore not only be defeated, but destroyed, and so must the system he represents. God – or at least history – must *hate* him, and not just wish to see him go home.

Despite a persistent tendency to identify Schmitt's friend/enemy distinction automatically with this absolutist position, his commentary on St Joan's response indicates an alternative, one that not only emulates St Joan's modesty regarding knowledge of God's likes and dislikes, but also one that is carefully agnostic with regard to the feasibility of the Marxist project. Emphasizing, as Schmitt does, the essentially agonistic aspect of politics is not the same as equating it with revolution. When Schmitt originally advanced the friend/enemy pair in his *The Concept of the Political*, he explicitly dissociated it from moral, aesthetic, or other categories (Schmitt, 1976, pp 25–27). Far from being cynical, this disassociation was itself ethically motivated, since Schmitt felt that excesses of violence could only be limited by acknowledging conflict as an existentially inevitable and thus a thoroughly legitimate feature of all genuine political activity. He defines politics as conflict, not to glorify violence, but to regulate it.[7] Thus Schmitt's notion of the political – to continue with the imagery introduced by St Joan – assumes that God respected the distance that separates the Heavenly from the Earthly City, or at least assumes that there is no one on earth who has exclusive and privileged access to the heavenly vision. Consequently, in the absence of an ultimate judge who could decide the outcome of mortal disputes, politics becomes the structure by which shape is given to the unavoidable necessity of conflict. Politics is not the means by which the universally acknowledged Good is actualized, but the mechanism that negotiates and limits disputes in the absence of any universally acknowledged Good. Politics exists because the just society does not. It soon becomes apparent, therefore, that if political struggle is an ever-shifting alliance of friends confronting an ever-shifting alliance of enemies, if politics is more Sisyphean than millennial, then the aim of revolution is precisely the abolition of politics, the abolition of conflict and dissent, all done in the name of a universal principle that is enunciated by a privileged particular instance. In other words, from *within* a given framework, from within a given social order, politics-as-conflict cannot be seen as the revolutionary *destruction* of the system, but rather as the activity that *reproduces* the system. Enemies are as much a part of this reproduction as friends. Thus, from the perspective of a thoroughly agonistic politics, the demand for revolution can only be seen as an eschatological appeal to a singular vision of the good life, the actualization of which would eventually preclude further political conflict. In a just society, we must all be friends, because there are no *actual* enemies, only *absolute* ones. And these must be absolutely eliminated.[8]

*

These two visions of the political are mutually exclusive. Either one defines politics as conflict immanent to a given system, or one aims at violently transforming the world by transcending the system's limits. One cannot inhabit both realms, nor can one decide on the validity of one view over the other from a neutral, third position. Indeed, the choice of one radically cancels the other. Thus, the definition of the political as a structure of controlled and regulated conflict not only runs counter to the self-understanding of Brecht's agitators, but must appear as an ideological manifestation of the order they wish to abolish. The world in which they work knows only one legitimate conflict, a total and absolute battle that will give birth to a new, conflict-free society. What is therefore required of them is faith in the absolute and unquestioned good of the revolution. 'Your work has been successful', the Control Chorus affirms at both the beginning and the end of the play. 'The revolution marches forward even in that country. The ranks of the fighters are well organized even there' (Brecht, 2001, p 9). But once the ultimate battle is won and the revolution is successful everywhere, not just in Mukden, what happens to these fighters? Must not the successful revolution renounce politics-as-conflict and therefore strive to pacify the oppositional impulse, even the critical spirit? If politics is reduced to tactics, does it not disappear once the end is achieved?

In asking this question, I do not mean to re-open the debate on the fate of the Young Comrade, but rather the debate on the relationship of the spectators to the action on stage. Contrary to conventional, post-Steinweg wisdom, the pedagogical impulse, the desire to suspend the difference between thought and deed, observation and action, has very little to do with progressive political behavior, despite (or perhaps because of!) its seeming affinities with Marx's 'Theses on Feuerbach'.[9] Indeed, in its extreme form, the ideal *Aufhebung* of the actor/audience distinction, as advocated in some of Brecht's fragments, can more correctly be seen as the cancellation of all critical and political distance. We can see this renunciation of politics *in nuce* in perhaps the most famous *Lehrstück* fragment, the one distinguishing a *Große* (great) from a *Kleine Pädagogik* (minor pedagogy) (Steinweg, 1976, p 51). The latter, identified with the 'time of transition of the first revolution' – that is, the democratic, bourgeois order – maintains the traditional distinction between actor and audience, though the spectators are to be 'activated', encouraged to engage their intellect, rather than their emotions, in order to take a definitive, political stand. The passive, sympathetic identification of old is to be replaced by an active, inquisitive and aggressive attitude. In short, the spectator is to be transformed into a 'statesman', a critical, political being. As we know, the 'great pedagogy', on the other hand, takes an extra step in that it dissolves the distinction altogether, '[it] cancels the system of actor and audience completely'. This new state of affairs is no longer bourgeois, but post-revolutionary. It is both the mode of theater and mode of being appropriate to a society in which 'the interest of the individual is the interest of the state'. In such a society, the antinomy between the individual and the general will, the antinomy 'naturalized' in Kantian, bourgeois morality, is overcome. As a result, the participants, both actor and spectator (who are now one in any case), need no longer exercise the same type of critical attitude that had to be learned during the 'time of transition'. They no longer need to be political in the sense defined above, for they have arrived in the post-political state. Opposition is traded in for cooperation and consensus. Individuals are now enjoined to learn the 'comprehended gesture' that determines their new 'way of acting'. Thus, though the action of *The Measures Taken* depicts the early stages of revolutionary agitation in the imaginary space of Mukden, the behavior modeled and the theoretical apparatus that surrounds the play are decidedly post-revolutionary. Here, the political stance of a critical audience is replaced by the cooperative efforts of a revolutionary party that both seeks to raise the consciousness of those not yet in its fold and mold the consciousness of those already there. It has, in other words, a two-fold task: it works politically when confronted with the class enemy and post-politically when dealing with dissent within its own ranks. If the teaching play can be said to have a lesson, then, it would be that in a post-revolutionary society the political is to be superseded by the pedagogical.

The above claim is extreme, seemingly hostile, and perhaps only partially tenable. I propose first to justify it, then see whether there are mechanisms inherent in the text that would allow us to reintroduce the political moment. To do so, I will focus on the transition the Control Chorus undergoes in its interactions with the agitators they are called upon to judge. If, ideally, the sublation of the actor/audience distinction can only be played out on stage by a coterie of participant observers, nevertheless, as readers of the text or as non-participating spectators in a traditionally staged production (the only kind possible, it would seem, when the music is included), we can still observe the portrayal of this desired sublation in the gradual transformation of the function of the Control Chorus. Far from being the representatives of a centralized party apparatus, as hostile criticism has repeatedly asserted, the members of this body epitomize, at the beginning of the play, the behavior of a critical audience, observing and judging the actions of the agitators in their recapitulation of the events in Mukden. Thus, just as the Chorus is invited by the agitators to judge their actions, we, the 'real' audience, are also invited to adopt the role of judge in order to learn the proper mental and physical movements of critical observation. As we follow the progress of this Chorus through the course of the play, however, we learn that the attitude we were first asked to assume must eventually be unlearned, for our critical attitude is at first supplemented and then transformed by the pedagogical impulse. Through questioning we learn, but once we learn, we no longer question.

Except for the occasional, if significant, intervention in the agitators' re-enactments, the Control Chorus engages primarily in the 'Discussion' sections at the end of scenes, or performs set songs that punctuate the action that the agitators depict. Though their words are always accompanied by music, these two activities serve different functions. Whereas the songs ('In Praise of the USSR', 'In Praise of Illegal Work', 'Change the World: It Needs It', and 'In Praise of the Party') reinforce the actions or decisions of the agitators (as opposed to those of the Young Comrade), the questions raised during the discussions are meant to probe the motives for and wisdom of these actions. Thus, with all due apologies to Herbert Marcuse, we might say that the explicitly titled songs represent the 'affirmative' moment of the Control Chorus's presence in the play, while the 'Discussions' display the Chorus in its 'critical' mode. It will, therefore, be instructive to trace, however briefly, the withering away of one of these functions and the ultimate triumph of the other.

The members of the Chorus appear at the very opening of the play in their full authority. They are called upon to receive the returning agitators and recognize their successes in Mukden. When they are told of the death of the Young Comrade, they assume their judicial responsibility. 'Describe how it happened and why,' they command, 'and you will hear our verdict.' The agitators present themselves honestly and confidently, but they agree to accept their apparent superiors' verdict: 'We will submit to your verdict', they reply (Brecht, 2001, p 9). This is the first of four quasi-judicial scenes. At the end of Scene 3, 'The Stone', the Control Chorus cross-examines the agitators regarding the Young Comrade's sympathy for the coolies – 'But isn't it right to aid the weak/ To help the oppressed and exploited/ In his daily affliction/ Wherever he is?' – but accepts their explanation – 'He didn't help us; he hindered us from using our propaganda in the lower part of the city' – with the simple 'We agree' so familiar to readers of Brecht's other teaching plays (Brecht, 2001, p 18). Thus ends the first lesson regarding the relative merits of feeling and understanding in revolutionary action. The situation is the same in the 'Discussion' section of Scene 4 ('Justice'). First comes the Control Chorus's question (this time about the correctness of combating injustice wherever it may appear), then the agitators' explanation (distinguishing greater from lesser injustices), and, finally, agreement (Brecht, 2001, pp 21–22). Indeed, by now we should recognize that the Chorus has no choice but to agree with the reasoning of the agitators, for it conforms to the relativization of morality laid out by the Control Chorus itself at the end of Scene 2. There is only one virtue, and that virtue is advancing the cause of revolution, no matter what other virtues may suffer in the process. Consequently, when, in Scene 5 ('What is Man'), the question is posed – 'But isn't it right to place honour above all else?' – an abrupt and unelaborated negation suffices – 'No' (Brecht, 2001, p 24). No explanation is needed, neither for the Chorus nor for us. Rather than repeating the by now customary 'We agree', the Chorus directly launches into song, 'Change the World: It Needs It', ending their plea for change and revolution with a confession: 'We shall not listen to you much longer as/ Judges. But/ As students' (Brecht, 2001, p 25). From here on out, there are no more 'Discussions'.

In following the progress of the Control Chorus, we witness the collapse of critical distance. At this point in the play, we might say that the so-called 'minor pedagogy', enacted by the critical cross-examinations of the Control Chorus as the embodiment of an 'activated' audience, transforms itself into the 'great pedagogy', the self-transcendence and negation of the audience's critical and oppositional function. It is not by chance that this transformation is punctuated by an explicitly titled song, that is, in the affirmative mode of the Chorus's way of being in the play, for the shift from critical judge to understanding pupil marks the end of debate. With the elimination of divisive individual interest, the potential for conflict is also fully canceled. Consequently, the Control Chorus does not understand the Young Comrade's death as the universal liquidation of the particular nor as the tragic subordination of inclination to abstract duty, but rather as a 'beautiful death', a self-sacrificing affirmation of the objectivity of the collective good. 'It was not you', the Chorus tells the agitators, 'who sentenced him, but/ Reality' (Brecht, 2001, p 33), and one cannot argue with reality. It is this transformation of law into fate and the abdication of the Control Chorus's juridical responsibility that marks the final disappearance of the political from *The Measures Taken*.

*

To observe this disappearance of political distance, however, we, the spectators, must retain our own. That opportunity is afforded us not only by the historical distance we enjoy – the fact that the 'the time of transition of the first revolution' is still with us, or, as the case may be, with us once again – but also by what can only be called a strategic 'verbal blunder' on the part of the Control Chorus. As it affirms its support of the measures taken by the agitators at the very moment that these measures are about to be re-enacted, the Chorus states: 'Continue your story. We/ Sympathize with you' (Brecht, 2001, p 33). Sympathize? How odd! Why should the agreement that is based on rationally accepting the better argument, to evoke a more recent adherent of agreement and consensus – why should that rationally arrived-at approval now be reduced to sympathy? It is reality, according to the Control Chorus, that condemns the Young Comrade, a reality that the emotional, humanist, new recruit failed to perceive in time, because he was a victim of his senses and his sympathy. Now, after numerous examples which are meant to show that cool, calculating, tactical reason triumphs over affective sincerity and ethical purity, why would this Chorus all of a sudden lose its own cool? Is our acceptance of the agitator's measures to be based on sympathy? Is our sympathy for the agitators' deeds meant to trump the more classical, bourgeois sympathy for the fate of the young lad about to lose his life? But how can that be? The battle over means and over ends cannot be fought with dueling sympathies. If we, as readers and spectators, have followed the progress of the Control Chorus and have seen it as a model to be imitated or tried on for size, if we have seen in its actions a type of training for right behavior in a revolutionary situation, then we must stumble over this word, and therefore also stumble over the apparent transformation the Chorus undergoes. If we have been good students, in other words, we are driven to question the lesson presented to us. As the Control Chorus learns to overcome the distance that separates it from the agitators, we re-learn the value of that distance. We may find that we no more wish to overcome the audience/actor distinction than we wish to sublate the difference between theory and practice. The political, as the possibility of conflict and opposition, resides in the space that separates these very different agencies with their very different functions. Our caution, here, may not suit the post-revolutionary, pedagogical Brecht; however, it may well be very much in line with the ironically skeptical Brecht of our persistent, very secular, and seemingly non-transcendable time of perpetual transition.

Notes

1   *The Measures Taken* (German: *Die Massnamhe*) is the most well known of Bertolt Brecht's *Lehrstücke* (teaching plays). These short libretti (for they were set to music, first by Paul Hindemith, then by Kurt Weill, and eventually by Hans Eisler (who composed the music for *The Measures Taken*)) were written for workers' choirs, school groups, and other amateur acting troupes that were part of Berlin's burgeoning proletariat culture in the early 1930s. Ideologically, they addressed problems associated with perceived capitalist exploitation and they 'practiced' or 'tried on' the attitudes and actions deemed necessary for a successful Marxist-Leninist revolution. In *The Measures Taken*, agitators are sent from Moscow to prepare the way for revolution in 'Mukden' in China. On their way, they enlist the aid of a Young Comrade newly converted to the cause. His thoughts and deeds reveal him to be of the bourgeoisie. The play depicts the conflict between the Young Comrade's desire to alleviate immediately and directly the exploitation and injustices he witnesses and the agitators' mission to educate dispassionately and deliberately the peasants and workers about their conditions and what to do about them. Each premature and emotional action by the Young Comrade precipitates disaster and threatens the revolution, which can only come about after the workers have achieved class consciousness. So as not to jeopardize the revolution completely, the Young Comrade (who has made himself recognizable to the authorities and thereby threatens the further actions of the agitators associated with him) must acquiesce to his own death. Upon return to Moscow, the agitators must justify their actions to the Control Chorus. Their justifications (in the form of re-enactments of what happened in each instance) and the Chorus's judgments form the action of the play.

2   See Steinweg, 1972 and Steinweg, 1976. Steinweg's famous thesis is challenged by Krabiel, 1993, and made further problematic by the September 1997 production of *Die Maßnahme* by the Berliner Ensemble, which makes only one gesture (a five minute silence, inviting audience members to think of a different solution to the

problem) in the direction of audience participation, a gesture that would be embarrassing to take seriously.

3 The word (*'gefühlsmäßig'*) comes from a characterization of the purpose of the play by Brecht. See Steinweg, 1976, p 92.

4 Gillian Rose's reading of the Kantian antinomies and their inevitable replication in neo-Kantian sociology (eg Weber) equally locates them in unresolved bourgeois property relations. The ability to resolve antinomies (between concept and intuition as well as between theoretical and practical reason) presupposes the ability to transform social relations, just as the ability to transform social relations presupposes the ability to resolve antinomies, that is, to think the absolute. Hers is the most brilliant contemporary attempt to think the philosophical (Hegelian) foundations of 'revolutionary practice'. For a summary statement of her position, see Rose, 1981, pp 204–20.

5 What Schmitt would call the 'Jacobin logic' of an 'educational dictatorship'. See Schmitt, 1985a, especially chapter 3.

6 The term ('operational closure') is Niklas Luhmann's. See Luhmann, 1997, pp 92–120.

7 This view is most thoroughly and famously advanced in Schmitt, 2003. See, for example, the passage on p 187 (cited above, Chapter 1).

8 'The end result of all this is certainly disconcerting. It reminds us of the deathbed scene of a 19th-century potentate. Asked by his spiritual advisor: "Do you forgive your enemies?" he answered with a clear conscience: "I have no enemies; I have killed them all"' (Schmitt, 1987, p 89).

9 See the famous fragment, 'Theorie der Pädagogien', and the literature Steinweg refers to in Steinweg, 1976, pp 70–71.

PART 2
SOVEREIGNTY AND ORIGINAL SIN

Chapter 4
Guilt as religion: Benjamin

Is capitalism religion, as Walter Benjamin claimed (Benjamin, 1996, pp 288–91)? As the name given to the modern economic system, or, quite simply and generally, to modernity itself, capitalism is not supposed to be a religion. It is supposed to be the great worldly other of religion. It is supposed to be emancipated from religion and from all religious or moral controls, as shown, for instance, by the medieval Catholic ban on usury. Is it then more appropriate to ask whether capitalism is secularized religion? Capitalism may very well be religious asceticism transferred onto an inner-worldly plane; it may, like religion, forsake dissipative pleasure, but not for the sake of saving the soul in an eternal afterlife. Rather, pleasure, too, and its denial, may be transformed under capitalism, for the dissipative excess of libidinous, luxurious, courtly delight may become the refined, bourgeois satisfaction with the austere accumulation of productive wealth over time, and in this way the religious condemnation of pleasure would be secularized and made useful for a rationalized, consumer society. After all: 'Time', as the puritanically inspired saying goes, 'is money'. So: 'Waste not, want not'.

If this is the case, then what Carl Schmitt said, in 1922, of the modern state – 'All significant concepts of the modern theory of the state are secularized theological concepts' (Schmitt, 1985b, p 36) – could also be said of the modern economy, indeed, *had* already been said of the modern economy by Max Weber, who, of course, charted the emergence of the capitalist ethos out of the psychological terrors of extreme Protestant theories of predestination. According to Weber's familiar thesis, the Calvinist Puritan's anxiety about the fact that one can do nothing to further one's own salvation, neither in the public arena of good works nor in the private realm of faith, can be assuaged only if one looks upon one's honorably earned and dutifully husbanded earthly fortune as a material sign – not guarantee, but comforting sign – of God's grace. Soon this enigmatic sign, this ethic of well-deserved material prosperity, becomes the worldly end in itself as salvation recedes further and further into the distant horizon. Thus, eventually, and for better or worse, such transfers and transformations of practices and signs are thought to be in the service of the modern, secular, liberalized, and wholly immanent world. So, to say, as Schmitt does, that there is an analogy between the legal state of exception and the religious miracle is *not* to say that the legal system is based on divine intervention in worldly affairs, or that God is the ultimate lawgiver, but rather and simply to speak in terms of functional equivalencies. Theology perhaps provides the tropes, but no longer the ground for any other social practice or system. Neither law nor God follows a rational design; therefore both law and God must escape the paradox of their own origins by way of a decision – Niklas Luhmann would say distinction – from whose consequences both law and God exempt themselves. God creates the universe, but not Himself. Law creates laws, but not legality *per se*. The sovereignty of any autonomous, operationally closed, self-reproducing system is the same as, and as paradoxical as, God's own sovereignty. Once this is realized, God disappears, having done His job. This is what we call secularization.

But if Walter Benjamin tells us that we should look upon capitalism *as* religion, that we should look upon modernity not as emancipated from religion but as an exemplar of it, then secularization would appear to be a failed project, or at best an unfinished one. In Benjamin's fragmentary account, religion seems to be not the skin of the snake that is sloughed off and left behind, but the snake itself, a snake that returns with the vehemence of the repressed. Perhaps, then, instead of assuming that the secularization process is somehow final, a historical trajectory with modernity as its *telos* and legacy, we ought to revive and revise a revered trope bequeathed to us by the Frankfurt School and speak of the 'dialectic of secularization'. Were we to do so, we would have to speak of two moments of this peculiar dialectic: the first, when the absolute transcendence of monotheistic religion spills over into the absolute immanence of the thoroughly rationalized, secular world; and the second, when, in turn, this absolute immanence becomes its own transcendence, as it were, by becoming its own religion. In the terms made familiar by Weber and echoed in Benjamin's fragment, the purported dialectic in question *first* describes the emergence of the psychological and ideological spirit of capitalism out of the cold, cold ashes of a very cold Protestant work ethic that was originally designed to counter the effects of the bleak doctrine of unremitting predestination; and then, as its *second* moment, the dialectic describes the transformation of this spirit of capitalism itself back into a guiding ethic, a type of ersatz yet universally compelling religion, which harnessed the tightly wound self-discipline of inner-worldly asceticism for the accumulation of productive wealth. God is dead! Long live God! Only now let us call that deity 'Man'; or, better yet, let us simply call it Money.

If we wish to keep with our image of the dialectic of secularization, then, seen structurally, the historical process of secularization would have to be a paradoxical intensification of radical transcendence until it transforms itself, as if by logical necessity, into its absolute other, radical immanence. This is precisely how Marcel Gauchet sees secularization in his study, *The Disenchantment of the World*. Rather than viewing the great monotheistic religions, especially Judaism and Christianity, as the epitome or culmination of religious development, he sees monotheism, with its absolutely transcendent and therefore absolutely other God, as the final stage in the total secularization of the world. The essence of religion, he writes, is in its origin, and that origin is characterized by what he calls radical dispossession. By dispossession he means that we humans 'owe everything we have, our way of living, our rules, our customs, and what we know, to beings of a different nature – to Ancestors, Heroes, or Gods. All we can do is follow, imitate, and repeat what they have taught us'. Everything, in other words, has been '*handed down to us*' (Gauchet,

1997, pp 23–24). The world, according to this essentially religious view, is not something we create, but something we inherit, and those from whom we inherit it, though they are wholly other than we are, are still present in our lives – they dictate our everyday practices and beliefs. The essential religious distinction, then, is that between the human community on the one hand and those beings on the other who serve as the imperious foundation for all human life. If one wishes to use a formal figure devised by George Spencer Brown and popularized by Luhmann, it is not difficult to see that this original distinction – between the human and the divine – re-enters the human community and separates one group from the other. According to Gauchet, with the rise of the ancient State (such as Egypt), the subordination of the human community to the divine order is replicated as the subjugation of one segment of society, the ruled, by the other, the rulers, who act as representatives, as it were, of the divine principle. Finally, with European Christianity, this social hierarchy is overcome, but in an extremely counterintuitive way, namely, through the absolute transcendence of the divine principle. With the establishment of the complete separation of the City of God and the Earthly City, Gauchet claims, all attempts to maintain a hierarchical relationship between them are doomed to failure. It is true; the desire that accompanied the dichotomy of the two cities was the desire to organize the human City according to the principles of the transcendent City of God. The aim of the 'true Christian community', Gauchet writes, was to 'unite all the faithful within a City-World, where the executive mechanisms and the wheels of authority would be subordinate to eternal aims, under the leadership of a single shepherd, who was himself closest to God'. However, 'as soon as one of the two possible hegemonic claims – in this case, the primacy of the spiritual – was openly asserted, it literally provoked the expression of an opposed claim, the autonomy of the temporal. The structural outcome was that the desire to subjugate everything to the beyond disclosed the irreducible independence of the here-below; this very desire legitimated its opposite' (Gauchet, 1997, p 153). In other words, a final re-entry occurs, one that now creates a division not *between* humans, that is, not between rulers and ruled, but *within* the individual human. This final distinction, this 'inner split', Gauchet maintains, 'opens up a *fracture in being*, which allows an illuminating access, from within, to more truth than is given by communal existence', such that 'meaning' is no longer the product of destiny, but 'could now be found here-below in a voyage of inner discovery' (Gauchet, 1997, p 47). The absolute separation of the two cities allows, then, for a space of human reflection and human deliberation, a human *re*-possession of thought and autonomy. As a result, an absolutely unknowable and invisible God is seemingly pushed back into the unmarked space that we simply call absolute transcendence because we have no way any more of imagining what or where this deity could possibly be. This, then, is the extreme dialectical moment, the point where the thesis – absolute transcendence – tips over and becomes its own negation – absolute immanence. 'The paradox', to quote Gauchet one last time:

is that an increase in a figurative or experienced otherness corresponds to a decrease in an actually implemented otherness; strengthening the image of the Other involves an actual decline in dependence on it ... One could almost devise a law to apply to this situation, a law of human emancipation through divine affirmation. It could be summed up as follows: the greater the gods, the freer humans are. (Gauchet, 1997, p 1)

Thus, God's infinitely remote otherness abandons us to our own devices and we learn to create a world in our own image and according to our own needs.

Gauchet's narrative of secularization, at least as presented here, is clearly a triumphalist, Enlightenment account of human emancipation. As one American reviewer of his book put it: 'There is a stubborn kernel of truth here. It is that a liberal order may find a friend in religion because God's otherness is what makes us free: free to believe and free not to believe. Western history is the unfolding of this irony.'[1] God, on this view, is functionalized for the better working of the liberal political order. We do not serve Him, He serves us. One could, however, also view the secularization narrative tragically, for it could be said to represent the loss of our communal foundation. With Heidegger, for example, one could say that the absolute otherness and transcendence of God, His retreat into the unmarked space, signifies nothing less than our forgetfulness of Being. With Heidegger, then, and with Heidegger's Hölderlin, we might see our contemporary fate to be nothing other than the fate of waiting for the return of the gods, those heroes and ancestors who laid the foundations of the human community in which we find our rightful and proper place. The question to be asked of Benjamin's fragment is whether his account of capitalism as religion in any way fits either the triumphant or the tragic model of modernity. If capitalism is a religion, does this mean that the gods have returned, or that they never left? And if they have returned, if they are still among us or among us once again, should we be pleased with their continued presence?

*

Although Max Weber's *The Protestant Ethic and the Spirit of Capitalism* is the clear impetus for Benjamin's speculations on the nature and structure of capitalism, his fragment, 'Capitalism as Religion', is presented not as an elaboration of Weber's thesis, but as the refutation of it. Capitalism is not merely a 'formation conditioned by religion', as Weber insisted, but is 'an essentially religious phenomenon' and thus has a 'religious structure' (Benjamin, 1996, p 288). It is this structure Benjamin wishes to investigate. And if we are to take Benjamin's claim seriously, then our first task is to ask: To which, if any, of the three structures of religious life outlined above, does capitalism conform?

Benjamin claims to be able to locate three aspects of the structure of capitalism. In fact, he identifies four features, but all four can be reduced to two overriding categories: the cultic nature of capitalism and the centrality of the notion of guilt within this cult. I will save the discussion of guilt for later and concentrate first on what Benjamin means by cult.

For Benjamin, a cult organizes every aspect of a person's life, leaving no time and no space untouched. Though, as he says, a cult has no single dogma or theology, it provides the central meaning to which each member has to refer. And it provides this meaning at all times. There is no 'weekday', he says, only the oppressive perpetuity of the *Festtag*: the holiday, the feast day, the holy day. Cults, therefore, demand the 'utter fealty of each worshiper' (Benjamin, 1996, p 288). There is no escape. These characteristics of the cult could be taken directly from the opening passages of Weber's classic text in which he describes the Calvinist Protestant attempt to reassert the church's control over all aspects of the lives of its members. The Reformation, Weber reminds us, was not interested in eliminating the Church's control over our private and public lives, but rather was interested in increasing that control, even substituting for an older, primarily formulaic and rather lax form of control a far more stringent and unbearable form, driven by the internal pangs of conscience and enforced by the external authority of what we would today call a totalitarian, theocratic society (Weber, 1958, pp 36–37). One need only think of the history of the 17th-century Massachusetts Bay Colony, with its inquisitions, religious persecutions and the double bind of its witch hunts, to understand what such a Puritan society looked like. Yet, despite – or rather because of – this psychological severity, there was, as Weber acknowledges, a kind of rare heroism in middle class self-discipline, a courage and perseverance that gave rise to the so-called heroic age of early capitalism. By the beginning of the 20th century, however, that heroism had become routine, even compulsory. 'The Puritan wanted to work in a calling', writes Weber; 'we are forced to do so' (Weber, 1958, p 188). Voluntary self-overcoming becomes involuntary self-numbing. Today, then, we are left with the robotic subjects of Weber's famous Nietzschean-sounding phrase, 'Specialists without spirit, sensualists without heart' (Weber, 1958, p 182). These latter, post-heroic 'specialists' are the inhabitants of Benjamin's cult of capitalism.

It is important to distinguish Benjamin's cult from what Weber defines as a sect. A sect, Weber writes elsewhere, 'wants to be an association of the religiously qualified and only them, not an institute of mercy like a church, which wishes to shed its light over the just and the unjust alike and indeed wants most of all to expose sinners to the discipline of God's commandments. The sect incorporates the ideal of the *ecclesia pura* (hence the name "Puritan"), the visible community of the holy, from whose midst the mangy sheep are to be cast lest they cause offense in the sight of God' (Weber, 1991, p 348). Benjamin's cult has no such pretensions. Indeed, it is interesting to see that in the final paragraph of his fragment, Benjamin explicitly equates capitalism with the religion of the 'first heathens', that is, with those whose interests were practical and who had not yet reached a state of self-reflection or self-observation that would lead to moral or transcendental ideals. A follower of the religion of these early heathens, Benjamin writes, 'regarded individuals who were irreligious or had other beliefs as members of its community, in the same way that the modern bourgeoisie now regards those of its members who are not gainfully employed' (Benjamin, 1996, p 290). All are included, precisely because dogmatic uniformity remains unimportant. What is important is membership in the community. Besides the idle poor and the unemployed – those, that is, whose lack of success advertizes their flawed faith and absent grace – one could add to the list of unbelievers numerous others, including explicit opponents searching for alternatives, like Benjamin perhaps, or academic Marxists, who, with their salaries, pension plans, mortgages, car loans, credit card debts, and private school tuition for their children, are every bit as much voluntary or involuntary members of the cult of capitalism as any investment banker. The unbeliever may not join a sect, but he or she cannot escape the cult.

As a cult, as a continuous sacral feast, capitalism is a community from which one cannot flee. It guides and controls our lives, whether we believe in its mechanisms or not. Confronted with so-called commodity fetishism and mass consumerism, do we nevertheless cling to notions of authenticity, use value, non-alienated labor? No matter, for we worship at the altar of exchange value every time we cash our paycheck, draw money out of an ATM machine, tip the waiter a few extra dollars. As the name given to the modern money economy and as the name given to the social order in which this economy functions, capitalism 'commands the utter fealty of every worshiper', and every member of modern society is by necessity a worshiper, whether or not he or she intends to be. Is this secularization? Not according to Benjamin. Indeed, we can now see that for Benjamin, capitalism is religion in its purest form, in its *Urform*. The collapse of transcendence, charted by Gauchet and documented by Weber with reference to Calvinist Protestantism, is not a collapse into godless immanence, but a collapse back into the primeval immanence controlled by the gods – those mysterious beings who tell us how the world works. To question these gods, to question their revelations, as they appear in the *Wall Street Journal*, the *Financial Times*, or the *Frankfurter Allgemeine Zeitung*, is not to present an alternate vision or philosophy of history, but to question reality itself.

*

If the cult of capitalism has no dogma, what is it that has such a hold on the community, such that it can hold the community together? Benjamin's answer is 'guilt', an all-pervasive guilt that is created by the cult and that implicates God. 'Capitalism', he writes, 'is probably the first instance of a cult that creates guilt, not atonement.' Therefore:

> A vast sense of guilt that is unable to find relief seizes on the cult, not to atone for this guilt but to make it universal, to hammer it into the conscious mind, so as once and for all to include God in the system of guilt and thereby awaken in Him an interest in the process of atonement. This atonement cannot then be expected from the cult itself, or from the reformation of this religion ... or even from the complete renouncement of this religion. (Benjamin, 1996, pp 288–89)

It is tempting, indeed, it seems inevitable, that one should focus both on the historical uniqueness of capitalism and on the double sense of the German term for guilt (*Schuld*) – meaning both *guilt*, in its theological sense, based on the burden of original sin, and *debt*, a form of economic guilt, based on the lack of credit, and thus the lack of credibility, the material sign of good faith, which is an equally universal burden, for without debt there could be no growth, no capitalist expansion. If one followed the secularization thesis, in other words, and saw the spirit of capitalism as a form of secularized Calvinism, one could see debt (*Schuld*) as secularized sin, a version of guilt (*Schuld*) that is carried to all corners of the globe and to all corners of the soul by money; and money, in turn, could be seen as both the cause of the debtor's guilt (*des Schuldners Schuld*) and the means by which the debtor can be potentially redeemed. And, in English, at any rate, one can continue to investigate the play in terminology by noting both the economic and the theological sense of the term 'redemption'. Certainly, to include God in the world's guilt would be to put God in our debt. It is, as I say, tempting to read Benjamin's fragment in this way, but it makes remarkably little sense to do so.

Why does it make little sense to play these word games? Because 'capitalism' for Benjamin seems not to be a historical category. Despite the historicity of the phenomenon capitalism – which Weber, for instance, insists upon when he distinguishes traditional economies, with their profligate attitude toward wealth, from capital, which is disciplined, even chastised wealth that is put to good work – Benjamin seems to use the term loosely, much the way Horkheimer and Adorno use the notion of the bourgeois subject in their *Dialectic of Enlightenment*. Although Benjamin insists that capitalism is 'entirely without precedent', he also maintains that capitalism, by the very fact that it creates, rather than compensates for guilt, 'is caught up in the headlong rush of a larger movement' (Benjamin, 1996, p 288). What this great movement may be is not specified. Historically, it could simply be identified as 'modernity', but then the term 'capitalism' would be restricted to being used as the description of modernity's economic system, and one would have to wonder how Benjamin envisioned, in 1921, capitalism's integration into this larger whole, especially considering its putative cult status. It may, therefore, be more useful to identify this movement structurally with the creation of guilt as such. It may be that money is the koine of the realm in which guilt is worshiped, but capitalism may not be the first or only force that brings guilt into being. A key to understanding this text, in other words, is to understand what Benjamin believes to be the correct view about the true origin of guilt in the human world.

Benjamin's reference to Sorel's *Reflections on Violence*, the first of a number of literary sources cited near the end of the text, may point us in the right direction; for here, Benjamin's reference to the 'heathen character of law' reminds us of his similar characterization of capitalism in the very last paragraph, the passage that notes capitalism's resemblance to the religion of the 'first heathens'. It presents no leap of the imagination, then, to glance at a much more famous and often discussed text, written and published in the same year (1921), Benjamin's 'Critique of Violence', for guidance.

The latter part of Benjamin's 'Critique' is structured around a set of distinctions with clear positive and negative values. The prime distinction is one between a negatively marked mythic force or violence and its positive other, divine violence. Mythic violence is equated with law. It is both law-positing and law-preserving. In Carl Schmitt's terms, one could say that mythic violence is both legitimacy and legality. To give a modern, liberal example: mythic violence is both the legitimizing force that establishes a constitution – a political revolution, for instance – and the legal force – the code of laws – that that constitution underwrites. Consequently, mythic violence creates a legal-political order. But Benjamin thoroughly condemns such a legal and political order, finding the mythical violence that constitutes that order both an 'executive' and an 'administrative' force, thus utterly reprehensible and in need of destruction (Benjamin, 1996, p 252). The force charged with opposing, even destroying mythic violence and the order it establishes is the 'pure immediate violence' that is labeled 'divine'. In a famous and oft-quoted passage, Benjamin contrasts the two manifestations of force as follows:

> If mythic violence is lawmaking, divine violence is law-destroying; if the former sets boundaries, the latter boundlessly destroys them; if mythic violence brings at once guilt and retribution, divine power only expiates; if the former threatens, the latter strikes; if the former is bloody, the latter is lethal without spilling blood. (Benjamin, 1996, pp 249–50)

Divine violence and its effects, in other words, cannot be positively defined, but only delineated by what it is not. It is simply destructive of the given order without promising anything new except the promise of the new itself.

Despite the religious language, it is important to remember that the model for this distinction between a mythic or legal violence, on the one hand, and a quasi-utopian, extra-legal and extra-political, divine violence, on the other, is Sorel's distinction between the political general strike, which simply replaces one political order with another, and the revolutionary or proletariat general strike, the aim of which is purely and directly destructive. What disturbs Benjamin about mythic violence is what disturbed Sorel about the coercive violence of the political strike, namely, that it transfers political power from one elite group to another, without altering the nature of political power as such. Mythic violence simply reproduces the structure of power and violence, whereas divine violence, by being essentially anarchical, is said to usher in a new historical epoch that potentially holds the promise of an order not based on the necessary perpetuation of legal or any other form of force. Mythic violence, in other words, *produces* guilt; divine violence delivers us from it. The relationship of mythic violence to guilt is intimated in the following enigmatic and philologically difficult passage:

> For blood is the symbol of mere life. Though it cannot be shown in detail here, setting legal violence in motion stems from the guilt of mere natural life, which consigns the living, innocent and unhappy, to an atonement that expiates the guilt of mere life – and doubtless also frees the guilty, not from guilt, however, but from law. For with mere life, the rule of law over the living ceases. Mythic violence is bloody power over mere life for

its own sake; divine violence is pure power over all life for the sake of the living. The first demands sacrifice; the second accepts it. (Benjamin, 1996, p 250; translation modified)

For Benjamin, and, more recently, for Giorgio Agamben, whose book *Homo Sacer* could be said to be an extended elaboration of this passage, the bloody violence to which mere life is exposed comprises the state of exception upon which the sovereign rule of the law is founded. Thus the realm of mere life and the realm of the political constituted by legal violence are intimately bound together. Mere life is not the condition of pre-political innocence to which one returns, but the condition of politically induced guilt that must be overcome. To accept the condition of mere life is to accept the condition of a socially and historically produced guilt; therefore, to accept the guilt of valuing mere existence over just existence, that is, 'the not-yet-attained condition of the just man' (Benjamin, 1996, p 251), is to embrace nihilism. To think the existing political order from within the existing political order, even if one attempts to alter that order, is to think nihilistically, for, in so doing, one can never free oneself from the guilt that this political order produces. As Agamben writes, 'Guilt refers not to transgression, that is, to the determination of the licit and the illicit, but to the pure force of the law, to the law's simple reference to something'. Therefore, 'until a completely new politics – that is, a politics no longer founded on the *exceptio* of bare life – is at hand, every theory and every praxis will remain imprisoned and immobile, and the "beautiful day" of life will be given citizenship only either through blood and death or in the perfect senselessness to which the society of the spectacle condemns it' (Agamben, 1998, p 11). But that 'completely new politics' cannot be planned or anticipated, it can only occur as the result of the absolute destruction of the present order by a purely immediate and bloodless divine violence.

If we keep this mythically, this legally and politically and socially, this humanly induced guilt in mind, we can see, I think, a form of divine violence make its presence felt in Benjamin's 'Capitalism as Religion' as well. Indeed, to avoid what I rather facetiously called the dialectic of secularization above, to avoid the apparent oscillation of immanence and transcendence that Gauchet describes, in which religion moves from its primal, immanent condition to a quasi-transcendence mediated by state authority, and finally to an absolute transcendence which, as if automatically, collapses back into the primal immanence of the gods and their omnipresent guilt – to avoid all this, the pure catastrophe of divine violence would seem to be necessary. Benjamin explicitly states that capitalism, as a cult of guilt, cannot simply be willed away. The cult makes guilt universal, yet no reformation or even renunciation of this cult, no *political violence*, reform, or revolution can atone for this guilt. Faced with such power, even God is made impotent. But this is precisely the point. The universality of guilt that capitalism imposes is pushed to such an extreme that despair turns to hope, the hope for the complete destruction of the world-as-we-know-it.

> The nature of the religious movement which is capitalism entails endurance right to the end, to the point where God, too, finally takes on the entire burden of guilt, to the point where the universe has been taken over by that despair which is actually its secret hope. Capitalism is entirely without precedent, in that it is a religion which offers not the reform of existence but its complete destruction. It is the expansion of despair, until despair becomes a religious state of the world in the hope that this will lead to salvation. God's transcendence is at an end. But he is not dead; he has been incorporated into human existence. (Benjamin, 1996, p 289)

God is the agent of the destruction of this world, but he does it by way of self-annihilation. He is not the omnipotent angry god who causes the flood, nor the sacrificial god who offers his own life for our sins. He is the god reduced to the plane of human activity, the god who is also destroyed by the violence that goes under his name. What remains will only be known when the time comes, and that time has obviously not yet come.

*

Is, then, Benjamin's critique of capitalism a critique of the secularization process, or an attempt to re-think it? Does Benjamin, in other words, propose a theological, indeed, a famously messianic alternative to the failed project of secularization? If guilt is introduced by the gods, including the gods that serve secular capital, it would seem that what will save us from guilt is neither a return of the gods nor their ultimate extermination. If a return is at all implied, it must be a return to a time and a space *before* the gods. Secularization – if that is what one would still want to call it – is therefore not the culmination of a historical process; rather, it comes as the denial of all process, as the absence of all history. Emancipation from the gods occurs, can only occur, before the gods ever make their appearance, in a space opened up by an absolute and absolutely cleansing destruction. Only then, Benjamin seems to say, can the new historical era begin.

Note

1   Jean Bethke Elshtain, cited on the back cover of the American paperback edition of Gauchet, 1997.

adding in parenthesis: '(There is not, as Russell thought, a special law of contradiction for each type; one law is enough, since it is not applied to itself)' (Wittgenstein, 1961, pp 62–63). Accordingly, it is not so much that the proposition 'All propositions are either true or false' falls *outside* the set of all propositions; rather, remaining inside, the proposition excludes itself from its own workings. It simply cannot be subject to the same judgment that it exercises – which is to say that, for the law of the excluded middle to operate, it must *be* the excluded middle, neither true nor false. Thus, self-exemption 'solves' the paradox of totalizing propositions by rudely and insolently *becoming* the paradox. The barber who shaves only and all those who do not shave themselves is not only *not* excommunicated from his Sicilian village, he is chosen to *rule* it. He is, at one and the same time, *of* the town and *over* it.

In a word, the barber is sovereign, for the paradox that both Russell and Wittgenstein ponder is the neat trick of sovereign self-exemption, which makes a necessary asymmetry out of an impossible symmetry. The sudden emergence of this figure – the figure of the sovereign – at first seems arbitrary and mysterious. When personified as an individual, an institution, or a general will, sovereignty appears as if it *precedes* the law, giving the law its force. Yet, the sovereign is simply the name given to a logical effect. Rather than prior or opposed to the law, the sovereign is law's shadow, its included and excluded double. In the set we call 'Sicilian village', law is universal. All are equal before the law. Whoever applies the law is also subject to the law. But the law itself is not subject to the law. The law lays down the law and demands obedience in exchange for protection *under* the law. In a world organized hierarchically, this Sicilian law might be subject to a 'higher' law, a 'natural' or 'moral' law, but such a world must eventually arrive at God, who then becomes the sovereign source of law by the selfsame self-exemption that hierarchical ordering means to avoid. Without God, deferral to higher levels must eventually lead to a classically bad infinity of provisional sovereigns whose sovereignty is forever relative to the next higher, yet equally provisional, equally relative sovereign. Ironically, then, for law to be absolute, it must be limited, it must be immanent to the set in which it rules and stand in no hierarchical relation to the outside. The distinction of levels is displaced – or rather – re-placed, re-entered into the set itself. The result is not a hierarchy of sets, but a simultaneous symmetry and asymmetry of propositions within the set of all propositions. The law does not derive its power from an external source, but rather achieves its power by distinguishing itself from itself – an act, as it were, of logical nuclear fission. Thus, the proposition that maintains that all propositions are either true or false claims for itself the *authority* of truth precisely by refusing to subject itself to the mechanism of truth-testing. It is sovereign simply because it is sovereign.

... and the rule of law

The figure of the sovereign makes those who are democratically inclined nervous, because the democratically inclined hope to avoid asymmetry at all

Chapter 5

From sovereign ban to banning sovereignty: Agamben

The logic of sovereignty …

Poor Bertrand Russell, what a mean father. He was such a splendid procreator of paradoxes, but he cared so little for his offspring, always wishing they would deny their own existence or acknowledge their illegitimacy. But they have not gone away, and they still entertain us today. Who can forget – as some compiler of Russell's greatest hits might say – who can forget the Sicilian barber, the barber who shaves only and all those in his village who do not shave themselves?[1] Does the barber shave himself? If he does, then he does not *only* shave those who do not shave themselves; and if he does not, then he does not shave *all* those who do not shave themselves. So what does the perplexed Russell do with our paralyzed barber? He exiles him and condemns him to live outside the city walls, up in the foothills, alone, traveling to town everyday to shave those who do not shave themselves. Poor Barber of the Outskirts of Town, he loses his birthright and his citizenship. Poor Bertrand, what a mean father – he subjects yet another of his unruly children to the paternal law of the excluded middle.

But what about that law itself? To what is the law of the excluded middle subject? Even asking the question raises the specter of another paradox, as Russell clearly recognized. Stated in the form of a proposition, the law of the excluded middle is a proposition about all propositions. It says: 'All propositions are either true or false.' The law, then, would seem to include itself within the set it adjudicates. It would seem to require that the law undergo its own scrutiny and pass judgment on itself. This Russell finds to be a vicious and therefore meaningless and illegitimate circle. 'If from this law', he and Whitehead write in the *Principia Mathematica*:

> we argue that, because the law of excluded middle is a proposition, therefore the law of excluded middle is true or false, we incur a vicious-circle fallacy. 'All propositions' must be in some way limited before it becomes a legitimate totality, and any limitation which makes it legitimate must make any statement about the totality fall outside the totality. (Whitehead and Russell, 1910, p 40)

But where such a fallen statement lands remains a problem. Russell recommends his theory of types,[2] to the effect that statements about totalities must be made from a hierarchical level higher than the level occupied by the now limited totality under discussion – from the extra-urban foothills, as it were. A totality of totalities, therefore, becomes incommunicable. To many observers, however, including Russell himself eventually, the arbitrary and ad hoc nature of the theory of types has always been disquieting.[3] Indeed, favoring self-exemption over endless stairways to heaven, Wittgenstein provocatively points to the superfluity of the theory of types. 'Clearly', he writes at 6.123 of the *Tractatus*, 'the laws of logic cannot in their turn be subject to laws of logic', costs. They do so by replacing sovereignty with the rule of law, as if the rule of law had no need of the personified sovereign because it made use of impersonal reason, that is, as if reason were not itself another name for the figure of sovereign self-exemption. As if, in other words, the operation of even the most basic law, such as the law of the excluded middle, were not a sovereign operation. Therefore, that the domestic and international rule of law replaces an older reliance on both state and, to a lesser degree, popular sovereignty, is a commonplace of 20th-century liberal, constitutional thought. In its most basic form, the rule of law, as opposed to the rule of men, allegedly supplants the naked and arbitrary force of a willful sovereign power or majority mob. The subjects of the rule of law are individuals who are said to form a collective entity called humanity. As late as 1934, the American legal scholar, James Brown Scott, could still unhesitatingly claim that what we now call 'humanity' is but an extension of an older, inclusive community of Christian believers. With the discovery of the New World, Scott wrote, the old European, Christian community was 'replaced by an international community today universal and embracing all peoples of all continents; the law applicable to members of the Christian community was found to be applicable to non-Christians; and the law of nations, once confined to Christendom, has become international' (Scott, 1934a, pp 1–2). More recently, and in a more secular vein, liberal theorists like Jürgen Habermas and John Rawls have grounded popular will formation and a Law of Peoples on liberal human rights, such that, ideally, we are left, in Habermas's words, with a 'cosmopolitan law' that 'bypasses the collective subjects of international law [ie states] and directly establishes the legal status of the individual subjects by granting them unmediated membership in the association of free and equal world citizens' (Habermas, 1998, p 181). In other words, a global legal order based on human rights, which, as Rawls states, form a 'proper subset of the rights possessed by citizens in a liberal constitutional democratic regime' (Rawls, 2001, p 81), is but a near seamless, universal extension of the liberal domestic sphere. Instead of the traditional anarchy of sovereign states jealously guarding their autonomy, we have a single community of individuals who obey the law – not because of its arbitrary and authoritarian sovereignty, but because the law is said to represent every individual's reasonable interests. With human rights established as the normative origin of all law, war is outlawed, rogue states policed, and violations of these rights punished in a global domestic sphere. The rule of law, we are told, governs all human relations.

Against this background, Carl Schmitt's famous definition – 'Sovereign is he who decides on the exception' (Schmitt, 1985b, p 5) – sounds, at best, anachronistic. After all, the decision has already been made, and that decision dictates that there will be no more decisions, that decisions will be replaced by universally valid, because rationally achieved, norms. Under the law, there will be no exception, just rule. Thus, from the universalist point of view, the concept of sovereignty, with its recognition of an irreducible and indeterminate conflict of state interests, is not just an outdated but also an outlaw concept, for it attempts to subvert the normative order that enlightened modernity is said to embody. But Schmitt's definition, though unpopular, is not all that anachronistic. And if it is illegal, it is not because it *opposes* the liberal order so much as it *exposes* it. Indeed, it seeks to explain it *as* an order, as one possible order among many – in short, as a political reality, and not merely a legal or moral ideology. 'Like every other order', Schmitt writes, 'the legal order rests on a decision and not on a norm' (Schmitt, 1985b, p 10). It can therefore be said that Schmitt's definition of sovereignty – again: 'Sovereign is he who decides on the exception' – is itself an answer to a question, namely: When push comes to shove, who decides? Who is this he, she, or it? Accordingly, the liberal denial of sovereignty necessarily prompts the paradoxical query: What or which sovereign power determines that there will be no sovereign power? Or, more politically theological: What or which sovereign power declares, 'Thou shalt have no other sovereign powers before me'?

Why is decision unavoidable? It is unavoidable, Schmitt answers, because of the limits of logic. Simply put, Schmitt argues against the possibility of determining logically or rationally a 'highest, legally independent, underived power', because any attempt to do so leads, as our Sicilian barber showed us, to either infinite regress or paradox. It leads to infinite regress because reality is governed by the law of causality, and the law of causality is infinite. Every cause is the effect of a prior cause. It is paradoxical because if the highest, underived power is the norm that establishes the rule of law, it too must be under the law, it must be in the field of its own operations – else it would commit the same self-exemption characteristic of sovereignty. But if it too is under the law, it cannot be the highest, underived power, because its actions can then be determined (By what? By whom?) to be legal or illegal. The problem cannot be solved logically. It must be solved 'existentially'. To cut the chain and fix a point of origin to serve as an underived norm, or, to establish procedures for determining where to cut the chain, or, to establish discursive rules for establishing procedures for determining where to cut the chain, is, ultimately, to commit a political act. More important than the question of where the chain is cut, is the question of who cuts. Liberal human rights, from which Habermas and Rawls wish to derive popular will formation and the Law of Peoples, are precisely what they say they are – liberal – because they are the manifestation of a liberal political order, and *not* because liberal ideology vibrates at the same frequency as the dynamo at the heart of the universe. The universality of human rights is directly linked to the extent of the political hegemony that serves as *their* starting point. Establishing norms does not precede politics and evade sovereignty; it *is* politics, sovereign politics.

When, therefore, Giorgio Agamben, following Schmitt, states that the 'paradox of sovereignty consists in the fact the sovereign is, at the same time, outside and inside the juridical order' (Agamben, 1998, p 15), he does not exclude the force of law from this rule. Classically, the paradox of sovereignty is resolved – but certainly not solved – by the distinction between a constituting and a constituted power, a distinction that Schmitt endorses and that constitutional liberals attempt to evade. As Agamben says, 'Today, in the context of the general tendency to regulate everything by means of rules, fewer and fewer are willing to claim that constituting power is originary and irreducible, that it cannot be conditioned and constrained in any way by a determinate legal system and that it necessarily maintains itself outside every constituted power' (Agamben, 1998, pp 39–40). Liberal theorists, like Hans Kelsen in Schmitt's time and Habermas in our own, try to derive the rule of law painlessly from norms that are said to be objectively, consensually and/or procedurally universal. They assume that objectivity or universality takes the sting of sovereignty out of constitutional rule, that, because necessary and thoroughly internalized, their norms exert no force, but only instantiate freedom. Thus, a liberal constitution simply embodies in legal form what, in Habermas's words, 'could be *jointly* accepted by *all* concerned without coercion' (Habermas, 1996a, p 42). Agamben replies that '*the constitution presupposes itself as constituting power* and, in this form, expresses the paradox of sovereignty in the most telling way' (Agamben, 1998, pp 40–41). Though written as law, it is as if the constitution existed outside the law in a state of nature. It legitimizes the rule of law but cannot itself be legitimized except by way of a sovereign self-exemption – the sovereign self-exemption of norms or procedures that are deemed (again: By whom?) universal and thus incontestable.

Like Schmitt, Walter Benjamin also saw through this liberal sleight of hand and recognized that if one wished to transcend sovereignty, one needed to transcend law itself. For this reason, Benjamin analyzed the force of law in terms of a dual, but linked, violence that is but another version of the distinction between constituting and constituted power. The violence that demands obedience to the existing law is *rechtserhaltend* (law-preserving), while the violence that founds the law, that establishes the necessary asymmetry by means of self-exemption, is *rechtsetzend* (law-positing). This latter violence opens up an ordered space that the former preserves. Benjamin names both types of legal violence mythic. Taken together, they sovereignly establish a historically given social, legal and political order (Benjamin, 1996). Regarding Benjamin's distinction, Agamben notes: 'If constituting power is, as the violence that posits law, certainly more noble than the violence that preserves it, constituting power still possesses no title that might legitimate something other than law-preserving violence and even maintains an ambiguous and ineradicable relation with constituted power' (Agamben, 1998, p 40). Benjamin, it can therefore be said, emphasizes the unity of the distinction between constituting and constituted violence by labeling them collectively 'mythic'.

There is, however, a second type of violence, categorically different from mythic violence. Divine violence, which cannot be defined positively, is nonetheless all that mythic violence is not. In Benjamin's words: 'If mythic violence posits law, divine violence destroys it; if the former sets boundaries, the latter destroys them boundlessly; if mythic violence brings with it guilt and atonement, divine violence redeems; if the former threatens, the latter strikes; if the former is bloody, the latter is bloodless in a lethal way' (Benjamin, 1996, p 199). Accordingly, mythic violence is mundane. It establishes a contingent political order that is built on the forced, provisional suspension of the originary paradox. It can define that ordered space only from within that ordered space. It is, for example, an order in which something called 'justice' prevails, not because justice is absolutely just, but because justice is an effect of the sovereign self-exemption and thus a necessary component of the contingently determined political order. In the court of reason, all propositions are judged to be true or false, except the proposition that states that the court is a court of reason. Divine violence, on the other hand, comes as if from the outside to limit the space of the political, indeed, to mark that space for demolition. It too recognizes that the paradox at the origin of the mythical world cannot be solved peacefully, but it assumes that the perplexing knot of asymmetry at the source of the political can be cut by a single, simple act of violence that will 'found a new historical age' (Benjamin, 1996, p 202), one in which the sovereign self-exemption will be rendered null and void. Divine violence does not replace one political order with another; it replaces one order of *the political*, based on the sovereign self-exemption, with another yet to be determined manifestation of the political beyond all exception.

The state of nature as the state of the political

On this, then, they all agree: that the paradox of sovereignty, no matter how resolved, is the common structure of all modern political life – indeed, perhaps all political life since Aristotle. Where they differ – where, that is, Agamben, taking Benjamin with him, differs from Schmitt – can be seen in this complaint: 'The problem of sovereignty', Agamben writes, 'was reduced to the question of who within the political order was invested with certain powers, and the very threshold of the political order itself was never called into question' (Agamben, 1998, p 12). Where they differ, then, is over the possibility of calling the logical structure of sovereignty into question; for calling into question the very structure of sovereignty is what Agamben wishes to do, and it is what he says Benjamin wishes to do. But calling sovereignty into question is not what Schmitt is after. Thus this is the great distinction that organizes the work of Schmitt, Benjamin and Agamben – not totalitarianism vs democratic rule of law, but the metaphysics of the West, which is characterized by the ontology of sovereignty, vs a post-metaphysical ontology of the political yet to be realized. Whereas Schmitt locates himself firmly within the political as defined by the sovereign exception, both Benjamin and Agamben imagine the possibility of a politics that exceeds the political. Yet neither Agamben nor Benjamin can say what the grand Other of the structure of sovereignty may be, only that it *ought* to be; that if and when it comes, it will come with an all consuming but bloodless violence that, in Benjamin's terms, will be divine, not mythic, neither lawmaking nor law-preserving; and that if and when it comes, it will institute a new, post-sovereign, post-rule-of-law, historical epoch. It will be, as Agamben, referring to Benjamin, intimates, 'capable of releasing man from guilt and of affirming natural innocence' (Agamben, 1998, p 28).

Agamben translates what we have treated as logical inevitability into a metaphysical mistake, or rather, into the mistake of metaphysics itself. The fall into metaphysics is occasionally historicized and talked of as the sin of modernity. When Agamben writes that the 'inclusion of bare life in the political realm constitutes the original – if concealed – nucleus of sovereign power', and when he then goes on to assert that it *'can even be said that the production of a biopolitical body is the original activity of sovereign power'* (Agamben, 1998, p 6), one can think of Bodin, absolutism, and eventually the French Revolution, with its inclusion of the 'social question', as Hannah Arendt called it – that is, the introduction of poverty and happiness into the realm of the political.[4] One can, and Agamben does, refer to *The History of Sexuality*, where Foucault notes 'the entry of life into history' in the 18th century. 'For the first time in history', Foucault writes at the end of the first volume, 'biological existence was reflected in political existence; the fact of living was no longer an inaccessible substrate that only emerged from time to time, amid the randomness of death and its fatality; part of it passed into knowledge's field of control and power's sphere of intervention'; indeed, 'it was the taking charge of life, more than the threat of death, that gave power its access even to the body' (Foucault, 1990, pp 142, 143). But when Agamben laments the '24 centuries' within which 'Western politics' has not been able to 'heal the fracture' that lay exposed and bare already in Aristotle (Agamben, 1998, p 11), then we know the argument is structural, foundational and historical only in the most apocalyptical sense. What reveals itself in the sovereign ban, as Agamben calls the move of self-exemption, is the long, slow, but inevitable *telos* of the West, an ingrained imperfection that inheres as much in the democratic tradition as it does in absolutism or 20th-century totalitarianism.

Agamben's claim, briefly, is this: The sovereign decision, exception, or ban – the sovereign self-exemption, in other words – places the sovereign (again, as person, institution or collective will) both within and without the space or system that the sovereign decision demarcates. Recall: The proposition about the set of all propositions both is and is not a proper member of that set. But this ambiguous zone of inclusion and exclusion in which the sovereign finds himself is also occupied by the sovereign's logical or structural analog, the enigmatic figure of *homo sacer* – sacred life – who incorporates bare life in all its exposed fragility. 'The sovereign sphere', Agamben writes, 'is the sphere in which it is permitted to kill without committing homicide and without celebrating a sacrifice, and sacred life – that is, life that may be killed but not sacrificed – is the life that has been captured in this sphere' (Agamben, 1998, p 83). Thus we have 'two symmetrical figures' in this sovereign space 'that have the same structure and are correlative: the sovereign is the one with respect to whom all men are potentially *homines sacri*, and *homo sacer* is the one with respect to whom all men act as sovereigns'. This space, Agamben notes, is 'the first properly political space of the West distinct from both the religious and the profane sphere, from both the natural order and the regular juridical order' (Agamben, 1998, p 84). This claim – namely, that the Western notion of the political is both historically and logically marked by a master/slave relationship far more radical than any Hegel imagined, one that is devoid of recognition and doomed to unavoidable death – is a claim in need of examination.

If one turns to Hobbes, surely the most interesting and influential early-modern philosopher of sovereignty, one notices that what Agamben calls the political, Hobbes calls the 'state of nature', that is, the pre-political and pre-historical situation that calls the political into being in the first place. In the Hobbesian state of nature, each person has the same right, the right to self-preservation, thus each person has the same absolute power over the other – and, of course, each person is also subject to the same absolute power of the other. The condition of the human individual in the state of nature is the condition of war. In this war of all against all, nothing is unjust because there is no law, no distinction between good and evil, right and wrong, justice and injustice. The state of nature, it could therefore be argued, is the state in which 'life may be killed but not sacrificed', indeed, the sphere in which the roles of sovereign and *homo sacer* are forever interchangeable. Agamben dehistoricizes the Hobbesian construction.[5] The state of nature, Agamben says, 'is not a real epoch chronologically prior to the foundation of the City but a principle internal to the City' (Agamben, 1998, p 105). Thus, the realm of the political is not, as in Hobbes, founded on a contract in which rights are transferred to a sovereign in exchange for peace and protection. Rather, the state of nature as the state of war is directly constituted by the political. 'It is not so much a war of all against all', Agamben writes, 'as, more precisely, a condition in which everyone is bare life and a *homo sacer* for everyone else' (Agamben, 1998, p 106). The political, that is, does not replace nature; it creates it. The state from which Hobbes's sovereign rescues us is the state into which Agamben's sovereign plunges us.

The contrast is instructive. The primal scene in Hobbes shows man in a fallen state. Or rather, a natural state is one in which nature is indifferent and man is left to fend for himself. Any attempt to overcome this natural state and create a political commonwealth for mutual security is forever threatened with failure, and failure is defined as the return of the state of nature in the form of a catastrophic and bloody civil war. Thus, the political, however temporary and flawed it may be, is cherished because it establishes the hope for civil peace. The principle of sovereignty, based on a constitutive asymmetry, is consequently seen as a necessarily imperfect but nevertheless still *necessary* solution to a perpetual problem. In the absence of divine intervention and an ultimate theory of types leading back to the sovereignty of an immortal God, the *mortal* God produced by the sovereign self-exemption will have to do. Left by an absent God to our own devices, we create the political. For Agamben, on the other hand, the problem that Hobbes thinks he solves is in reality the *product* of the political space he creates and the *consequence* of the sovereign ban. The existence of *homo sacer*, the life that may be killed but not sacrificed, is not a political problem, but a problem of the political. Consequently, any strictly political action undertaken in the space defined by the sovereign ban is undertaken in vain. 'Until a completely new politics ... is at hand', he writes, 'every theory and every praxis will remain imprisoned and immobile, and the "beautiful day" of life will be given citizenship only either through blood and death or in the perfect senselessness to which the society of the spectacle condemns it' (Agamben, 1998, p 11). Much like Adorno and Horkheimer, on the one hand, and Heidegger, on the other, Agamben sees the trajectory of the political in the West heading inexorably toward totalitarianism or facile consumerism. In either case, thoughtless political action simply replicates and expands the horrific space of the modern. To think the political from within the political, in Agamben's view, is to 'remain inside nihilism' (Agamben, 1998, p 60).

It is a fascinating dilemma that we are faced with. Hobbes's pessimistic view of human nature, his belief in natural or anthropological evil, allows, oddly enough, for human fallibility, but only at the expense of accepting human incorrigibility. The fact of original sin compels tolerance of imperfection. The political is the realm in which the effects of fallibility are contained and minimized. Sovereign self-exemption is the mechanism by which this containment is achieved. To Agamben, however, this toleration of the political as defined by the sovereign ban can be nothing but a fatalistic acquiescence in the *creation* of the social nightmare called the state of nature. In order to transcend this nihilism, we are urged to embark on a quest for metaphysical transfiguration. Intolerant of what we are, or what we have been forced to become, we are charged with becoming other than what we are, becoming, perhaps, truer to what we *really* are, or what we ought to be. Consequently, we are faced with a staggering Heideggerian task – no mere reconfiguration of the political, but a thorough rethinking of Being. Simply to think 'the form of law', Agamben tells us, 'does nothing other than repeat the ontological structure that we have defined as the paradox of sovereignty (or sovereign ban) ... Only if it is possible to think the Being of abandonment beyond every idea of law ... will we have moved out of the paradox of sovereignty toward a politics freed from every ban' (Agamben, 1998, p 59). If mythic violence establishes and preserves the law, then a 'politics freed from every ban' must arrive, if and when it does arrive, on the wings of a thoroughly divine, thoroughly bloodless but lethal violence.

Messiah or *katechon*?

The line is clearly drawn between the presumption of guilt and a fallen politics on the one hand, and, on the other, a reclaimed innocence based on being abandoned by the law. Agamben marks this distinction with a neat contrast between Walter Benjamin and Carl Schmitt – between, that is, the Messiah and the *katechon*. 'For Benjamin', Agamben notes:

> the state of demonic existence of which law is a residue is to be overcome and man is to be liberated from guilt (which is nothing other than the inscription of natural life in the order of law and destiny). At the heart of the Schmittian assertion of the juridical

> character and centrality of the notion of guilt is, however, not the freedom of the ethical man but only the controlling force of a sovereign power (*katechon*), which can, in the best of cases, merely slow the dominion of the Antichrist. (Agamben, 1998, p 28)

For Benjamin, according to Agamben, guilt does not precede law and call it into being; rather, guilt is introduced into the world with the demonic rule of law. Thus, to be liberated from the structure of sovereignty is to be returned to a natural state of innocence. Agamben's Schmitt, on the other hand, is a firm believer in both the priority and the irreducibility of original sin. Sovereignty is the result of and compensation for guilt, not its cause. In short, Benjamin's messianic, divine violence would bring us back to the garden from which we have strayed. Schmitt's *katechon*, on the other hand, condemns us to a long, lonely vigil, a fearful wait first for the Antichrist and then the eventual cataclysmic redemption, a redemption that does not restructure political life on earth, but relieves us from having to live on earth at all.

The theological scene of battle evoked by Agamben is not gratuitous, for we are reminded of medieval debates concerning natural law (*ius naturale*), debates that culminate in a 13th-century battle between the pope and radical Franciscans. Roman legal theorists of the early Church held the view that in the state of nature there was no dominion, no private property and no mastery of one human over another. Rather, everything was held and used in common. It is only with the introduction of the law of nations (*ius gentium*) that private property and the political sphere, with its separation of nations and resultant wars, come into being. By espousing 'apostolic poverty', which stated that one had the right to use the earth and its products for survival but had no rights of dominion, no property or ownership rights, the Franciscans wished to re-occupy this state of nature and thereby reclaim a measure of innocence, even in the midst of a fallen and sinful world. But, as Richard Tuck in his study of the origin of natural rights theories states, the Franciscan theory of apostolic poverty was not just the self-justification of a religious order, but had 'a normative point: if it was possible for some men to live in an innocent way, then it should be possible for all men to do so' (Tuck 1979, p 22). The image of the entire world as an enormous commons, open to all and owned by none, has nourished utopian thought ever since, and continues to do so today. One need only think of Linebaugh and Rediker's *The Many-Headed Hydra* or Hardt and Negri's *Empire*.[6] And, I would add, one need only think of Agamben's work as well, his injunction to move 'out of the paradox of sovereignty towards a politics freed from every ban' and his evocation of a 'coming community' that has never heard the call of the law.

But one could ask: Why has this new community, freed from every ban, never been realized? It is, to be sure, an unfair question. Utopias should never be scrutinized. But it is a necessary question, for any answer will inevitably bring us back to the issue of guilt.

As the melancholic and self-pitying champion of the *katechon*, the delayer, who preserves an imperfect social order in the absence of the *parousia*, Schmitt is made to stand for the political nihilism Agamben deplores. Schmitt becomes the embodiment of guilt, the guilty, disciplined body that waits for the Antichrist. But more: Agamben accuses him of a guilt of a higher order, for Schmitt is not simply the representative of an unavoidable guilt, he is not simply guilty; rather, he is guilty of his guilt. As the apologist for a natural or anthropological notion of evil, Schmitt, like Hobbes, finds humans to be fundamentally incorrigible. We live, to invoke again the language of Hobbes, in an indifferent state of nature in which the guilt of our imperfection manifests itself as violence. As a consequence, the political is constituted as a realm in which this violence can be contained, limited and redirected, but never abolished. The political, on this view, is not a utopian space of individual or social self-actualization, but an imperfectly human space of infinite negotiation. A natural or anthropological notion of original and ineradicable sin, therefore, relieves us from the impossible pressures of perfectibility and compels tolerance of imperfection. Guilty of our imperfection, we atone for our sins imperfectly within a social space that acknowledges our imperfection.

Thus, to argue for the political as currently configured, with its recognition of a social and legal order constituted by a necessary mythic violence, is to embrace the oddly comforting notion of guilt. This, the acceptance of a natural and inevitable guilt, is the *higher order* guilt Agamben labels nihilism. We are commanded therefore to deny the political as delineated by the sovereign ban, to free ourselves from guilt by rejecting the metaphysics that, in Agamben's view, supports it. Overcoming the metaphysics of the sovereign ban clearly cannot occur from within the political space of that metaphysics. Any step out of our fallen state must be a step initiated by a divine violence – this time a truly bloodless violence, because it is to take place in the non-corporeal world of thought. Ironically, if we do *not* reject the political and the metaphysics that grounds it, then we are burdened with an even greater guilt than the simple guilt of the political; if we do not reject the paradox of sovereignty, then we are charged with the guilt of accepting guilt, the theological guilt of rejecting redemption. It is as if willfully inhabiting the political were like staring into the face of God – and denying Him. The symbol of this greater guilt is Agamben's dramatic equation of modernity with Auschwitz – that is – his characterization of the camp – the death camp, the work camp, the internment centre – as the '*nomos* of the modern' (Agamben, 1998, p 166), the 'political space of modernity itself' (Agamben, 1998, p 174), where 'all life becomes sacred and all politics becomes the exception' (Agamben, 1998, p 148). With the essence of modernity reduced to a technological killing field, embracing the political is equivalent to building concentration camps while awaiting the Antichrist.

But denying God – or at least denying His intervention in the world of the political – is precisely what the *katechon* does. The word *katechon* refers to a perplexing figure in the Second Epistle to the Thessalonians, in which Paul attempts to dampen overeager expectations. Christ's return, Paul assures us, is imminent, but will be preceded by signs. Only after the Antichrist has usurped God's place in the temple will Christ come again to claim his own. Waiting for Christ entails waiting for the Antichrist, yet the time of the latter's arrival is also not known, for there is, Paul says, a *katechon*, a delayer or restrainer, whose task it is to prevent the Evil One's arrival. Christ will come at some unknown future time when the Antichrist has prevailed over the *katechon*. The unsolved riddle of the *katechon* lies not only in who or what this figure might be, but *why* Paul would want to delay the coming of the Antichrist when the coming of the Antichrist signals the final battle and the triumphant return of Christ. If we longed for the *parousia*, should we not be impatient with the interference of the *katechon*?

But what if, after two thousand years and untold promises, we have lost our faith in the *parousia* and grown weary of waiting for the arrival of divine violence? Then would not delaying the Antichrist be what we should hope for? What if the *katechon* were not primarily a theological figure, but a political one, or rather a figure of the political itself? Attempting to come to terms both with the seemingly infinite deferral of the Second Coming and with the existence of a universal yet non-Christian, secular authority, the early Church assumed that the *katechon* represented the Roman Empire. Thus, in the absence of any imminent ascendancy into the City of God, the mundane space of the political as such is designed to prevent the coming of the Antichrist, and with him, the end of the world. The political on this early Christian view must be imperfect but beneficial – were it perfect, it would not be the *katechon*, but Christ, and were it demonic, to use Agamben's term, it would be the Antichrist, which is precisely what the political attempts to hold at bay. The *katechon*, as a figure for the political, rejects the promise of the *parousia* and protects the community from the dangerous illusions of both ultimate perfection and absolute evil. Embracing the political, therefore, can only be considered nihilistic if one entertains the hope of replacing the City of Man with the City of God here on earth itself.

So, if we commit what in Agamben's eyes can only be seen as the sin of embracing the political, perhaps it is because we do not fear the arrival of the Antichrist as much as the arrival of Christ Himself. We are like the stubborn Pharisees who denied Christ, and perhaps we can now see that they were right! In an odd but compelling way, we know that Christ and the Antichrist are really the same – figures who promise us perfection, figures who offer us redemption and bestow upon us the guilt of failing perfection or rejecting their offer. The *katechon*, the political, those human institutions that keep us human, that keep us ensnared in our many, ordinary guilts – perhaps this is all we have. And to long for the divine destruction of the imperfect world of the political – perhaps this is the greater nihilism.

Coda

Agamben offers us an alternate vision of the political, a vision of the political that cannot be recognized as such by one who seeks to delay the Antichrist. In his book, *The Coming Community*, Agamben confronts us with a fascinating theological question: What happens to the souls of unbaptized babies who have died in ignorance of both sin and God? What is their punishment? 'According to Saint Thomas', Agamben reports:

> [t]he punishment of unbaptized children who die with no other fault than original sin cannot be an afflictive punishment, like that of hell, but only a punishment of privation that consists in the perpetual lack of the vision of God. The inhabitants of limbo, in contrast to the damned, do not feel pain from this lack: since they have only natural and not supernatural knowledge, which is implanted in us at baptism, they do not know that they are deprived of the supreme good … The greatest punishment – the lack of the vision of God – thus turns into a natural joy: Irremediably lost, they persist without pain in divine abandon. God has not forgotten them, but rather they have always already forgotten God. (Agamben, 1993, pp 5–6)

This, then, is the state of the ideal community, the community based not on identity or law, but on being blissfully abandoned.

> Like the freed convict in Kafka's *Penal Colony*, who has survived the destruction of the machine that was to have executed him, these beings have left the world of guilt and justice behind them: the light that rains down on them is that irreparable light of the dawn following the *novissima dies* of judgment. But the life that begins on earth after the last day is simply human life. (Agamben, 1993, pp 6–7)

Simple, human life is not bare life; it is not the life that is constructed by the sovereign ban, nor the life that is structured, as Schmitt's, by the primacy of the friend/enemy distinction. It is not sacred life, thus not exposed life. Rather, in this description of limbo we have the vision of a community that has never heard of the gods and thus is in no need of the law; a community that knows no friendship, has no need of friendship, because it has never known enemies; a community that cannot conceive of innocence because it has never experienced guilt. In limbo we await no one and wait for nothing.

It would be nice to be one of those dead and unbaptized babies who float, in limbo, between the polarities that trigger the paradox and the guilt of sovereign logic. But I wonder: Can they remain suspended indefinitely? How long would it take for the sin of the political to make its presence felt again? After all, what would the members of this community do if at their borders – and those borders could be internal as well as external – a messenger arrived, an apostle with an apple, as it were, who spoke of God and Satan, of good and evil, of salvation and damnation, of friend and enemy? What would they do? Would they listen to this emissary from another world? Could they *avoid* listening to this tempting apostle? Would it be possible to close one's ear to the sound of the political coming as if from the outside? Would it be possible to forget what one has heard immediately upon hearing it? If not, would it be possible to close the mouth of this political emissary in a non-political way? Or can the political only be silenced politically? Do you suppose that in an attempt to protect itself from this message, the community of abandoned souls would be tempted to silence the messenger? Do you suppose these souls would be tempted to kill the messenger for the sake of the community, much like the Young Comrade must be killed, and must agree to his killing, in Bertolt Brecht's *The Measures Taken*? If so, what kind of killing would this be? Would it be a sacrifice? A homicide? Or would it be a killing that was neither a sacrifice nor a homicide?

Notes

1   On Russell's barber paradox see Kline, 1980, p 205, and Sainsbury, 1995, pp 2, 108.

2   See Russell, 1908.

3   In his Preface to the First American Edition of his *Laws of Form*, George Spencer Brown claims the following: 'Recalling Russell's connexion with the Theory of Types, it was with some trepidation that I approached him in 1967 with the proof that it was unnecessary. To my relief he was delighted. The Theory was, he said, the most arbitrary thing he and Whitehead had ever had to do, not really a theory but a stopgap, and he was glad to have lived long enough to see the matter resolved' (Spencer Brown, 1979, pp xiii–xiv). For a resumé of Spencer Brown's purported proof, see pp xiv–xv.

4   See Arendt, 1990, pp 22–24, 59–114.

5   Or, put the other way around, Hobbes historicizes the conditions that obtained in the New World following the Spanish, English and French conquests. See, for example, Schmitt, 2003, pp 95–97.

6   Linebaugh and Rediker chart the destruction of the commons and the rise of slavery in the 17th century, but also celebrate those pockets of resistance created by hybrid societies of sailors, ex-slaves, and others in the various nooks and crannies of the 'revolutionary' Atlantic of the time. The memory of the various forms of the commons animates today's struggles, to which the closing lines of their study bear witness: 'The globalizing powers have a long reach and endless patience. Yet the planetary wanderers do not forget, and they are ever ready from Africa to the Caribbean to Seattle to resist slavery and restore the commons' (Linebaugh and Rediker, 2000, p 353). For Hardt and Negri, the commons are not a space, but desire: 'It is sufficient to point to the generative determination of desire and thus its productivity. In effect, the complete commingling of the political, the social, and the economic in the constitution of the present reveals a biopolitical space that ... explains the ability of desire to confront the crisis. The entire conceptual horizon is thus completely redefined. The biopolitical, seen from the standpoint of desire, is nothing other than concrete production, human collectivity in action. Desire appears here as productive space, as the actuality of human cooperation in the construction of history. This production is purely and simply human reproduction, the power of generation. Desiring production is generation, or rather the excess of labor and the accumulation of a power incorporated into the collective movement of singular essences, both its cause and its completion' (Hardt and Negri, 2000, pp 387–88).

One cannot argue for one ontological view of the world over another, because one's ontology, even if it is uttered as the rejection of ontology, is the basis for, not the result of, one's arguments. One cannot ground one's ontology logically, because belief in the truth of logic presumes a particular ontological view of the world – that there is *a* world, for instance, that it can be known, and that the structure of logic, its bivalent notion of truth and falsehood, is not just an adequate but rather the necessary tool for deciphering the presupposed structure of this world. One's ontological commitments, therefore, are either openly embraced or tacitly assumed; they are either the emphatic object of one's faith or they reveal their basic outline gradually in the structure of one's epistemological, aesthetic, political, moral, religious, and other arguments. One cannot argue for one's ontology, but one can explicitly or implicitly offer one's ontological presuppositions up for inspection.[1]

However, instead of merely displaying one's assumptions, one can claim that one's own view is morally or politically superior to rival views and thus aggressively attempt to persuade others that one's own ontological presuppositions are superior to those which seem to have dominated the philosophical tradition in the past and which seem to continue to dominate today. As we have so often heard over the past century or more, the flawed ontological assumptions and metaphysical commitments of the Western philosophical tradition have failed us. More specifically, modernity, with its obsessive mind/body, subject/object, culture/nature dualisms and the political and ecological terrors these dualisms are said to have unleashed (from Auschwitz to factory farming, to use Heidegger's famous comparison), is but the logical conclusion, if not cruel and vicious parody, of the tradition we all apparently want to escape. Thus, one is implored to cast the old faith aside and adopt a faith in an unknown future, an ontology that is yet to be fully realized. Giorgio Agamben, as we saw in the last chapter, can maintain that the structure of sovereignty informs all aspects of the Western political tradition, including – indeed, especially – its emphasis on the rule of law. Thus, he contends, 'the task that our time imposes on thinking' is to move beyond the simple recognition of the form and force of law. 'Every thought that limits itself to this does nothing other than repeat the ontological structure that we have defined as the paradox of sovereignty (or sovereign ban)' (Agamben, 1998, p 59). And, as the blueprint of the barracks at Auschwitz that adorns the cover of the American edition of *Homo Sacer* is meant to remind us, the 'logical structure of sovereignty' is evil. We are thus called, in true Heideggerian fashion, to experience an abandonment (*Seinsverlassenheit*) that is

> freed from every idea of law and destiny. ... This is why it is necessary to remain open to the idea that the relation of abandonment is not a relation, and that *the being together of*

the being and Being does not have the form of relation. This does not mean that Being and the being now part ways; instead, they remain without relation. But this implies nothing less than an attempt to think the politico-social *factum* no longer in the form of a relation. (Agamben, 1998, p 60)

To hear and accept this call to think the non-relation of Being and the being would necessarily be a leap of faith. Neither Heidegger nor Agamben can *describe* this positive form of *Seinsverlassenheit*, because language is nothing if not infinitely relational; and neither can *demonstrate* logically or empirically that to think of abandonment in such a way would release us from the nihilism in which we now so hopelessly dwell, because logic too is necessarily tied to relation, and empirically such abandonment has yet to be experienced. Each, however, like a modern day Dante, entices us to leave the sinful world we inhabit and embark upon a path that will lead us to a place that even Beatrice would feel comfortable calling home.

Gilles Deleuze and Félix Guattari offer a similar invitation. Our task – which is to say, philosophy's task – is, finally, once and for all, to overcome the time honored but world-distorting distinction between transcendence and immanence. It is the philosopher, the true philosopher, and only the philosopher, who can institute the infinite plane of immanence we are to inhabit. That plane, which is, of course, not physical and not explicable according to 'spatiotemporal coordinates' (Deleuze and Guattari, 1994, p 37), can only be described by way of evocative similes and metaphors. If, for example, 'concepts are like multiple waves, rising and falling', then 'the plane of immanence is the single wave that rolls them up and unrolls them'. Or, if 'concepts are the archipelago or skeletal frame', then 'the plane is the breath that suffuses the separate parts'. And again: 'Concepts are events, but the plane is the horizon of events, the reservoir or reserve of purely conceptual events: not the relative horizon that functions as a limit, which changes with an observer and encloses observable states of affairs, but the absolute horizon, independent of any observer, which makes the event as concept independent of a visible state of affairs in which it is brought about' (Deleuze and Guattari, 1994, p 36). This last, of course, defines ontology as such. The world *is*, independent of its observers. Thus the world, or, in this case, the plane of immanence, 'constitutes the absolute ground of philosophy, its earth or deterritorialization, the foundation on which it creates its concepts' (Deleuze and Guattari, 1994, p 41). Nor is it unusual that the plane of immanence and what it grounds are described as absolute ('Concepts are absolute surfaces or volumes, formless and fragmentary, whereas the plane is the formless, unlimited absolute, neither surface nor volume but always fractal' [Deleuze and Guattari, 1994, p 36]), unadulterated ('the plane of immanence is always single, being itself pure variation' [Deleuze and Guattari, 1994, p 39]), and infinite ('That is why there are always many infinite movements caught within each other, each folded in the others, so that the return of one instantaneously relaunches another in such a way that the plane of immanence is ceaselessly being woven, like a gigantic shuttle. … Diverse movements of the infinite are so mixed in with each other that, far from breaking up the One-All of the plane of immanence, they constitute its variable curvature, its concavities and convexities, its fractal nature as it were. ... The plane is, therefore, the object of an infinite specification so that it seems to be a One-All only in cases specified by the selection of movement' [Deleuze and Guattari, 1994, pp 38, 39]). All these images can be elucidated intelligently; or they can at least provoke further evocations that can make a powerful claim on our philosophical imagination. Yet, to repeat, none can demonstrate its own accuracy, and none can be demonstrated to be logically correct or empirically accurate. Nor should that be demanded of them.

Of interest to us in the context of this study, however, is not the validity of these ontological claims, but the political world they imply or the political positions explicitly derived from them. The call for philosophy to constitute an infinite plane of immanence as a radically new ontology is made from within a particular narrative – in the case of Deleuze and Guattari, from within a rather Manichean philosophy of history. The characters in this world drama are Immanence, played by Philosophy (at its best), and Transcendence, portrayed, in all its evil disguises, by The Priestly Caste, which can include Philosophy (at its worst). 'The Greeks', Deleuze and Guattari write, 'were the first to conceive of a strict immanence of Order to a cosmic milieu that sections chaos in the form of a plane. ... In short, the first philosophers are those who institute a plane of immanence like a sieve stretched over the chaos'. And it was Spinoza (with Nietzsche's help) who showed us that the plane of immanence is 'surrounded by illusions', 'thought's mirages', like the 'illusion of transcendence', the 'illusion of universals', the 'illusion of the eternal', and the 'illusion of discursiveness' (Deleuze and Guattari, 1994, pp 49–50). But alas, such true philosophy has its enemies, and even within philosophy its false friends. From without, there is the priest, for instance, or the sociologist; there is the epistemologist, the linguist, the psychoanalyst, and the logician; and now, closest to home, there comes the 'most shameful moment', the moment of 'computer science, marketing, design, and advertising, all the disciplines of communication' (Deleuze and Guattari, 1994, p 10). And from within, there is the desire 'to think transcendence within the immanent', to think the functional equivalent of transcendence in the transcendental. This philosophic fall from grace (punctuated only by the above mentioned protests of a Spinoza or a Nietzsche) follows a fairly consistent trajectory marked by Plato, Christianity, and the modern invention and development of the transcendental subject by Descartes, Kant and Husserl (Deleuze and Guattari, 1994, pp 44–48). Nevertheless, despite these philosophic Quislings, the world-historical battle is essentially conducted by Philosophy and Religion. The religious sage conceives of 'the institution of an always transcendent order imposed from outside by a great despot or by one god higher than the others. ... Whenever there is transcendence, vertical Being, imperial State in the sky or on earth, there is religion; and there is Philosophy whenever there is immanence. ... Only friends can set out a plane of immanence as a ground from which idols have been cleared' (Deleuze and Guattari, 1994, p 43).

The irony – or is it tragedy? – of this radical immanence lies, of course, in the clearing away of these idols, for this 'clearing' is anything but friendly. If philosophy and only philosophy, if only *true* philosophy can institute immanence, then philosophy, perhaps in the personified guise of a Philosopher-King or, more romantically, a Philosopher-Revolutionary, must wage war against its enemies, those usurpers of its role coming from the realms of religion, the human sciences and social engineering. Radical immanence, it seems, can only be achieved by radically eliminating competing spheres of belief and knowledge, or, ironically, by instituting again a proper hierarchical relationship in which philosophy reigns supreme. Thus, the institution of a new, correct ontology and the new, infinite plane of immanence that that ontology allows cannot wait for the withering away of the state of transcendence, but must be put in place by revolutionary warfare, even if the revolution in question is 'bloodless'. The post-revolutionary state is one in which the enemies of immanence have been defeated and in which all traces of the Gulag have been made to disappear. It is a state which friends and *only* friends can call home. That is, after all, what friends are for.

If the enemy of pure immanence is transcendence, then within immanence the transcendental symbol of this impure, undesired and hierarchical political distinction is the feared and maligned notion of sovereignty. To maintain, as was done in the previous chapter, that sovereignty is the consequence of unavoidable logical paradox would seemingly confirm the putative poverty of Western metaphysics and thus the need for a radically new ontology (and 'a completely new politics') in which such paradox could never arise, or, at any rate, would be forever rendered invisible and ineffective. While the old metaphysics posits the primacy of violence ('original sin') and thus calls sovereignty into being as a kind of lightning rod, the new ontology would presuppose that sovereignty and the transcendental dominance it stands for *causes* the negative effects of social life. Thus the elimination of transcendental sovereignty will introduce a new social order that is precisely *not* an order, but a benevolent self-organization of all productive human endeavors.

Though this attempt to delete sovereignty from political actuality has emerged with a vengeance in recent years, it is not new. Indeed, it was thought that the task had been successfully completed. Have not, after all, liberal individualism, pluralism, and most importantly the division of power supplanted the arbitrary willfulness of the absolute sovereign? Alas, we are told, though it now wears new clothes, the beast remains the same; only, the old dragon slayers have become the new dragons. Whereas the proto-liberal John Locke in the 17th century denounced monarchical absolutism in the name of parliamentary power, and whereas liberal theorists from the late 18th to the early 20th centuries, theorists like Wilhelm von Humboldt, John Stuart Mill and Harold Laski, denounced state supremacy in the name of the individual and the pluralism that would allow this individual to flourish, the new critics of sovereignty, which, in addition to Agamben, include Michael Hardt and Antonio Negri, do not excoriate it in the name of liberalism, but rather condemn liberalism itself as the new form of sovereignty; for as it turns out, what liberalism replaced was not sovereignty as such, but particular modes of state sovereignty that characterized modern Europe up through the 19th century. Accordingly, the question Hardt and Negri ask is whether and how the modern, transcendental logic of sovereignty can *now, finally*, be supplanted by a universally benign immanence in which transcendently imposed order is replaced by egalitarian self-organization. Their book, *Empire*, assumes from the outset a positive answer to the question of whether such self-organization is possible, even if it leaves us little with which to answer the question of how such a transformation is to come about. To challenge their initial supposition – that pure immanence can exist without its constitutive other – may indeed indicate to the prophets of a new ontology that one is still mired in the nihilistic swamp of metaphysics. Nevertheless, the chiliastic spirit of the overly hopeful has its chilling moments as well. Thus, the question I propose to address here asks whether the logic of sovereignty can be expelled from the realm of the political, or whether its expulsion must ultimately also assume the expulsion of the political altogether. Can one desire, in other words, the overcoming of sovereignty from within the political, or must that desire always express itself as a quasi-theological longing for a post-political state, a New Jerusalem? My tentative answer to that question is: Though the 'solution' to the paradox of immanence that we call sovereignty – precisely because it is no solution – may take varied forms and can be re-fashioned in an incalculable number of ways, some more desirable than others, the paradox of sovereignty itself cannot be sublated; or rather, *the logical paradox that sovereignty contingently and imperfectly solves is the logical paradox that radical immanence itself imposes on the modern structure of the political*. The question that the concept of sovereignty answers and that therefore we must confront reads: In a world, in which order is not divinely ordained, how is order nevertheless possible?

*

According to Niklas Luhmann, the monotheistic religions all 'seem to have a common underlying element, namely a salvation perspective. They thereby contemplate access to transcendence as a corrective for the suffering from distinctions. They propose that every distinction can be sublated in a realm beyond all distinctions. This is the form in which the distinction between immanence and transcendence is made manifest' (Luhmann, 2000, p 150). The essence of religion, then, its originary moment, is one of paradox. Religion introduces a distinction between immanence and transcendence, between a realm of distinctions and a realm of pure indistinction, in order to express the desire to transcend all distinctions. Yet, this distinction between distinction and non-distinction can be made only from the mundane world of distinction itself. The desire for perfect indistinction can express itself only in the imperfect form of a discrete distinction. The desire for non-distinction, therefore, can do nothing but replicate what it wishes to transcend, namely, distinction. To live in space and time is to be forced to live in the profane, 'sinful' world of distinctions, the world opened up, as the first book of the Bible tells us, by the knowledge of the difference between good and evil. It is only in time out of mind, in the beyond, the after-life or at the end of history, that the perfect state of indistinction can be achieved.

A politics wishing to pattern itself on this religious desire would not be content with a-historical, transcendent solutions, but would attempt to actualize the realm of indistinction within history. It would attempt, as the saying goes, to establish a paradise on earth. Within history and on earth, however, transcendence of distinctions is, by definition, impossible. A theologically oriented politics, then, would seek to establish on earth the *functional equivalent* of paradise, a secular paradise that at least in its formal aspects would neutralize the malignancy of distinction. This, for example, is precisely how Fichte formulates it in his eighth lecture to the German nation. Because of unique historical circumstances, Fichte tells us, early Christianity was forced to institute a realm of absolute transcendence, outside of terrestrial time and space, in which eternal life could be found. This rigid separation of immanence and transcendence, however, is a false separation. 'In the regular order of things,' Fichte writes, 'this earthly life itself is intended to be truly life.' That is: 'The natural impulse of man ... is to find heaven on this earth, and to endow his daily work on earth with permanence and eternity; to plant and to cultivate the eternal in the temporal ... in a fashion visible to the mortal eye itself' (Fichte, 1968, pp 112, 113). For Fichte, of course, the island of indistinction in the sea of difference is called the *Vaterland*, and the spirit that imbues this island with eternal life is the love of the fatherland expressed by the self-constituting *Volk*. 'People and fatherland', in other words, are the 'support and guarantee of eternity on earth' (Fichte, 1968, p 118). But just as the moral individual is infinitely perfectible and never complete, so too is the self-perfection of the people and the fatherland eternally under construction. The political project Fichte imagines, then, is both the constitution of a plane of radical immanence, to steal the Deleuzean phrase used so often by Hardt and Negri, and the projection of infinite perfectibility on that infinite plane. Thus the nation-state becomes both the desired goal and the site of an eternally unfinished project of self-improvement. The distinction between transcendence and immanence that the idea of the fatherland was said to overcome is thus reintroduced as the distinction between lesser and greater perfection; or worse, between an improper and a proper constitution of a *Volk*, an improper and proper expression of its spirit.

One has here the beginnings of a philosophy of history, since the distinction between transcendence and immanence unfailingly re-enters each new plane of immanence that politics attempts to institute. Ironically, each attempt to eliminate distinction becomes the source of a new opposition, thereby transforming the politics that attempts to eliminate the distinctions of history into the very engine of history itself. Once relocated in the temporal realm of society, the initial distinction between the profane and the sacred is continuously repeated as the difference between the world as it is and the world as it ought to be. A theologically conceived politics, then, exists at the cusp of every replicated manifestation of this initial, paradoxical distinction between distinction and non-distinction. In attempting to annihilate distinctions, politics also forever aims at eliminating its own necessity. 'This time', it says to itself as it projects its cure for 'the suffering from distinctions' into the future – 'This time will be the last time'. With final ascension into the absolutely just society, political theology completes its task and both religion, as compensation for worldly misery, and politics, as its cure, cease to exist.

If we can make the term 'theodicy' mean both reconciling the human to the world as it is and reconciling the world to the needs and nature of the human as she is, then political theology is a theodicy, 'dialectically' harmonizing the most basic desires of the human as a *Gattungswesen* (species-being) with the malleable constraints of an essentially accommodating world. As Raymond Geuss has recently stated, much of modern, post-Kantian (German) philosophy can best be understood as theodicy. Starting with the decidedly non-Aristotelian assumption that the perceived (natural and social) world falls far short of our reasonable expectations, modern philosophy's duty has been to show that this discrepancy between reality and expectation is either the fault of our perception of the world's constitution, or arises from the fact that the world is out of sync with itself and in need of correction. As Geuss explains, using Hegel as his main witness, modern theodicy assumes that 'as human beings we have a fundamental – in fact Hegel calls it an "absolute" – human need to be genuinely "at-home" (either "*zu Hause*" or "*bei sich*") in the world, where "the world" includes not just the natural universe, but also the social, cultural and political world in which we live' (Geuss, 1999, p 80). To be at home in the world, according to Geuss's reading of Hegel, the world must actually *be* (and not, as in Kant, just conditionally posited to be)[2] both rationally comprehensible and commensurate to our absolute needs. Thus it is the duty of philosophy (and art) to make this inherent comprehensibility and commensurability evident to us so that we can become 'reconciled' to the world. Our happiness is no longer contingent upon our ability to exercise a 'subjectively' reflective teleological judgment (Kant), but rests upon the ability of philosophy to demonstrate to us how the modern, post-1789 world has become so constituted as to welcome us home if only we had eyes to see and ears to hear, or to demonstrate to us how it *can* become so constituted if only we could make the surface manifestations of the given world conform to its essential deep structure. In its most intricate form, theodicy is 'dialectical', changing the either/or into a both/and, such that modern, ameliorative theodicy finds fault with our perception of the world *because* the social structure – especially property relations – has distorted and perverted that perception. It is therefore philosophy's duty to reconcile us to the world as it really is by getting us to recognize the truth of the world so that we may help it become what it – and thereby we – is meant to be.

Consequently, as a theodicy, political theology serves as the vehicle by means of which social reality can be so altered as to match deep human expectations. That is, as a theodicy, the political becomes the instrument of perfectibility and thus a path to secularized salvation. With salvation, however, comes extinction, the extinction of the political; for as a theodicy the political must be fashioned as a self-consuming artifact. Once the human and the world are 'reconciled', the purpose of the political has been fulfilled and ceases to exist. On this view, even if the process of reconciliation is thought of as infinite and never to be completed, the political must be viewed theoretically as a non-essential feature of a longed-for reconciled world, since its only object is to effect this reconciliation. At the imagined end of history, politics, along with the other sins of the world, simply vanishes. Or, put succinctly: In a world that sees perfection as its goal, the end of politics is the end of politics.

*

Though perfectibility as such makes no special appearance in *Empire*, Hardt and Negri are every bit as interested in overcoming the distinction, and the paradox of the distinction, between immanence and transcendence. Yet, rather than projecting the perfection of transcendence onto an immanent plane, they simply seek to eliminate the transcendent altogether, for the potential for perfection inheres immanently and needs only to be released. It is not that this world must achieve the perfection of the beyond; rather, *natural* perfection, which the order imposed from the outside has repressed, must be reclaimed. The world *is* so structured that we may be truly at home in it, if only that which perverts the structure, and perverts *our* structure, could be excised. To effect this scission, Hardt and Negri construct an Armageddon-like narrative, one in which immanence is pitted against transcendence in an ultimate clash of good versus evil, though now the 'multitude' replace Fichte's *Volk* and Marx's proletariat (Hardt and Negri, 2000, pp 394, 395). It is tempting to read Hardt and Negri ironically here, that is, to read their claim that 'the world of modern sovereignty is a Manichaean world, divided by a series of binary oppositions that define Self and Other, white and black, inside and outside, ruler and ruled' as a sly and modest comment on the fact that Hardt and Negri themselves divide modernity neatly into a morally good and a morally bad version by using the binary opposition of immanence and transcendence. The irony, however, escapes them, for they seem to be deadly serious about their distinction. Modernity emerges, in their narrative, as a revolutionary rejection of the past and a radically new institution of immanence. 'It develops knowledge and action as scientific experimentation', they claim, 'and defines a tendency toward a democratic politics, posing humanity and desire at the center of history' (Hardt and Negri, 2000, p 74). In language – partly liberal, partly communitarian, if qualified in a Deleuzean manner – that reflects the pathos of high modernist manifestos, they ring the changes on the list of positive attributes of humanism's incipient revolution without tarrying to tease out the substantial qualities or necessary nuances of these attributes. They talk of 'nomadism and exodus' and the 'desire and hope of an irrepressible experience'. They claim that 'Renaissance humanism initiated a revolutionary notion of human equality, of singularity and community, cooperation and multitude, that resonated with forces and desires extending horizontally across the globe, redoubled by the discovery of other populations and territories' (Hardt and Negri, 2000, p 76). They champion the humanist triad *vis-cupiditas-amor* (strength-desire-love), asking: 'Why cannot knowledge and will be allowed to claim themselves to be absolute?' Their answer: 'Because every movement of self-constitution of the multitude must yield to a preconstituted order, and because claiming that humans could immediately establish their freedom in being would be a subversive delirium. This is the essential core of the ideological passage in which the hegemonic concept of European modernity was constructed' (Hardt and Negri, 2000, pp 78, 79).

But such revolutionary activity triggered, of necessity, a counterrevolution. This reactionary second stage or second tradition of modernity, this 'Thermidor of the Renaissance revolution' (Hardt and Negri, 2000, p 140), posed 'a transcendent constituted power against an imminent constituted power, order against desire' (Hardt and Negri, 2000, p 74). Order, here, designates an attempted medieval restoration of an imposed hierarchy. The specifics of the restoration fail, largely because the unity, and therefore the sovereignty, of Christianity can no longer be represented theologically or politically. But the principle of order perseveres and finds its new home in state sovereignty (Hardt and Negri, 2000, p 70). Desire, on the other hand, is the emotive if vaguely defined term that designates something Michael Hardt elsewhere (Hardt, 1993) calls organization – a type of anarchical self-organizing power that results in democracy. Desire, it seems, takes on the duty formerly discharged by the concept 'nature' and fuses it seamlessly with the concept 'society'. In Hardt's elucidation of Deleuze's reading of Spinoza, the state of nature consists of bodies, human bodies, seeking to expand their powers. These bodies inevitably encounter one another and an unrestrained, emergent civil society, rather than suspending or canceling the state of nature, organizes the exhilarating self-expansion of the body in nature for maximum efficiency. 'Natural right', Hardt claims, 'is not negated in the passage to civil right ... but rather it is preserved and intensified, just as imagination is fortified in reason. In this transformation the multiplicity of society is forged in a multitude. ... The multitude is multiplicity made powerful. Spinoza's conception of civil right, then, complements the first notion of freedom with a second: from the freedom from order to the freedom of organization; the freedom of multiplicity becomes the freedom of the multitude. And the rule of the multitude is democracy'. From the anarchy of (negative) liberal freedom necessarily arises, when allowed to, the (positive) communal freedom of the self-organized *demos*. 'In the passage of freedom, then, from multiplicity to multitude, Spinoza composes and intensifies anarchy in democracy. Spinozian democracy, the absolute rule of the multitude through the equality of its constituent members, is founded on the "art of organizing encounters"' (Hardt, 1993, p 110). Thus, the battle between the two opposed modernities, between order and desire, becomes the war of a natural organization of human self-assertion in a state of innocence against the willfully perverse imposition of a repressive hierarchy designed to thwart our natural flourishing. For reasons left to the (theological) imagination, that which comes naturally excites the impulse in those with a sovereign disposition to contravene the normal intensification of will and intellect that occurs in the state of nature and that would otherwise lead to their perfect completion in civil society. The 'new emergence' of radical immanence provokes this war. How could it not? 'How could such a radical overturning not incite strong antagonism? How could this revolution not determine a counterrevolution' (Hardt and Negri, 2000, p 74)? Indeed, faced with pure innocence, Satan is always angered.

Though the overriding flavor is liberal, this reading of Spinoza is not without Marxian elements in their most idealist guise. Civil society, self-organized according to the unfettered natural needs of the human as species-being, explodes the historically contingent order imposed by ec-centric, asymmetrical, perverse property relations. The liberal anarchy of the multiplicity raises itself to the collective, gathered in the commons. In *Empire*, labor, productivity and re-productivity are added to desire, and the multitude, as naturally formed social being and historically privileged political subject (Hardt and Negri, 2000, p 394), is charged with forging a new constituent power. I quote: 'This notion of labor as the common power to act stands in a contemporaneous, coextensive, and dynamic relationship to the construction of community. ... We can thus define the virtual power of labor as a power of self-valorization that exceeds itself, flows over onto the other, and, through this investment, constitutes an expansive commonality. The common actions of labor, intelligence, passion, and affect configure a *constituent power*' (Hardt and Negri, 2000, p 358). Hardt and Negri play variations on this theme throughout the final sections of their book. For instance: 'When the multitude works, it produces autonomously and reproduces the entire world of life. Producing and reproducing autonomously mean constructing a new ontological reality. In effect, by working, the multitude produces itself as singularity ..., a singularity that is a reality produced by cooperation, represented by the linguistic community, and developed by the movements of hybridization. ... Standing the ideology of the market on its feet, the multitude promotes through its labor the biopolitical singularizations of groups and sets of humanity, across each and every node of global interchange' (Hardt and Negri, 2000, p 395). Finally, a near ecstatic crescendo is reached when they claim: 'The movements of the multitude designate new spaces, and its journeys establish new residences. ... A new geography is established by the multitude as the productive flows of bodies define new rivers and ports. The cities of the earth will become at once great deposits of cooperating humanity and locomotives for circulation, temporary residences and networks of the mass distribution of living humanity' (Hardt and Negri, 2000, p 397). Though the notion of a (as yet achieved) common language plays a part in gathering the multiplicity together into a multitude (Hardt and Negri, 2000, pp 56–57), and the multitude into an effective 'political power' (Hardt and Negri, 2000, p 398), the vocabulary describing this gathering is naturalistic, the imagery luxuriantly excessive, the locale bucolic. It is as if radical transformation of society were akin to a tropical rainforest reclaiming abandoned villages or formerly industrialized cities.

As appealing as these images may be, the social and political world they evoke is based on a typical evasion of the democratic paradox. In its most obvious form, the paradox reveals itself as the identity between the ruler and the ruled. How are 'the people' to be thought of as both? There are a variety of ways of contingently and always temporarily resolving the paradox, including the notion of representation – one rules oneself through representatives – and temporal differentiation – today's rulers are tomorrow's ruled (eg the distinction between government and opposition that Luhmann sees as the political's defining feature). The solution Hardt and Negri implicitly propose, or so it seems to me, has more to do with Rousseau's distinction between private and general will, and this despite their explicit critique of Rousseau.[3] Let us return to a passage cited previously, the one that pits order against desire by referring to a 'transcendent *constituted* power against an immanent *constituent* power' (Hardt and Negri, 2000, p 74; emphasis added). The distinction is as old as the French Revolution and was codified by Sieyès. In discussions of sovereignty (popular or other), constitutions and law, the two notions are necessarily linked. A *constituent* power (the pope, the emperor, the people) inaugurates a political order (a legal code or constitution, say) that serves as the *constituted* power that regulates our daily lives in the public arena. We can think of the distinction, for instance, as that between legitimacy and legality. What makes laws legal is the 'legitimacy' of the political order that institutes them. To separate legitimacy from legality, constituent power from constituted power, allows for logical or chronological 'solutions' to the problem of political organization. The law of the land is 'grounded' in a constitution that was drafted by (representatives of) the 'people'. The sovereignty of the law is, so to speak, founded on the sovereignty of the people. Hardt and Negri critique such logical justifications. Sovereignty is the name they give to constituted order. It is absolutism, the rule of law, or the rule of capital – it makes no difference. Such order seeks 'legitimacy' and searches for it elsewhere, outside of itself. The liberal rule of law and capital, in other words, looks for a 'democratic' founding. 'The precarious power of sovereignty as a solution to the crisis of modernity', they write,

> was first referred for support to the nation, and then when the nation too was revealed as a precarious solution, it was further referred to the people. In other words, just as the concept of nation completes the notion of sovereignty by claiming to precede it, so too the concept of the people completes that of nation through another feigned logical regression. Each logical step back functions to solidify the power of sovereignty by mystifying its basis, that is, by resting on the naturalness of the concept. The identity of the nation and even more so the identity of the people must appear natural and originary. (Hardt and Negri, 2000, p 102)

Thus, to avoid infinite logical regression, they sever the terms; or rather, they overlay the first distinction with a second one: good/bad. Constituted power is bad – much like Benjamin's mythic violence – and is to be disposed of; constituent power – which serves as a divine violence in all its eschatological glory – is good and to be embraced. The empire of capital as constituted 'order', no matter its legitimating fictions of 'nation' and 'people', is reprehensible and to be replaced by the *constituent* power of the multitude, for the multitude, unlike the people, are not one. 'The multitude', they remind us, 'is a multiplicity, a plane of singularities, an open set of relations, which is not homogeneous or identical with itself and bears an indistinct, inclusive relation to those outside of it. ... Whereas the multitude is an inconclusive constituent relation, the people is a constituted synthesis that is prepared for sovereignty' (Hardt and Negri, 2000, p 103).

One question remains, however: How will the constituent power of the multitude produce a political space that avoids being marked by the evil logic of sovereign order? If liberal doctrine trumped absolutism by claiming that subjects would become participants in the new order constituted by *popular* sovereignty, what trumps the liberal political order, which has become defined by the sovereignty of capital? What, in other words, does this new 'constituent' power of the multitude do, and how does it do it differently? What type of political 'organization' does the multitude, as *'political subject'* (Hardt and Negri, 2000, p 394) – What would be the right verb here? Constitute? – 'constitute'? This question remains deliberately unanswered. 'What specific and concrete practices will animate this political project? We cannot say at this point' (Hardt and Negri, 2000, pp 399–400). Neither could Sorel. Neither could Benjamin. Neither can Agamben. To give an answer to this question would, of course, enmesh the constituent power of the multitude in the logic of sovereignty that Hardt and Negri wish to avoid. Thus, the distinction between constituent and constituted must rely on the *position* of that power, much like the distinction Georges Sorel made between violence and force relies on the pathos of authority and resistance. 'Sometimes', Sorel wrote,

> the terms 'force' and 'violence' are used in speaking of acts of authority, sometimes in speaking of acts of revolt. It is obvious that the two cases give rise to very different consequences. I think that it would be better to adopt a terminology which would give rise to no ambiguity, and that the term 'violence' should be employed only for the second sense; we should say, therefore, that the object of force is to impose a certain social order in which the minority governs, while violence tends to the destruction of that order. The bourgeoisie have used force since the beginning of modern times, while the proletariat now reacts against the middle class and against the State by violence. (Sorel, 1999, pp 165–66)

For Sorel the proletarian general strike performs the 'clearing' Deleuze speaks of, and what succeeds proletarian violence is pointedly left open. To forecast the future would be utopian. Rather, one expresses one's faith in the myth of the general strike, in the myth, to return to Hardt and Negri, of the multitude, their desire and their singularities. This faith comes from the basic assumption that once evil is cleared away, only the good will remain. 'Rousseau said that the first person who wanted a piece of nature as his or her own exclusive possession and transformed it into the transcendent form of private property was the one who invented evil. Good, on the contrary, is what is common' (Hardt and Negri, 2000, p 303). Good, in the theodicy of Hardt and Negri, is the default drive of the cosmos.

Yet, when we look at the language used to describe the (non-violent) acts of violence of the multitude as they assert their constituent power, one is struck by the traditional rhetoric of political empowerment. Even if the community of the multitude is thought as a gathering of singularities, a collective will seems to emerge that takes on the political role all collective wills take on, namely, the representative role of unavoidable sovereign decision-making and implementation of political goals and realities. So, while excoriating the sovereignty of Empire, Hardt and Negri assert a fairly common notion of unmediated popular sovereignty, neither realizing nor caring about the traditional cautions regarding the excesses of radical democracy and the tyrannies of the general will. Thus, when they state that 'the action of the multitude becomes political primarily when it begins to confront directly and with an adequate consciousness the central repressive operations of Empire' (Hardt and Negri, 2000, p 399), or when they emphasize that *the general right to control its own movement is the multitude's ultimate demand for global citizenship'*, or again when they claim that 'great collective means must be mobilized' and that the 'constituent power of the multitude' is the 'product of the creative imagination of the multitude that configures its own constitution' such that it has a basic *'right to reappropriation'* of, among other things, the means of production (Hardt and Negri, 2000, pp 400, 405, 406), then one cannot help but observe the multitude assert itself *as* a sovereign entity in opposition to the sovereign entity of its enemy. The enemy is not sovereignty, is not, in other words, the ability to organize and execute political power. The enemy here is capital; the enemy is Empire. And 'violence' or – to translate the term into the register of this volume – conflict is what brings the enemy sharply into view.

Accompanying this not so surprising re-emergence of a familiar form of popular sovereignty is its often observed and never eliminated paradox, namely that the people – or in this case the multitude – both rule and are ruled, both are the 'collective means' and 'mobilize' the collective means, both are the constituent power that institutes the constituted power of a general strike or that which follows such a cataclysm, and are at the same time the subject of control (of 'their' own movement) of that constituted power ('constitution') and its various administrative and policing agencies – the vanguard party, if you will, or the philosopher, who reminds us of philosophy's duty to institute a new, correct ontology. The appeal to immanence in no way does away with this paradox because this paradox only fully emerges when the plane of immanence is fully instituted. Sovereignty, or the paradox that sovereignty imperfectly solves in order that the political may exist, is the result of immanence, not its enemy. Sovereignty appears as the necessity of making distinctions where none seems to exist 'naturally'; where, that is, no divine or natural order presents us with a pre-ordained hierarchy. And when such a natural order is asserted, it reveals itself to *be* a distinction, not as that which replaces distinction. Without the immanence of distinctions, there is no immanence.

Hardt and Negri state that the multitude constitutes itself politically when it confronts Empire. I would like to ask the question that is generally not asked: What happens to the political subject that is the multitude after Empire is defeated? To this question they have no answer, stating explicitly that they are in no position 'to point to any already existing and concrete elaboration of a political alternative to Empire' (Hardt and Negri, 2000, p 206). But since the post-Empire political state (condition) is presented as a *telos*, a quasi-natural outgrowth of desire, labor and productivity, one cannot help but wonder whether political opposition will be at all possible. Are all singularities submerged in the multitude, or will it be possible to oppose the multitude? If what the constituent power of the multitude mobilizes and puts into effect is nothing but a reflection of the Good that is left after Evil is cleared away, will new, different singularities and multitudes be able to emerge, ones who may wish to mobilize against the *new* Empire? Or will all future opposition be deemed unnatural, morally perverse, reactionary, counterrevolutionary, and counterproductive – that is, counter to the best interests of life and the productivity of the body? Instead of just assuming that a post-catastrophe order of things will resemble at all the fantasies of the pre-catastrophe imagination, one might do well to read Carl Schmitt's description of Rousseau's *volonté générale* as at least a warning, if not as a more accurate indicator of the future. 'The *volonté générale*', Schmitt writes:

> is Rousseau's most fundamental political concept. It is the will of the sovereign and constitutes the state as a unity. This characteristic gives it the conceptual quality that distinguishes it from every particular will. With this concept, what is always coincides with what should be. Just as God unites might and right within Himself and what He wants is always good and what is good is always what he really wants, in Rousseau the sovereign, that is, the *volonté générale* appears by its very existence to be what it should be. ... The *volonté générale* is always right, it cannot make a mistake, it is reason itself and is stamped with the same necessity as the natural law that rules the physical. (Schmitt, 1994a, pp 117–18)

If this is the terrifying image that Hardt and Negri oppose when they oppose sovereignty and 'the people' who constitute the state (Hardt and Negri, 2000, pp 85, 102–03), it may, tragically, also be the terrifying image Hardt and Negri leave us with when they sing the unqualified and incautious praises of the multitude who dwell in the purported indistinction of radical immanence. For my part, I prefer the realm of distinctions over this dream of perfection. And I prefer acknowledged sovereignty, a sovereignty one can at least hope to oppose, over a sovereignty that pretends that it has, once and for all, transcended the evils of sovereignty.

Notes

1   I offer up my explicit and implicit presuppositions for inspection in Rasch, 2000b, and Rasch, 2002.

2   In the second half of his *Critique of Judgment*, that section dealing with the 'Critique of Teleological Judgment', Kant informs us that the 'highest good' consists in the combination of morality and 'universal happiness, ie the greatest welfare of the rational beings of the world' (Kant, 1987, p 343). Morality, or the act of living in conformity with the moral law, which makes us *worthy* of being happy, is a product of our freedom and our faculty of practical reason; but the condition of universal happiness rests on the assumption that the world is so constructed as to be commensurate with our understanding and thus in conformity with our needs. Kant states that we have no way of cognitively *knowing* that such is the case, but we may exercise our faculty of non-determinate, teleological judgment in order to act *as if* there were a 'moral cause of the world', which is to say, as if there were a god who constituted the world in such a way as to satisfy our most basic desires. For a person to be 'righteous', she need only 'actively rever[e] the moral law' (Kant, 1987, pp 341–42) and follow her duty; but for this morally 'righteous' person to be happy in the world, she must act as if she knew that the world had been intentionally created to provide for the needs and desires of the human race.

3   'Rousseau's social contract guarantees that the agreement among individual wills is developed and sublimated in the construction of a general will, and that the general will proceeds from the alienation of the single wills toward the sovereignty of the state' (Hardt and Negri, 2000, p 85).

PART 3
EVEN UNTO THE END
OF THE WORLD ...

Chapter 7

'For there is no difference between the Jew and the Greek': the legacy of St Paul

'Go ye therefore, and teach all nations, baptizing them in the name of the Father, and of the Son, and of the Holy Ghost: Teaching them to observe all things whatsoever I have commanded you: and, lo, I am with you always, even unto the end of the world' (Matthew 28, 19–20). So ends the gospel of Matthew, recording Jesus' final words to his disciples. The gospel of Mark reports a similar exhortation. 'Go ye into all the world, and preach the gospel to every creature' – upon which, Mark tells us, the disciples 'went forth, and preached every where' (Mark 16, 15, 20). Whatever else may or may not be true about the Biblical account of the life of Jesus, that a group of devoted Jewish and non-Jewish followers of this Jewish sectarian spread a message beyond the boundaries of its origin, 'unto the end of the world', cannot be denied. One need only recall the history of this formerly Celtic, Germanic and Slavic forest called Europe – not to mention the Christian conquest of the Western Hemisphere and large parts of Africa and the Pacific – to be reminded of the propagandistic power of this universal message. And this is remarkable, for the Jewish religion, like the other religions of the day, was a civic religion, based on laws and practices that consolidated national, ethnic or tribal identity. The Jewish religion, like the other religions of the day, was a way of distinguishing friend from stranger. As the biblical scholar Elaine Pagels writes:

> Had Jesus' followers identified themselves with the majority of Jews rather than with a particular minority, they might have told his story very differently ... They might have told it, for example, in traditional patriotic style, as the story of an inspired Jewish holy man martyred by Israel's traditional enemies, foreign oppressors of one sort or another. (Pagels, 1995, p 14)

Had they done so, their mission would not have been cosmopolitan and they would have had no more of a desire to go 'unto the end of the world' as they would have had a desire to go to Mars. Jesus' followers, however, did *not* choose this narrative strategy, or were constrained by circumstance from choosing it. Rejected by the Jewish majority for their contrary doctrines, Jesus' followers rejected the Jewish majority – not by rejecting the world, like the Essenes, who retreated into the desert in order to preserve the pure essence of Judaism, but by rejecting Judaism itself and going out into the world in search of pagan converts. They thus invented a new language, a universal language of love, redemption and salvation, but also a universal language of eternal damnation, that has had a lasting impact – not only on the religion that came to be known as Christianity, but also on the universalist and expansionist religion that has come to be known as liberalism.

What I wish to do in the following is examine certain rhetorical features of the Apostle Paul's Epistle to the Romans and show how they become a model for similar moves made by key figures of 17th- and 18th-century

Enlightenment. A Jew who felt himself called to preach Christ's message both among his fellow Jews and among the Gentiles, Paul re-draws lines of difference, obliterating the particularity of both Jews and Gentiles in the name of a higher, spiritual, and non-corporeal unity. That this gesture, this move from material – ie physical and geographical – bases of identity to formal, spiritual ones has had notable political consequences is clear. What these consequences are, however, remains a point of contention. Therefore, as we have entered yet another millennium with no second coming in sight, it behooves us to examine the appeal of formal universality, for it is not at all clear whether the globalization of our sectarian messages is to be thought of automatically as universally good.

*

In the New Testament, the coming of Jesus represents both the fulfillment of Old Testament prophecies and the cancellation of the Jewish world within which these prophecies originated. Thus the fulfillment of God's promise to the Jews, coming, as it does, during a time of political crisis and foreign occupation, ironically 'saves' the Jews by dissolving their religious and national specificity. Believe in Jesus, Jews are enjoined, and you may enter a global community in which you will no longer have to establish ethnic or national identity by means of outward signs. Believe in Jesus, and in the very moment that you cease following the law of your fathers you will fulfill the promise of that law. Though the roots of Western anti-Semitism are clearly located in this Jewish-Christian break with the law and community, or more specifically, with Jewish-Christian resentment directed against the Jewish establishment, the impulse itself, at least according to Jacob Taubes, is quite traditionally Jewish. The apostle Paul, as Taubes sees him, deliberately styles himself after Moses, deliberately styles himself as one who is called to mediate between an angry God and His people, for what Paul desires is 'the establishment and legitimation of a new people of God' (Taubes, 1995, p 42). The Jewish denial of Jesus triggers God's anger, as it has been triggered in the past, and signals the possibility of the total destruction of his people. Paul, like Moses, intercedes, therefore, and pleads both with God and with his people for a new contract. This new contract, however, is no longer restricted to the historical Jews, the Jews who identify themselves by circumcision and the Mosaic law of the first contract, and this break with the past, Taubes believes, causes Paul great anguish. Paul's Judaism, his Jewish-Christianity, transcends the historical particularity of the Jewish people by proclaiming the universality of Israel. Paul, in Taubes's words, 'is a fanatic … a zealot, a Jewish zealot', for whom this step beyond the borders of the law is painful and momentous. Despite the fact that Paul is a Roman citizen (Acts 16, 37; 22, 25–28), and despite the fact that his special mission is the conversion of the Gentiles (Galatians 1, 15–16; 2, 7–8), Paul is no Josephus, no upper-class believer in a Jewish-Roman-Hellenist synthesis. 'The spiritual costs he had to pay', Taubes forcefully proclaims, 'were not made for some blah blah in this great liberal world order'. Paul *is* a universalist, Taubes acknowledges, but his universalism 'is however a universalism that points to the special election of Israel, but only after Israel is transfigured in the end into a *"pas* Israel"', a pan-Israel (Taubes, 1995, p 38). The irony of Paul's undertaking lies in the transfiguration, for once this new, transfigured and universalized Israel is established, the old, particular and national Israel disappears – indeed, quite literally only a few years after Paul's death.

What interests us, what lingers, is the linguistic transfiguration that Paul effects. The universalization of Israel does not entail the universal extension of Jewish law to the Gentiles, but rather its 'pneumatization', as Taubes puts it, its 'spiritualization' (Taubes, 1995, pp 64, 65). The motif is familiar. The 'letter' of the law – its 'positivity', to speak with Hegel, or, in the current vernacular, its 'materiality' – is denied so that its 'spirit' may prevail. To follow the law, then, is to deny it; and to deny it is to follow it. The letter/spirit distinction makes this paradox both visible and soluble. To follow the *letter* is to deny the *spirit*, so that *denying* the letter leads to an *affirmation* of the spirit. Yet, denying the letter also means denying the particularity of one's identity. The real Jew, the really righteous Jew, cannot be the pious Jew who is loyal to the law of his fathers. In his Epistle to the Romans, Paul repeatedly describes the dilemma of the Jews in terms of this paradox. 'That the Gentiles, which followed not after righteousness, have attained to righteousness', he writes. 'But Israel, which followed after the law or righteousness, hath not attained to the law of righteousness' (Romans 9, 30–31). Follow the law, affirm Judaism in all its outward manifestations, he seems to say, and you are lost; but transgress the law, deny your specificity, and you shall be saved. Why? Because to be a dutifully lawful member of the nation of Israel does not automatically make one a benefactor of the promise that God made to the nation of Israel. 'For they are not all Israel, which are of Israel', Paul warns, and 'neither, because they are the seed of Abraham, are they all children' (Romans 9, 6–7). The form/matter distinction – by which the law, or the traditional rites and practices of the people of Israel, is depreciated – allows Paul to distinguish an authentic inner *faith* from the deceptive external performance of meaningless *works*, and thereby allows Christianized Jews to dis-embed themselves from the material aspects of their heritage and yet still claim to be Israel's true heirs, the true seed of Abraham. 'For the promise', Paul claims, 'that he should be the heir of the world, was not to Abraham, or to his seed, through the law, but through the righteousness of faith' (Romans 4, 13). This internalization and formalization of what makes a Jew a Jew extends all the way to circumcision, 'For', to quote Paul again, 'he is not a Jew, which is one outwardly; neither is that circumcision, which is outward in the flesh: but he is a Jew, which is one inwardly; and circumcision is that of the heart, in the spirit, and not in the letter' (Romans 2, 28–29). Mosaic law – even that shibboleth of all shibboleths, circumcision – proves to be illusory, and Paul declares it null and void. 'But now we are delivered from the law, that being dead wherein we were held; that we should serve in newness of spirit, and not in the oldness of the letter' (Romans 7, 6).

Taubes insists that Paul's polemic against the law is a politically motivated double-edged sword, aimed, with one swing, against the established Jewish deniers of the Messiah, and, with the other, against Roman imperial rule. Thus, two types of law are opposed: (1) Jewish law as a codification of customs and practices that separates nation from nation, people from people, and (2) Roman law, the imperial extension of which purports to unite the many under the rule of the one. The former establishes borders; the latter obliterates or reconfigures them. Paul advances a third law, one that seemingly transcends all borders because it is a law that offers no outward, material signs by which identity and difference can be established; a law that suspends both the Jewish state and the Roman empire because it is a law that, as he says in an oft quoted passage, is 'written in their hearts' (Romans 2, 15). When thus emancipated from the dead letter of the law, we rise above the external world of signs and the old world of nations, for, as Paul now pointedly proclaims, 'there is no difference between the Jew and the Greek' (Romans 10, 12).

As a consequence of the law being written in our hearts, there is no longer any difference among nations. Paul's immediate political aim, of course, is to unite Jewish and Gentile converts to Christ's message under the umbrella of a higher unity – faith – than the one represented by national or imperial law. Jewish and 'Greek' – that is, pagan – identity are to be traded in for a 'Christian' identity, a universal community of believers based on the invisible law of the heart. That such a formal, 'pneumatisized' and transfigured law, a law that we all have unmediated access to, could appeal to later generations and thus be incorporated into their political ideologies is not at all surprising. Indeed, we can hear in Paul's transfiguration of the Jewish law the program of a much more general enlightenment of all laws. Consequently, what I would like to do now is briefly examine three philosophical receptions of Christianity that secularize, as it were, Paul's mode of argumentation. What we will see is that the universal transfiguration of law is always accompanied by the unquestioned and unquestionable demand to assimilate to the new law, a demand that hastens the obliteration of particular identities.

*

Like Paul, the 17th- and 18th-century enlightenment thinkers, from Spinoza to the young Hegel, also wish to subvert 'positive' legal codes that are expressed in figurative language and are based on an external authority provided by a historical narrative. In their stead, we are urged to follow the sure and necessary dictates that come with the use of a clear and transparent reason. Spinoza, for instance, explicitly pits the ancient Mosaic ceremonial laws against a universal, de-materialized, divine law, which is neither grounded in a legitimizing narrative nor demands the performance of rituals or ceremonies. 'Christ', he writes,

> who taught only universal moral precepts … was sent into the world, not to preserve the state nor to lay down laws, but solely to teach the universal moral law.

... His sole care was to teach moral doctrines, and distinguish them from the laws of the state; for the Pharisees, in their ignorance, thought that the observance of the state law and the Mosaic law was the sum total of morality; whereas such laws merely had reference to the public welfare, and aimed not so much at instructing the Jews as at keeping them under constraint. (Spinoza, 1955, pp 70–71)

The divine law, therefore, is aimed not at guiding specific conduct, but rather at the free attainment of an unconstrained knowledge and love of God. Spinoza's message is similar to Paul's – faith as knowledge and love of God – but the metaphysics are quite different, for the knowledge and love of God is now expressed in the rational language of clear and distinct ideas arranged logically and according to the geometric method. Appealing to a distinction that will become increasingly important within the Western tradition, Spinoza notes that people are swayed either by arguments that appeal 'to the facts of natural experience, or to self-evident intellectual axioms'. The more convincing, powerful and long-lasting of the two methods is the latter – the appeal to rational deduction – but it is also the most tedious, 'usually requir[ing]', he notes, 'a long chain of arguments, and, moreover, very great caution, acuteness, and self-restraint – qualities which are not often met with; therefore people prefer to be taught by experience rather than deduce their conclusion from a few axioms, and set them out in logical order' (Spinoza, 1955, p 77). This distinction between experiential language and the language of logical deduction is not merely methodological, but also typological, for it divides humanity into the immature, who need 'stories' to aid their understanding, and the rationally mature. The second method, the rational method, which leads to universal and necessary truths of reason, befits a free and mature humanity. Thus, whereas 'knowledge of and belief in [the Scripture] is particularly necessary to the masses whose intellect is not capable of perceiving things clearly and distinctly', a person 'who is ignorant of them' – and here Spinoza speaks very much in the Pauline manner – 'and nevertheless knows by natural reason that God exists ... and has a true plan of life, is altogether blessed – yes more blessed than the common herd of believers, because besides true opinions he possesses also a true and distinct conception' (Spinoza, 1955, p 78). In Spinoza, Paul's universal law of the heart transforms itself into a universal law of the intellect – which is to say, the language of belief in an omnipotent but merciful God becomes the language of belief in an omniscient and unyielding reason.

As a consequence, universal Enlightenment brings with it not only the disappearance of *particular* narratives – such as the Old Testament stories of the prophets, which Spinoza can only read as allegories designed for a people in their collective infancy – but eventually also brings with it the disappearance of narrative *altogether*. Lessing is quite explicit in this regard, not only emphatically pointing to the 'ugly, broad ditch' (Lessing, 1957, p 55) that stands between the contingent truths of history and the necessary truths of reason, but also insisting that to continue to rely on historically contingent narratives long after their usefulness is 'harmful' (Lessing, 1957, p 91). During humanity's childhood, the Old Testament could be considered an appropriate primer, but once Christ, 'a better instructor' (Lessing, 1957, p 91) came along, he introduced us to 'the second, better primer' (Lessing, 1957, p 93), one appropriate to an increased, but not complete, maturity. To continue to worry over the allusions and allegories of our old primer, he warns, would give us 'a petty, crooked, hairsplitting understanding', and make us 'full of mysteries, superstitious, full of contempt for all that is comprehensible and easy' (Lessing, 1957, p 91). This more advanced primer is the New Testament, of course, and its virtue lies not only in its specific teachings (above all, the teaching of the immortality of the soul), but also in its universality, for it not only replaces the outdated Old Testament, but supersedes all locally based historical narratives the world over. 'It would have been impossible', Lessing writes,

> for any other book to become so generally known among such different nations: and indisputably, the fact that modes of thought so completely diverse from each other have turned their attention to this same book, has assisted human reason on its way more than if every nation had had its *own primer* specially for itself. (Lessing, 1957, p 93)

With this, Paul's Mosaic attempt to save the Jewish nation from the wrath of God by extending Judaism beyond its traditional borders becomes the European attempt to rouse the rest of the world from its self-incurred immaturity. Education replaces salvation, and thus, as Lessing well knows, even this second primer, written, in part, by Paul, has become dispensable. We now stand on the threshold of a 'new eternal gospel' (Lessing, 1957, p 97), he writes, one that does without narrative, because full maturity requires 'the development of revealed truths into truths of reason' (Lessing, 1957, p 26), and these necessary truths of reason will enjoy the same incontestable validity that Jesus' teachings once did, 'unto the end of the world'.

But, in a truly genial move, the young Hegel sublates this enlightened sublation of Christianity, in that for Hegel, Christ's apotheosis of love not only transcends the Jews' fate – a fate marked by their incorrigible sensuality and slavish obedience to external authority – but also resolves, *avant la lettre*, the Kantian antinomy of duty and inclination, thus, the antinomies of freedom and necessity and of the universal and the particular that plague Western Enlightenment. In his *The Spirit of Christianity and Its Fate*, Hegel writes: 'Since laws are unifications of opposites in a *concept*, which thus leaves them as opposites while it exists itself in opposition to *reality*, it follows that the concept expresses an *ought*.' When this concept, which is a law, is grasped as form, the ought, the command, is moral, but 'if we solely look at the content, as the specific unification of specific opposites, the command is civil' (Hegel, 1971, pp 209–10). The positivity of civil law characterizes the limits of the Jews (and others) who sunder themselves and their God from nature and thereby reify external authority. The formal and freely internalized moral law is Kantian, but, Hegel maintains, the distinction between an externally authoritarian, positive moral code, on the one hand, and an internalized, freely chosen moral law, on the other, is not as great as Kant made it out to be. 'Between the Shaman of the Tungus, the European prelate who rules church and state, the Voguls, and the

Puritans, on the one hand', Hegel writes, 'and the man who listens to his own command of duty, on the other, the difference is not that the former make themselves slaves, while the latter is free, but that the former have their lord outside themselves, while the latter carries his lord in himself, yet at the same time is his own slave' (Hegel, 1971, p 211). Thus, instead of obedience to the law, which presupposes the distinction between duty and inclination, Jesus offers fulfillment, which, with Hegel, we may call 'an inclination to act as the laws may command, ie a unification of inclination with the law whereby the latter loses its form as law' (Hegel, 1971, p 214). The Sermon on the Mount, Hegel tells us, 'does not teach reverence for the laws; on the contrary, it exhibits that which fulfils the law but annuls it as law and so is something higher than obedience to law and makes law superfluous' (Hegel, 1971, p 212). Reconciliation – a specifically non-Jewish notion, Hegel assures us (p 241) – makes law 'wholly superfluous' (p 215), such that love, which is to be thought of not as an 'ought' but as an 'is', as a simple modification and quality of life, emancipates us from both law and duty. Love is 'the sole principle of virtue', because: 'To complete subjection under the law of an alien Lord, Jesus opposed not a partial subjection under a law of one's own, the self-coercion of Kantian virtue, but virtues without lordship and without submission, ie, virtues as modifications of love' (Hegel, 1971, p 244).

There you have it: All you need is love!

*

So where does this leave us? Lessing's account of the *The Education of the Human Race* left us with an unacknowledged irony – it presents the end of narrative in the form of a historical narrative. Hegel, on the other hand, leaves us with a logic of reconciliation that is not the result of evolution, but rather the correction of a mistake. 'The state of Jewish culture cannot be called the state of childhood, nor can its phraseology be called an undeveloped, childlike phraseology', Hegel writes. Rather, Jewish culture is a 'consequence of the supreme miseducation of the people' (Hegel, 1971, p 256), a miseducation that is to be overcome. And this, ironically, brings us back to Paul, the Jew who wished to save his people from their own blindness, their own slavish obedience to Jewish civic law and the neglect of the law written in their own hearts. This law, as both Paul and Hegel tell us, is not duty, not even a freely chosen and self-imposed moral duty, but love. Yet, as the somewhat older Hegel would have recognized, love is not simply a transfigured unity, but one pole of a larger opposition, an opposition that Paul – and the Jewish-Christian world out of which he came – knew how to wield with particular skill. Let us recall Taubes's claim that Paul's 'pneumatization' of the law was a political act, a political theology, aimed at two targets: the Mosaic law of the Jewish world and the imperial legal expansion of the Roman world. Paul's war with the Romans may have been a simple rebellion against the tyranny of foreign occupation, but his argument with the Jews is a good deal more intimate. It is a civil war. Here, the forbearance of the Sermon on the Mount does not hold. In a civil war, one does not love one's political enemy; one hates him – one hates him 'unto the end of the world', as a matter of fact. With the promise of love and life everlasting comes also the promise of eternal damnation. As you will have noticed, at the beginning of this chapter I cited only part of Mark's account of Jesus' final instructions to his disciplines. The full passage reads: 'Go ye into all the world, and preach the gospel to every creature. He that believeth and is baptized shall be saved; but he that believeth not shall be damned' (Mark 16, 15–16). He who refuses to believe is not ignored, not merely pitied, not merely defeated and overcome; he who refuses to believe is condemned to eternal death. This is no longer a local war, a national war between Jews and Egyptians or Babylonians. This is a war in which one's enemy is a brother who has committed the greatest betrayal. He has not broken the law of the land, he has done much worse: he has violated the law that is written in his own heart. Once the message is universalized, once the material, earthly, distinct basis of any political program has become spiritualized and globalized, the enemy too becomes universal, global.

In her social history of Satan, Elaine Pagels shows how the identity of Satan was altered in the Jewish world during the time of Christ, in part as a result of ongoing sectarian battles. From one of God's many helpful angels, Satan is transformed into God's primary adversary, the principle of evil that is eternally at war with God's purposes. In this way, Pagels notes, immanent, sectarian, political battles were seen to have their spiritual, heavenly correspondence. The various first century battles between marginal groups (like the Essenes and the Jewish-Christians) and the Pharisees or other representatives of the Jewish establishment are thus 'pneumatisized', for what happens on earth is but a reflection of a divine conflict between Good and Evil as fought by God and Satan in the hearts of man. One's worldly enemies are also the enemies of God, for they carry out Satan's plans on earth. One begins, therefore, to fight universal, moral battles, not just political ones – indeed, one fights, in the words of Carl Schmitt, *absolute*, and not just *actual*, enemies. Let me just remind you again of the anecdote Schmitt relates concerning the trial of St Joan in the 15th century. 'When her ecclesiastical judge tried to trap her theologically by asking whether she claimed that God hated the English, she answered: I do not know whether God loves or hates the English; I only know that they must be driven out of France. Every normal partisan defender of the native land', Schmitt goes on to say, 'would have given this answer. With this basic defense, a fundamental limitation of the notion of enmity is given. The actual enemy is not made into the absolute enemy and therefore not into the ultimate enemy of humanity' (Schmitt, 1963, pp 93–94).

One of the great ironies of the 20th century is that though we, in the West, have become thoroughly secularized, St Joan's surprising modesty about her knowledge of God's intentions has been entirely lost. We no longer need God or Satan to construct absolute enemies; we have the true believers in rational discourse like Habermas, whose certainty about language's universal validity claims is downright God-like. With the simple formula – 'Just those action norms are valid to which all possibly affected persons could agree as participants in rational discourses' (Habermas, 1996a, p 107) – Habermas writes the dangerous because unavoidable law again into our hearts. If I disagree with it, then I too will be damned as an unbeliever – this time as one who denies the universal light of reason that uniquely illuminates legitimate dialog. It may be helpful to remind ourselves, however, that the Roman Empire, against which Paul aimed one prong of his attack on the law, soon made its peace with Christianity and found it extremely useful to combine the universality of a global religion with its own particular political and economic interests. Our contemporary Roman Empire – the United States – has also found it useful to combine its particular political and economic interests with a secularized universal discourse of human rights, democracy and liberal market values. When Paul proclaimed that there was no difference between Jew and Greek, he in effect erased the Jew from a world dominated by Greeks. A similar erasure of the 'childlike' or simply 'miseducated' Jew is affected by the universalist impulse of Spinoza, Lessing and Hegel. As we now go about Americanizing the globe – excuse me – as we now go about extending the benefits of universal human rights that have been discovered by a universally valid procedure of rational communication, perhaps we ought to be aware of which differences we silently obliterate, and perhaps we ought to remember that the universality of a cosmopolitan language is necessarily also accompanied by the universality of a global silence. Such a silence may in fact be unavoidable, but we ought not to delude ourselves. Our faith in our abilities to articulate a universal language of formal consensus and a 'pneumatized' universal law and moral code is every bit as much a political theology as Paul's, a political theology that seeks out and eternally damns its absolute enemies – unto the end of the world.

Chapter 8

Human rights as geopolitics: from Vitoria to Rawls

Dates, dates, dates. 1917, 1945, 1989. The wars of the world seem to have been reduced to a squabble about dates. For Jürgen Habermas, the year 1945 is pivotal. As he puts it, the Allied victory 'permanently discredited an array of myths which, ever since the end of the nineteenth century, had been mobilized against the heritage of 1789'. The unconditional surrender of Germany in 1945, then, stands for the unconditional surrender of *'all* forms of political legitimation that did not – at least verbally, at least in words – subscribe to the universalist spirit of political enlightenment' (Habermas, 2001, p 46). 1989 is merely an afterthought. If, in 1945, after the collapse of their fascist and militarist regimes, Germany, Italy and Japan were integrated into the new universalist order, then 1989 simply represents the year in which former communist regimes, which in any event paid the all important lip service to the ideals of 1789, were effectively and not just verbally integrated into that order. Ernst Nolte (1997) likes all three dates because they form the beginning and end dates of a series of consecutive civil wars, a European civil war between bolshevism and fascism from 1917 to 1945, and a global civil war between liberal capitalism and communism from 1945 to 1989. Thus for Nolte, 1945 is pivotal only in the sense that it represents a crucial transition, an intensification, not a culmination, that only finds its ultimate resolution at the end of the short 20th century. Nolte, in other words, conflates Nazi Germany and the Soviet Union by calling the defeated enemy of the 20th century 'totalitarianism', while Habermas persists in seeing communism as an admittedly imperfect Enlightenment ally in the fight against the uniquely evil, fascist counter-Enlightenment.

Carl Schmitt, who may be said to be the inspiration for those, like Nolte, who speak of European and global civil wars, witnessed the events of 1917 (which in Germany were the events of 1918–19) and 1945, but unlike some of his colleagues who celebrated 100 or more birthdays (Ernst Jünger, Leni Riefenstahl, Hans-Georg Gadamer), his long life did not quite stretch to the contentious year 1989. Nevertheless, it is clear that, for all their importance, neither totalitarianism nor fascism would have been his crucial terms. It is also clear that he would have been closer in his assessment to Habermas than to Nolte, for the year 1945 represents the final victory of a particular manifestation of the universalist spirit. In retrospect, 1989 was only a mopping-up operation. More specifically, for Schmitt the events of 1917, personified by Lenin and Wilson, signal the eclipse of a centuries-old Euro-centric world that had more to do with the events of 1492 and the ideas of 1648 (Peace of Westphalia) or 1713 (Peace of Utrecht) than those of 1789. Given the demise of this concrete, spatially articulated, Euro-centric order, the question he asks is simple: What will be the shape of the world to come? Writing in 1955, at the height of the friend/enemy conflict that we called the Cold War, Schmitt imagined three alternatives. First, one of the two contestants could win a clear-cut victory. 'The victor would then be the sole ruler of the world. He would take, distribute, and use the entire planet, land, sea, and air, according to his plans and ideas.' Second, under the hegemony of one or the other power (and Schmitt thought that this type of hegemony could only be exercised by the US), a managed, global balance of power could be established. That is, regional blocks would form, ultimately subject to American supervision. The realization of this alternative would represent a transfiguration of the 19th-century British form of global hegemony. Third, a truly symmetrical regional balance of power could be achieved. 'It could happen that several regional powers or blocks [*Großräume*] could be formed, which would bring about a balance of power and thereby a world order' (Schmitt, 1995, p 521). As the subjunctive phrase 'it could happen' [*es könnte sein*] reveals, Schmitt recognized the doubtful and quixotic nature of this option. Indeed, he did not need the events of 1989 to tell him what he already knew, namely, that a single power, the United States, would determine the shape of things to come.

The only power to emerge from the 20th century's first world war fresh and at the top of its game was the United States. Although it took another 70 years to subdue all its rivals fully, it was already clear then that this, the 20th, was to be the American century, perhaps the first of many such centuries. Not only was the US a new power, but there was also something distinctly new about its power. As Schmitt recognized in 1932 (Schmitt, 1988b, pp 184–203), America's legal mode of economic expansion and control of Europe – and by extension or ambition, the rest of the globe – was qualitatively different from previous forms of imperialism. Whereas, for example, Spain in the 16th century and Great Britain in the 19th justified their imperial conquests by asserting religious and/or cultural superiority, America simply denied that its conquests were conquests. By being predominantly economic – and using, as Schmitt says, the creditor/debtor distinction rather than the more traditional Christian/non-Christian or civilized/uncivilized ones (Schmitt, 1988b, p 186) – America's expropriations were deemed to be peaceful and apolitical. Furthermore, they were legal; or rather they presented themselves as the promotion and extension of universally binding legality *per se*. Because law ruled the United States, the rule of the United States was first and foremost the rule of law. For Schmitt, this widely accepted self-representation was neither merely 'ideological' nor simply propagandistic. It was in truth an intellectual achievement, deserving respect, precisely because it was so difficult to oppose. As the American geo-strategist Zbigniew Brzezinski has more recently concluded: 'The American emphasis on political democracy and economic development ... combines to convey a simple ideological message that appeals to many: the quest for individual success enhances freedom while generating wealth. The resulting blend of idealism and egoism is a potent combination. Individual self-fulfillment is said to be a God-given right that at the same time can benefit others by setting an example and by generating wealth.' He goes on to say: 'As the imitation of

American ways gradually pervades the world, it creates a more congenial setting for the exercise of the indirect and seemingly consensual American hegemony. And as in the case of the domestic American system, that hegemony involves a complex structure of interlocking institutions and procedures, designed to generate consensus and obscure asymmetries in power and influence' (Brzezinski, 1997, pp 26–27). To sum up, Brzezinski notes that 'the very multinational and exceptional character of American society has made it easier for America to universalize its hegemony without letting it appear to be a strictly national one' (Brzezinski, 1997, p 210). It seems, then, that to oppose American global hegemony is to oppose the universally good and common interests of all of humanity. This – the equation of particular economic and political interests with universally binding moral norms – *this* is the intellectual achievement Schmitt could not help but admire, even as he continuously embarked upon his disastrous attempts at fighting his elusive because non-localizable enemy, which proved to be mere shadowboxing in the end.

The *nomos* of the world

In 1950 – after, in other words, the pivotal year 1945 – Schmitt published his elegy to a lost world, *Der Nomos der Erde im Völkerrecht des Jus Publicum Europaeum*. The lost world in question was the world of European public law, the international law that regulated the affairs of the European sovereign states from, roughly speaking, the mid-17th century to the end of the 19th. It was an unusual time in which Europe, or Christendom, enjoyed a hegemony over a newly 'discovered' and conquered world, a time in which, as Schmitt says, the Christian nations of Europe were seen as the 'creators and representatives of an order applicable to the whole earth' and in which the term '[c]ivilization was synonymous with *European* civilization' (Schmitt, 2003, p 86). But it was also a time in which no single Christian religion and no single continental power enjoyed ultimate sovereignty over Europe itself. To cite Brzezinski one more time: 'The essential reality was that of Europe's civilizational global supremacy and of fragmented European continental power ... The geopolitically consequential fact was that Europe's global hegemony did not derive from hegemony in Europe by any single European power' (Brzezinski, 1997, p 19). Once, perhaps – during the High Middle Ages, for instance – European unity could represent itself as hierarchical with a dual sovereignty at the top (Emperor and Pope), and Europe's relations with the non-European world, primarily Islam to its south, could be seen as symmetrical, since neither civilization could claim cultural or military supremacy over the other. By the time of the 17th-century religious conflicts, however, the situation had radically changed. Because of the Reformation, and because of the rise of politically autonomous sovereign states, traditional European unity was threatened by the most vicious of civil wars, one based on ideological differences backed by identical truth claims. Seen from the inside, then, with Protestants accusing the Pope of being the Anti-Christ and Catholics identifying Protestantism with heresy, Europe had become irrevocably differentiated, both politically and spiritually. Its challenge was to reconstruct a more complex and comprehensive unity amid difference, and to do so it required a more global distinction than the one available during the Middle Ages.

During the 16th- and 17th-century European conquest of the Americas, that distinction was provided, Schmitt says, by the so-called Amity Line, which distinguished the newly discovered world from the old and thereby created a concretely localizable distinction between a zone of political and juridical exception and a space that served as the legal norm. 'At this "line"', he writes, 'Europe ended and the "New World" began. At any rate, European law, ie, "European public law", ended here … Beyond the line was an "overseas" zone in which, for want of any legal limits to war, only the law of the stronger applied'. This seemingly lawless zone, however, served to establish, or maintain, a particular legal order, for Schmitt sees the quality of the political equilibrium on the European side of the line to be directly dependent on the disequilibria that existed beyond it. Indeed, he views these zones of exception as a kind of 'tremendous *exoneration* of the internal European problematic' (Schmitt, 2003, p 94). How that 'exoneration' (German *Entlastung* [Schmitt, 1988a, p 62]) worked can be glimpsed in the following remarkable passage:

> The significance of amity lines in 16th and 17th century international law was that great areas of freedom were designated as conflict zones in the struggle over the distribution of a new world. As a practical justification, one could argue that the designation of a conflict zone at once freed the area on this side of the line – a sphere of peace and order ruled by European public law – from the immediate threat of those events 'beyond the line', which would not have been the case had there been no such zone. The designation of a conflict zone outside Europe contributed also to the limitation of European wars, which is its meaning and its justification in international law. (Schmitt, 2003, pp 97–98)[1]

It is ironic, then, that 16th-century European observers were so outraged by Aztec human sacrifices, since on this view, the entire Western Hemisphere can be said to have been sacrificed, after a fashion, to maintain a European civilized order. From a legal standpoint, the laws or conventions that regulated European international relations were not – or at least were not *only* – derived from divine or natural law, but rested on the ability to locate spatially concrete zones of exclusion that are exempt from the very laws and conventions they enable. As Schmitt points out, the consequences of the conquest's catastrophic reordering of the world picture 'challenged all traditional intellectual and moral principles' and 'affected all new theories and formulas of the 17th century', especially those of Pascal Hobbes, and Locke (Schmitt, 2003, p 95). The seemingly paradoxical relationship between the realms 'this side' of the line and the excluded zones 'beyond' had to be explained.

The language of *Entlastung*, an 'un-burdening' that points toward the compensatory release of pressure, tempts one, of course, to read this justification of the European occupation of the New World in a psychological and anthropological manner. On this reading, civilization is represented by the higher powers; lack of civilization by uncontrolled animal drives. Natural drives cannot be eliminated, but they can be neatly disentangled and dissociated from the mental and spiritual faculties. To their European conquerors, early reports of the Indians' sensuality and licentiousness, their lack of the 'correct' forms of social intercourse, and their purported 'cannibalism', seemed to confirm their 'animal' nature. Therefore Europe sublimates its animality by establishing the Americas as an extra-legal zone in which bestial deeds can be 'acted out' far away from polite company. It is as if a 'violence brothel' had been created so that chaste relations could be preserved at home. Schmitt reads Pascal's famous phrase – *'Un Méridien décide de la vérité'* (A meridian decides the truth) – *not* as a general expression of relativism or skepticism, but rather as a reflection on

> a fact almost inconceivable to a person of Pascal's mind, ie, that in certain areas Christian princes and peoples had agreed to disregard the distinction between justice and injustice. Pascal's meridian is nothing other than the amity lines of his time, which had created an abyss between freedom (the lawlessness of the state of nature) and an orderly 'civil' mode of existence. (Schmitt, 2003, p 95)

And indeed, the discovery of America meant the discovery of the state of nature, a distinctly Hobbesean state in which *homo homini lupus* (man is a wolf to man). Hobbes too Schmitt reads in light of the line. Hobbes's 'state of nature is a *no man's land*, but this does not mean it exists *nowhere*. It can be located, and Hobbes locates it, among other places, in the New World' (Schmitt, 2003, p 96). Both the supposed wolf-like character of the native inhabitants and the atrocities committed by the Spaniards contribute to the composite vision of a permanent civil war of all against all to which we – that is, all of Europe – could be returned if we do not carefully maintain the proper boundaries.

But Schmitt is far more concerned with a different kind of release (*Entlastung*), a logical release, if that bizarre combination of terms may be admitted. We are dealing here not so much with a sublimation of drives as with a 'dialectic' of inclusion and exclusion. By virtue of their explorations and conquests, Spain, France, England and the other imperial powers, though fundamentally at odds with each other both religiously and politically, could still represent the unity of Christendom and civilization over a heathen and barbarian external world. The non-European, one might say, functioned as the 'environment' that guaranteed the overall unity and identity of the internally differentiated 'system' that was Europe. Furthermore, the inclusion within a self-identical Europe of equal sovereign states, self-regulated by public law without the benefit of a supreme secular or spiritual executive, relied not only upon an exclusion of the non-European, but also on the exclusion of European colonial rivalry. The warfare between European powers in the New World (between illegal British privateers and Spanish galleons, for example) was different in kind from continental warfare and was to be kept as separate as possible from the way European power politics was conducted. And finally, whereas in the New World Europeans and their descendants conducted wars of extermination against the indigenous populations, in Europe a golden age of limited and 'civilized' warfare lasted until 1914. Simply put, European unity manifested itself in the fact that European states felt obliged to conduct their inter-European affairs differently from how they conducted themselves when in contact with the 'un-' or 'lesser' civilized world under their control. Consequently, Europe could identify itself as 'civilized' in its asymmetrical relationship with the 'uncivilized' or 'half-civilized' rest of the world. If, in other words, internally, with the loss of the medieval 'organic' and hierarchical unity, there developed a symmetrically ordered, self-organizing and self-regulating system of sovereign states, a plurality of sovereigns with no sovereign over them, this was expressly *because* there existed a hierarchical European sovereignty over large parts of the rest of the world. 'The designation of a zone of ruthless conflict', Schmitt writes, 'was a logical consequence of the fact that there was neither a recognized principle nor a common arbitrational authority to govern the division and allocation of lands' (Schmitt, 2003, p 100). Had there still been a united Europe over which a single secular and/or spiritual sovereign ruled, the discovery and occupation of the New World could have been 'orderly' – that is, directed from the top, with the supreme sovereign (pope or emperor) granting particular rulers particular rights and privileges of colonization. Such a hierarchy, if effective, could have compelled obedience and brutally repressed dissention. The lack of such a clearly defined hierarchy, however, had as one of its consequences a 'rationalization, humanization, and legalization – a limitation – of war' within Europe itself. 'At least with respect to continental land war in European international law, this was achieved by limiting war to a military relation between states' (Schmitt, 2003, p 100). It is this self-regulated limitation of war that Schmitt considers to be 'the highest form of order within the scope of human power' (Schmitt, 2003, p 187).

Let us be clear on what Schmitt is saying. Order, no matter how structured, comes at a price. Hierarchical order brings with it a domination/subordination structuring principle. When hierarchies dissolve, either civil war ensues or a new ordering principle takes the old order's place. On the verge of disintegration through civil war, on the verge, as many feared, of a return to the 'bad' anarchy of unlimited violence in a state of nature, Europe – and Christendom – produced a 'good' anarchy of controlled violence. In place of *a* sovereign, there reigned *many* sovereigns, which left the ultimate position of authority open. It is around this void that the new order organized itself. To fill the void would be to re-establish the old principle of order, something that the remaining sovereign powers would refuse to accept. So, to return to the dates mentioned above, 1648 established the plurality of sovereign states, 1713 their relative balance. In a sense, the seemingly infinite regress of authority that always attaches to hierarchical orderings – positive law based on natural law based on divine law based on … what? God?, the rational structure of the cosmos? – was halted and replaced by an 'invisible hand' long before that description of origin-less emergence was theorized as such.

But this order too was bought at a price. Europe exerts its sovereignty over the New World by positing itself as the norm (culturally and legally) and relegating the regions beyond the line as the exception that establishes the norm. By making the 'state of nature', to which the regions beyond the line are condemned, a necessary logical component of the order that is the norm, Europe does not merely exclude the New World from the new legal order, but, as Giorgio Agamben states, the New World is 'included solely through its exclusion' (Agamben, 1998, p 18). Its exclusion from the realm of European public law is the means by which it is taken possession of. Furthermore, its exclusion is never complete. Though localized in the newly discovered realms overseas, the state of nature remains an ever-present, if invisible, threat within Europe itself. 'Sovereignty', Agamben notes – and sovereignty here simply means the state of exception that founds or supports the law – 'thus presents itself as an incorporation of the state of nature in society ... Hobbes, after all, was perfectly aware ... that the state of nature did not necessarily have to be conceived as a real epoch, but rather could be understood as a principle internal to the State revealed in the moment in which the State is considered "*as if it were dissolved*"' (Agamben, 1998, pp 35–36). What Europe momentarily 'achieved' and what Schmitt guardedly and with reservation celebrated is a spatial articulation of the exception. The state 'as if it were dissolved' was seen to exist 'over there' so that it would not occur 'over here'. What Schmitt also recognized, and bemoaned, is the breakdown of that spatial articulation. The world wars of the 20th century demonstrated that what was over there was over here as well. As early as the 1920s Schmitt saw, in Agamben's words, that 'the constitutive link between the localization and order of the old *nomos* was broken and the entire system of the reciprocal limitations and rules of the *jus publicum Europaeum* brought to ruin'. This breakdown continues to this day: 'What happened and is still happening before our eyes is that the "juridically empty" space of the state of exception ... has transgressed its spatiotemporal boundaries and now, overflowing outside them, is starting to coincide with the normal order, in which everything again becomes possible' (Agamben, 1998, p 38).

Clearly, neither Agamben nor Schmitt, despite the latter's nostalgia for the older, Euro-centric order, advocates a return of the hegemonic and genocidal relationship to the non-European world. But they do fundamentally differ in their evaluation of the sovereign exception. Schmitt, in his argument with abstract normativity, steadfastly maintains that, whether it is acknowledged or not, order is always spatially and concretely grounded. For him, the 'state of nature', from which the law is banished but upon which the law is based, can be managed, controlled, localized and limited, but never eliminated. Order is localizable and therefore so is the state of exception (*Ausnahmezustand*) upon which it is grounded. Agamben, on the other hand, implicitly believes in the possibility of a political order that would *not* be based on an exclusion. The insistence on localizing a putatively logically necessary exception is, in Agamben's view, what drives modernity. Indeed, it is what has driven us all straight to hell, because for Agamben, the *telos* or logical consequence of such localization is, quite simply, if melodramatically, Auschwitz. 'When our age', he writes, 'tried to grant the unlocalizable a permanent and visible localization, the result was the concentration camp' (Agamben, 1998, p 20). Thus, rather than merely 'limiting' or 'civilizing' the violence associated with a fatalistically necessary state of exception, Agamben wishes to eliminate it. Accordingly, his vision of the political is alternately nihilistic and utopian – that is – hopeless except for the one grand hope. 'Until a completely new politics … is at hand', he writes, 'every new theory and every praxis will remain imprisoned and immobile, and the "beautiful day" of life will be given citizenship only either through blood and death or in the perfect senselessness to which the society of the spectacle condemns it' (Agamben, 1998, p 11).

We will return to the issue of a 'completely new politics' later.[2] For now I wish to investigate a second trajectory that the sovereign ban traces, one that Agamben hints at but does not examine. Agamben focuses on the localization of the state of exception and its apotheosis in the camp. If the first successful modern localization of the sovereign exception is represented by the distinction between Europe and the New World, then its culmination as the internment, labor, concentration and death camps of the 20th century can be seen as a type of re-introduction of the initial distinction *within* Europe itself – and, of course, within the now 'civilized' Western Hemisphere as well. One thereby replaces the civilized/uncivilized distinction with Aryan/non-Aryan, white/black, native/immigrant, or – and though Agamben does not mention this possibility, some surely would – child/fetus. There is, however, a parallel if reverse way of dealing with exclusion, and the remainder of this study will focus not on localization, but on the *invisibilization* of the exception in the abstract moral and legal norm that informs the liberal rule of law and its extension as universal human rights. With Europe divested of its moral and political authority and integrated into a larger, potentially global order, the new American hegemony challenges us to imagine a total, exception-less inclusion of sovereign peoples (Rawls) or sovereign individuals (Habermas) with no enabling exclusion. Schmitt postulated that whether one likes it or not, the norm rests on an exception, inclusion on an exclusion. Schmitt would therefore ask: Can one think of the entire globe as a differentiated unity without an outside? The purpose of his much-maligned friend/enemy distinction was neither to glorify war nor justify the extermination of the heterogeneous, but to show that a total or global 'inclusion of the other', to use Habermas's threatening phrase (Habermas, 1998), could only occur if the *otherness* of the other, that which makes him what he is, is excluded from the world community. One cannot help but draw the friend/enemy distinction, then, when one recognizes in the handshake of the purported friend the surreptitious continuation of warfare by other means. Thus, the question we need to ask is: Upon what exclusion is the ostensive universal extension of human rights based? To repeat: It was Schmitt's contention that America's greatest achievement involved making this new exclusion invisible. If that is the case, then our task is to bring that exclusion back to light.

Barbarians

The Spanish conquest of the New World gave rise to two pressing and interconnected questions: What type of humans (if humans they were) occupied this strange world and what legal or moral justification was there for Spanish dominion over them and their possessions? The answer to the first question, and thus implicitly to the second, was simple, but needed further specification: They were barbarians.[3] When the Greeks coined the word, they used it to distinguish the foreign 'other' from themselves. If at first it merely meant the foreigner as such, by the fourth century BC it marked the foreigner as inherently inferior. By virtue of such an asymmetrical distinction between self and other, the qualities of the self are simply assumed, unstated, and silently equated with the norm, while the sub-standard properties of the other can be endlessly enumerated. To be Greek was to be in an ethnically, politically, culturally and linguistically defined closed community. All else was, and remained, outside, to be ignored, or, if noticed, to be dominated and used. When the early Christian Church took the term as their own to distinguish between believers and non-believers, they divested it of its ethnic, linguistic and geographic substance, for all humans had souls and all humans had the potential of being included in the Kingdom of Christ. That is, the distinction between the self and the other was no longer fixed, but fluid; the other could give up its otherness and become part of the larger and ever-expanding self – could, in a word, *assimilate* itself to the dominant group. Universalization, however, has its price. All peoples, not just Greeks, could now belong to an all-encompassing group and by virtue of that possibility all peoples could be part of something called 'humanity'; but because Christians are in possession of the one and only Truth and because inclusion is now based on the choice to accept that one and only Truth, to refuse to join was condemned as moral perversity. One was offered a choice, but rather than a neutral either/or, the alternatives were labeled 'right' and 'wrong'. Those who lived in vincible ignorance of Christ – those, in other words, who had heard but *rejected* the good news of the Gospel – committed a mortal sin and would face eternal damnation. While still on earth, such infidels could also be the targets of a 'just war', a 'crusade'. Thus, though all peoples are members of 'humanity', some – the non-believers – are lesser members than others, possessing fewer rights and deserving opprobrium.

If Anthony Pagden is correct in his assessment of the 16th-century Spanish response to the conquest of America, then one can say that first the Greek, then the Christian meaning of 'barbarian' was elaborated and used to justify the Spanish acquisitions. In his *The Fall of Natural Man*, Pagden argues that the initial Spanish response to the Amerindians, especially those encountered on the Caribbean islands, was to view them, following Aristotle, as 'natural slaves', incapable of ruling themselves and thus in need of masters. Like Aristotle's barbarians, the American Indians' natural function was to provide physical labor for those – the Spanish – whose nature it was to lead, thus it was unnatural for the former to roam free in their blissful ignorance (Pagden, 1986, pp 27–56). Upon discovering the highly complex Mexican and Inca civilizations, however, the notion that the indigenous populations could not rule themselves was rendered absurd. Therefore, to explain their inescapable difference – their idolatry, their 'barbaric' customs of cannibalism and human sacrifice, and their ignorance of the one, true religion – Francisco de Vitoria and his followers at the University of Salamanca developed the theory that later flourished in the Enlightenment and indelibly imprinted itself on 19th-century ethnology, namely that the Amerindians were, in Pagden's words, 'some variety of fully grown child whose rational faculties are complete but still potential rather than actual'. Therefore, 'Indians have to be trained to perceive what other men perceive without effort, to accept what other men regard as axiomatic without prior reflection' (Pagden, 1986, p 104). Pagden concludes that 'Vitoria and his successors were effectively claiming, as the great seventeenth-century natural law theorists – Puffendorf [sic] in particular – were to do, that any man who is capable of knowing, even in retrospect, that something is in his own interest may be said to have consented to it, even where there is no question of his having exercised any freedom of choice' (Pagden, 1986, p 105). To be capable of affirming the truth of the Gospel or the right reason of natural law when exposed to it is the same as accepting it – unless one willfully and perversely dissents.

I do not wish to cast Vitoria in an unjustly negative light; as every commentator has remarked, the dispassionate objectivity, honesty, clarity and scholastic rigor of his thinking is as refreshing to behold now as it must have been in the 16th century. His clear and logical defense of the rights of the American Indians effectively denied most – some say all – of the various Spanish claims over the New World, and his restrained but unmistakable condemnation of the excessive force employed by the conquistadors were used by Las Casas and others as ammunition in their fight against slavery and the harsh treatment of the native inhabitants. It has even been suggested that Vitoria, not Grotius, Pufendorf or Selden, is the true originator of the modern notion of international law.[4] Yet, it is the stated inherent *potential* in all humans, even barbarians, to know the truth that gave European Christians their irresistible and irreversible legal wedge. If, like every human, the peoples of the New World possessed the light of reason, then if only they could hear the good news, they would recognize the truth and accept their own salvation. Therefore, among the reasons for a possible 'just war' against the indigenous peoples of the Americas, Vitoria lists 'natural partnership and communication', 'spreading of the Christian religion', and the 'defense of the innocent against tyranny' (Vitoria, 1991, pp 278–91). In the first and third of these 'just titles' we can recognize versions, on the one hand, of the modern, liberal freedoms of travel and trade – though, as even one of Vitoria's students noted, it is absurd to view the conquistadors as tourists[5] – and, on the other, the modern, liberal propensity for 'humanitarian' interventions. It is the middle item, the freedom to preach Christianity, however, that gives one the moral authority to exercise the other two, for only by being in possession of the truth can one recognize the difference between innocence and tyranny, or turn travel to the land of the other into conversion to more of the same.

'To preach and announce the Gospel in the lands of the barbarians', Vitoria admonishes us, is not just a right; it is also a Christian duty. 'Brotherly correction is as much part of natural law as brotherly love; and since all those peoples are not merely in a state of sin, but presently in a state beyond salvation, it is the business of Christians to correct and direct them. Indeed, they are clearly obliged to do so' (Vitoria, 1991, p 284). Though it is wrong to convert the barbarians forcibly – here, as almost everywhere, Vitoria follows Aquinas – it is right and just to force them to *listen*, whether they accept the truth or not. Accordingly, if the barbarians obstruct or prevent the Spaniards in any way from exercising their Christian duty to spread the truth, then the Spaniards may 'take up arms and declare war on them, insofar as this provides the safety and opportunity needed to preach the Gospel'. They may even 'lawfully conquer the territories of these people, deposing their old masters and setting up new ones and carrying out all the things which are lawfully permitted in other just wars by the law of war, so long as they always observe reasonable limits and do not go further than necessary' (Vitoria, 1991, pp 285–86). It was Vitoria's sad and sincere belief that Spaniards had not observed 'reasonable limits', and had, in fact, 'gone beyond the permissible bounds of justice and religion', but their excesses neither canceled their rights to use force when necessary, nor vitiated the legal and moral principles involved (Vitoria, 1991, p 286). Christians had the right and the duty to travel wherever they pleased, take the gold and other goods that they found to be unused and unclaimed, and preach their way of life, by force if necessary, in order to bring the barbarians of the New World out of their self-imposed immaturity and into civic adulthood as full members of the Christian community.

Vitoria is careful to specify that the barbarians of the Americas had nearly all of the same rights as the Spaniards, for instance, the right to travel to Spain and receive the full protection of Spanish law. But, for all of Vitoria's concern with reciprocity – granting the Indians the same rights of travel and trade – he cannot grant them equal rights when it comes to religion. Here, as Schmitt is quick to point out, one finds Vitoria's, and Christendom's, central and inescapable asymmetry. The ultimate justification for the Spanish conquests lies in Christ's command to the apostles, to 'teach all nations, baptizing them in the name of the Father, and of the Son, and of the Holy Ghost: Teaching them to observe all things whatsoever I have commanded you … even unto the end of the world' (Matthew 28, 19–20). In more secular terms, the Church's evangelical mission becomes Spain's 'civilizing' mission, a mission for which, perhaps because of his lingering Catholicism and his adamant Euro-centrism, Schmitt cannot help but have some sympathy. It is worth listening to what Schmitt has to say here at some length:

> It is necessary to reiterate that Vitoria did not present the Spanish conquest of the Americas as 'unjust'. There is no need to discuss in detail all the 'legitimate legal titles' he explicates, but only to restate that his conclusions ultimately justified the *conquista*.

His lack of presuppositions, his objectivity and neutrality, have their limits, and do not go so far as to disregard the distinction between Christians and non-believers. On the contrary, the practical conclusion is completely consistent with Vitoria's Christian convictions, which found their true justification in Christian missions. It never occurred to the Spanish monk that non-believers should have the same rights of propaganda and intervention for their idolatry and religious fallacies as Spanish Christians had for their Christian missions. This is the limit of the absolute neutrality of Vitoria's arguments, as well as of the general reciprocity and reversibility of his concepts.

Vitoria may have been an Erasmian, but he was no advocate of the absolute humanity fashionable in the 18th and 19th centuries; he was no follower of Voltaire or Rousseau, no freethinker or socialist. For Vitoria, the *liberum commercium* was not the liberal principle of free trade and of free economy in the sense of the 'open door' of the 20th century; it was only an expedient of the pre-technical age. The freedom of missions, however, was truly a freedom – a *libertas* of the Christian Church. In the thinking and terminology of the Middle Ages, *libertas* was synonymous with law. Thus, for Vitoria, Christian Europe was still the center of the earth, both historically and concretely oriented to Jerusalem and to Rome.

(Schmitt, 2003, pp 113–14)

Yes, this passage attests to the anti-liberal prejudices of an unregenerate Euro-centric conservative with a pronounced affect for the counter-revolutionary and Catholic South of Europe. It seems to resonate with the apologetic mid-20th-century Spanish reception of Vitoria that wishes to justify the Spanish civilizing mission in the Americas.[6] But the contrast between Christianity and humanism is not just prejudice; it is also instructive, because with it, Schmitt tries to grasp something both disturbing and elusive about the modern world – namely, the apparent fact that the liberal and humanitarian attempt to construct a world of universal friendship produces, as if by internal necessity, ever new enemies.

For Schmitt, the Christianity of Vitoria, of Salamanca, Spain, 1539, represents a concrete, spatially imaginable order, centered (still) in Rome and, ultimately, Jerusalem. This, with its divine revelations, its Greek philosophy, and its Roman language and institutions, is the *polis*. This is civilization, and outside its walls lie the barbarians. The humanism that Schmitt opposes is, in his words, a philosophy of absolute humanity. By virtue of its universality and abstract normativity, it has no localizable *polis*, no clear distinction between what is inside and what is outside. Does humanity embrace all humans? Are there no gates to the city and thus no barbarians outside? If not, against whom or what does it wage its wars? We can understand Schmitt's concerns in the following way. Christianity distinguishes between believers and non-believers. Since non-believers can become believers, they must be of the same category of being. To be human, then, is the horizon within which the distinction between believers and non-believers is made. That is, humanity *per se* is not part of the distinction, but is that which makes the distinction possible. However, once the term used to describe the horizon of a distinction also becomes that distinction's positive pole, it needs its negative opposite. If humanity is both the horizon and the positive pole of the distinction that that horizon enables, then the negative pole can only be something that lies *beyond* that horizon, can only be something completely antithetical to horizon and positive pole alike – can only, in other words, be *in*human. As Schmitt says:

> Only when man appeared to be the embodiment of absolute humanity did the other side of this concept appear in the form of a new enemy: the *inhuman*. The expulsion of the inhuman from the human was followed in the 19th century by an even deeper division, between the *superhuman* and the *subhuman*. Just as the human presupposes the inhuman, so, with dialectical necessity, the superhuman entered history with its hostile twin: the subhuman. (Schmitt, 2003, p 104)[7]

This 'two-sided' aspect of the 'idea of humanity' (Schmitt, 2003, p 103) is a theme Schmitt had already developed in his *The Concept of the Political* (1976) and his critiques of liberal pluralism (eg Schmitt, 1988b, pp 151–65). His complaint there is that liberal pluralism is in fact not in the least pluralist, but reveals itself to be an overriding monism, the monism of humanity. Thus, despite the claims that pluralism allows for the individual's freedom from illegitimate constraint, Schmitt presses the point home that political opposition *to* liberalism is itself deemed illegitimate. Indeed, liberal pluralism, in Schmitt's eyes, reduces the political to the social and economic and thereby nullifies all truly political opposition by simply excommunicating its opponents from the High Church of Humanity. After all, only an unregenerate barbarian could fail to recognize the irrefutable benefits of the liberal order.

Though he favorably opposes 16th-century Christianity to 18th-century Enlightenment, Schmitt has no interest in re-establishing the hegemony of the Roman Church. Rather, he is in search of conceptual weapons with which to fight the contemporary enemy. But it is a failed search just as it is a failed contrast; for in Christianity, Schmitt finds not the other of humanism, but humanism's roots. In truth, what Schmitt calls humanism is but an intensification of the aspirations of the Roman Church. Unlike the Judaism from which it sprang, Christianity is not a tribal or national religion, but a religion of universal pretensions.[8] The distinction between believer and non-believer is not a distinction between tribe and tribe or nation and nation; it is not a distinction between neighbor and foreigner or even one between finite and localizable friends and enemies. Rather, ideally, in the Christian world, the negative pole of the distinction is to be fully and finally consumed without remainder. The differences between families, tribes, nations, friends and enemies are meant to disappear. In the final analysis there is no room for opposition, neither within the City of God nor against it, and the *polis* – call it Rome, call it Jerusalem – will encompass the entire world. *That* is precisely the purpose of its civilizing power. What Schmitt calls humanism is but a more complete universalization of the same dynamic.[9] Christianity and humanism are both civilizing missions. In neither case can there be barbarians left outside the gates, because eventually there will *be* no outside of the gates, and thus, no more gates. To live in the city, the barbarians must thoroughly give up their barbarian ways – their customs, their religion, their language. In the discourse that equates the *polis* with humanity, to remain a barbarian is not to remain outside the city, but to be included *in* the city as a moral and legal outlaw and thus to come under the city's moral and legal jurisdiction.

That liberal America's civilizing mission is an extension of Christian Europe's was clearly seen and approved of by James Brown Scott, who, during his life (1866–1943), had been Professor of international law and foreign relations at Georgetown, both Director and Secretary of the Carnegie Endowment for International Peace, President of three American and European societies of international law, editor and interpreter of Vitoria, Suarez and Grotius, active propagandist for the Allied cause during and after World War I, and loyal servant to President Woodrow Wilson. Scott recognized the link between the conquest of the New World and the splintering of the old. The 'discovery of America', he wrote in a volume devoted to Vitoria and Suarez, 'gave birth to a modern law of nations, Spanish in origin, lay in form, but Catholic in fact and capable of continued development under the control of that Christian morality of which all peoples, and therefore all nations, are beneficiaries' (Scott, 1934a, p 2). This birth of a new law out of the spirit of Christianity coincides with that religion's fragmentation, 'broken by the Reformation', as Scott puts it, and 'replaced by an international community, today [1934] universal and embracing all peoples of all continents; the law applicable to members of the Christian community was found to be applicable to non-Christians; and the law of nations, once confined to Christendom, has become international. Without ceasing to be Christian in fact, the law of nations became laicized in form' (Scott, 1934a, pp 1–2). In this way, Christianity survives its own secularization and the Greco-Christian West rises from its ashes, re-christened simply as the entire world. The 'international community', Scott writes, 'is coextensive with humanity – no longer merely with Christianity'; it has become 'the representative of the common humanity rather than of the common religion binding the States'. Therefore, the international community 'possesses the inherent right to impose its will ... and to punish its violation, not because of a treaty, or a pact or a covenant, but because of an international need' (Scott, 1934b, p 283). If in the 16th century it was the Christian Church that determined the content of this international need, in the 20th century and beyond it must be the secularized 'church' of 'common humanity' that performs this all-important service. 'Vitoria's idea', Scott reminds us, 'was to treat the Indians as brothers and as equals, to help them in their worldly affairs, to instruct them in spiritual matters and lead them to the altar by the persuasion of Christian life on the part of the missionary' (Scott, 1934a, p 2). Thus, with the secularization of the Christian mission comes also the secularization of the Christian missionary, who still shows his brotherly love by exerting brotherly correction.

Human rights and the inhuman other

In the past, we/they, neighbor/foreigner, friend/enemy polarities were inside/ outside distinctions that produced a plurality of worlds, separated by physical and cultural borders. When these worlds collided it was not always a pretty picture, but it was often possible to maintain the integrity of the we/they distinction, even to regulate it by distinguishing between domestic and foreign affairs. If 'they' differed, 'we' did not always feel ourselves obliged to make 'them' into miniature versions of 'us', to Christianize them, to civilize them, to make of them good liberals. Things have changed. With a single-power global hegemony that is guided by a universalist ideology, *all* relations have become, or threaten to become, domestic. The inner/outer distinction has been transformed into a morally and legally determined acceptable/unacceptable one, and the power exists (or is thought to exist), both spiritually and physically, to eliminate the unacceptable once and for all and make believers of everyone. The new imperative states: The other *will* be included. Delivered as a promise, it can only be received, by some, as an ominous threat.

In his *The Conquest of America*, Tzvetan Todorov approaches our relationship to the 'other' by way of three interlocking distinctions, namely, self/other, same/different, and equal/unequal. A simple superposition of all three distinctions makes of the other someone who is different and therefore unequal. The problem we have been discussing, however, comes to light when we make of the other someone who is equal because he is essentially the same. This form of the universalist ideology is assimilationist. It denies the other by embracing him. Of the famous 16th-century defender of the Indians, Bartolomé de Las Casas, Todorov writes:

> [his] declaration of the equality of men is made in the name of a specific religion, Christianity ... Hence, there is a potential danger of seeing not only the Indians' human nature asserted but also their Christian 'nature'. 'The natural laws and rules and rights of men', Las Casas said; but who decides what is natural with regard to laws and rights? Is it not specifically the Christian religion? Since Christianity is universalist, it implies as essential non-difference on the part of all men. We see the danger of the identification in this text of Saint John Chrysostrom, quoted and defended at Valladolid:[10] 'Just as there is no natural difference in the creation of man, so there is no difference in the call to salvation of all men, barbarous or wise, since God's grace can correct the minds of barbarians, so that they have a reasonable understanding'. (Todorov, 1984, p 162)[11]

Once again we see that the term 'human' is not descriptive, but evaluative. To be truly human, one needs to be corrected. Regarding the relationship of difference and equality, Todorov concludes: 'If it is incontestable that the prejudice of superiority is an obstacle in the road to knowledge, we must also admit that the prejudice of equality is a still greater one, for it consists in identifying the other purely and simply with one's own "ego ideal" (or with oneself)' (Todorov, 1984, p 165). Such identification is not only the essence of Christianity, but also of the doctrine of human rights preached by enthusiasts like Habermas and Rawls. And such identification means that the other is stripped of his otherness and made to conform to the universal ideal of what it means to be human.

And yet, despite – indeed, because of – the all-encompassing embrace, the detested other is never allowed to leave the stage altogether. Even as we seem on the verge of actualizing Kant's dream, as Habermas puts it, of 'a cosmopolitan order' that unites all peoples and abolishes war under the auspices of 'the states of the *First World*' who 'can afford to harmonize their national interests to a certain extent with the norms that define the halfhearted cosmopolitan aspirations of the UN' (Habermas, 1998, pp 165, 184), it is still fascinating to see how the barbarians make their functionally necessary presence felt. John Rawls, in his *The Law of Peoples*, conveniently divides the world into well-ordered peoples and those who are not well-ordered. Among the former are the 'reasonable liberal peoples' and the 'decent hierarchical peoples' (Rawls, 2001, p 4). Opposed to them are the 'outlaw states' and other 'burdened' peoples who are not worthy of respect. Liberal peoples, who, by virtue of their history, possess superior institutions, culture and moral character (Rawls, 2001, pp 23–25), have not only the right to deny non-well-ordered peoples respect, but the duty to extend what Vitoria called 'brotherly correction' and Habermas 'gentle compulsion' (Habermas, 1997, p 133).[12] That is, Rawls believes that the 'refusal to tolerate' those states deemed to be outlaw states 'is a consequence of liberalism and decency'. Why? Because outlaw states violate human rights. What are human rights? 'What I call human rights', Rawls states, 'are ... a proper subset of the rights possessed by citizens in a liberal constitutional democratic regime, or of the rights of the members of a decent hierarchical society' (Rawls, 2001, p 81). Because of their violation of these liberal rights, non-liberal, non-decent societies do not even have the right 'to protest their condemnation by the world society' (Rawls, 2001, p 38), and decent peoples have the right, if necessary, to wage just wars against them. Thus, liberal societies are not merely contingently established and historically conditioned forms of organization; they become the universal standard against which other societies are judged. Those found wanting are banished, as outlaws, from the civilized world. Ironically, one of the signs of their outlaw status is their insistence on autonomy, on sovereignty. As Rawls states, 'Human rights are a class of rights that play a special role in a reasonable Law of Peoples: they restrict the justifying reasons for war and its conduct, and they specify limits to a regime's internal autonomy. In this way they reflect the two basic and historically profound changes in how the powers of sovereignty have been conceived since World War II' (Rawls, 2001, p 79). Yet, what Rawls sees as a postwar development in the notion of sovereignty – that is, its restriction – could not, in fact, have occurred had it not been for the *unrestricted* sovereign powers of the victors of that war, especially, of course, the supreme power of the United States. The limitation of (others') sovereignty is an imposed limitation, imposed by a sovereign state that has never relinquished its own sovereign power. What for Vitoria was the sovereignty of Christendom and for Scott the sovereignty of humanity becomes for Rawls the simple but uncontested sovereignty of liberalism itself.[13]

So goes the contemporary refinement of the achievement that so impressed Schmitt in 1932. 'Time and again', wrote Schmitt back then, sensing what was to come,

> the great superiority, the amazing political achievement of the US reveals itself in the fact that it uses general, flexible concepts ... With regard to these decisive political concepts, it depends on who interprets, defines, and uses them; who concretely decides what peace is, what disarmament, what intervention, what public order and security are. One of the most important manifestations of humanity's legal and spiritual life is

the fact that whoever has true power is able to determine the content of concepts and words. *Caesar dominus et supra grammaticam*. Caesar is also lord over grammar. (Schmitt, 1988b, p 202)

For Schmitt, to assume that one can derive morally correct political institutions from abstract, universal norms is to put the cart before the horse. The truly important question remains: Who decides?[14] What political power representing which political order defines terms like human rights and public reason, defines, in fact, what it means to be properly human? What political power distinguishes between the decent and the indecent, between those who police the world and those who are outlawed from it? Indeed, what political power decides what is and what is not political? Habermas's contention that normative legality neutralizes the moral and the political and that therefore Schmitt 'suppresses' the 'decisive point', namely, 'the legal preconditions of an impartial judicial authority and a neutral system of criminal punishment' (Habermas, 1998, p 200), is enough to make even an incurable skeptic a bit nostalgic for the old Frankfurt School distinction between affirmative and critical theory. One could observe, for instance, that the 'universality' of human rights has a very particular base. As Habermas says:

> Asiatic societies cannot participate in capitalistic modernization without taking advantage of the achievements of an individualistic legal order. One cannot desire the one and reject the other. From the perspective of Asian countries, the question is not whether human rights, as part of an individualistic legal order, are compatible with the transmission of one's own culture. Rather, the question is whether the traditional forms of political and societal integration can be reasserted against – or must instead be adapted to – the hard-to-resist imperatives of an economic modernization that has won approval on the whole. (Habermas, 2001, p 124)

Thus, despite his emphasis on procedure and the universality of his so-called 'discourse principle', the choice that confronts 'Asiatic societies' or any other people is a choice between cultural identity and economic survival, between, in other words, cultural and physical extermination. As Schmitt said, the old Christian and civilizing distinction between believers and non-believers (*Gläubigern* and *Nicht-Gläubigern*) has become the modern, economic distinction between creditors and debtors (*Gläubigern* and *Schuldnern*).

But, while affirmative theorists like Habermas and Rawls are busy constructing the ideological scaffolding that supports the structure of the status quo, what role is there for the 'critical' theorist to play? Despite the sanguine hopes of Hardt and Negri (2000), that 'Empire' will all but spontaneously combust as a result of the irrepressible Ur-desire of the multitude, can we seriously place our faith in some utopian grand alternative anymore, or in some revolutionary or therapeutic result based on the truth of critique that would allow us all, in the end, to sing in the sunshine and laugh everyday?[15] Do not, in fact, such utopian fantasies lead to the moralizing hubris of a Rawls or a Habermas? In short: It is one thing to recognize the concealed, particular interests that govern the discourse and politics of human rights and quite another to think seriously about how things could be different, to imagine an international system that respected both the equality *and* the difference of states and/or peoples. Is it possible – and this is Todorov's question – to value Vitoria's principle of the 'free circulation of men, ideas, and goods', and still also 'cherish another principle, that of self-determination and noninterference' (Todorov, 1984, p 177)? The entire 'Vitorian' tradition, from Scott to Habermas and Rawls, thinks not. Habermas, for instance, emphatically endorses the fact that 'the erosion of the principle of nonintervention in recent decades has been due primarily to the politics of human rights' (Habermas, 1998, p 147), a 'normative' achievement that is not so incidentally correlated with a positive, economic fact: 'In view of the subversive forces and imperatives of the world market and of the increasing density of worldwide networks of communication and commerce, the external sovereignty of states, however it may be grounded, is by now in any case an anachronism' (Habermas, 1998, p 150). And opposition to this development is not merely anachronistic, it is illegitimate, not to be tolerated. So, for those who sincerely believe in American institutional, cultural and moral superiority, the times could not be rosier. After all, when push comes to shove, 'we' decide – not only about which societies are decent and which ones are not, but also about which acts of violence are 'terrorist', and which comprise the 'gentle compulsion' of a 'just war'.

What, however, are those 'barbarians' who disagree with the new world order supposed to do? With Agamben, they could wait for a 'completely new politics' to come; but the contours of such a politics are unknown and will remain unknown until the time of its arrival. And that time, much like the second coming of Christ, seems infinitely deferrable. While they wait for the Benjaminian 'divine violence' to sweep away the residual effects of the demonic rule of law (Benjamin, 1996, pp 248–52), the barbarians might be tempted to entertain Schmitt's rather forlorn fantasy of an egalitarian balance of power. Yet, if the old, inner-European balance of power rested upon an asymmetrical exclusion of the non-European world, it must be asked: What new exclusion will be necessary for a new balance, and is that new exclusion tolerable? At the moment, there is no answer to this question, only a precondition to an answer. If one wishes to entertain Todorov's challenge of thinking both equality and difference, universal commerce of people and ideas as well as self-determination and nonintervention, then the concept of humanity must once again become the invisible and unsurpassable horizon of discourse, not its positive pole. The word 'human', to evoke one final distinction, must once again become descriptive of a 'fact' and not a 'value'. Otherwise, whatever else it may be, the search for 'human' rights will always also be the negative image of the relentless search for the 'inhuman' other.

Notes

1   Translation modified. See Chapter 1, note 20.
2   For a more comprehensive critique of Agamben, see Chapter 5. On Schmitt and the new world order, see Kervégan, 1999.
3   See the discussion in Pagden, 1986, pp 15–26.

4   See for instance Scott, 1934b, p 9a. Pagden, however, finds such assertions 'anachronistic'. See Pagden in Vitoria, 1991, p xvi.

5   On this, see Todorov, 1984, pp 149–50.

6   See Pagden's comments in Pagden, 1986, pp 7–8.

7   For a further elaboration of this idea, see Koselleck 1985; see also Chapter 1 of this volume.

8   See the interesting observations in Todorov, 1984, pp 105–07, 162–65.

9   For the outline of a genealogy that starts with St Paul and moves through Spinoza, Lessing and the early Hegel, see Chapter 7.

10 Site of a debate in 1550 between Sepúlveda and Las Casas. See Todorov, 1984, pp 151–67.

11 The Las Casas quote is taken from Las Casas, 1975, p 42.

12 The German phrase reads 'sanfte Nötigung' (Habermas, 1996b, p 217) and has elsewhere (Habermas, 1998, p 186) been diplomatically softened in the translation to 'gentle pressure'. See Chapter 2, note 3.

13 Though the term 'liberalism' is contested and variously used, in contemporary debates the dominant trend is to justify its legitimacy and extension in terms of universally valid moral and/or legal principles. On the history and nature of liberalism and on his impatience with human rights discourse, see Geuss, 2001, pp 69–109, 138–46. Of interest to us here is the following: 'For a number of reasons and in a number of ways liberalism is conceptually and theoretically much more elusive than the state. … Liberalism is more like Christianity than like the state, that is, it is a complex of doctrines, ideals, suggestions for implementing those ideals, beliefs, and informal patterns of habitual action and thought. Liberalism, though, is both much more doctrinally amorphous and indeterminate than Christianity was, and has a much more indirect relation to any social reality. Christianity had its church buildings, rituals, *symbola*, public professions of faith, seminaries, catechisms, and, at least at some points in its history, inquisitorial tribunals, prisons, etc. The prisons of liberalism are prisons of the mind, and they operate by trapping the unwary in a shifting, labyrinthine hall of mirrors rather than by immobilization behind palpable brick and steel' (Geuss, 2001, p 69). On liberalism's blind spot regarding its relationship to its 'fundamentalist' or 'terrorist' other, see also Bolz, 2002. And for a salient and detailed critique of Rawls, see Mouffe, 2000, pp 17–35.

14 This, it would seem, is also the question implied in the following passage by Geuss: 'A "human right" is an inherently vacuous conception, and to speak of "human rights" is a kind of puffery or white magic. … "Group X has a natural right to Y" in contemporary political discourse, then, usually means that they do not have a (legal) right to Y but we think they ought to. To be sure, such things as the Universal Declaration of Human Rights are intended to establish a mechanism which *would* in fact bring it about that there were reliable consequences of suppressing free speech, preventing self-determination, incarcerating without cause, and so forth. However, it is important to realize that *even if* (and it is a cyclopean "if") it *were* to be or come to be the case that such Declarations had more than rhetorical effect, they would constitute not so much a vindication of the doctrine of human rights as a transformation of individual components of someone's moral beliefs into a system of *positive* rights. We would merely have begun to invent and impose on the nations of the world a new layer of positive (international) law' (Geuss, 2001, p 144).

15 On Hardt and Negri see Chapter 6.

Bibliography

Agamben, G, *The Coming Community*, Hardt, M (trans), 1993, Minneapolis: Minnesota UP

Agamben, G, *Homo Sacer: Sovereign Power and Bare Life*, Heller-Roazen, D (trans), 1998, Stanford: Stanford UP

Anderson, MH, *War and Society in Europe of the Old Regime, 1618–1789*, 1998, Montreal and Kingston: McGill/Queens UP

Arendt, Hannah, *Lectures on Kant's Political Philosophy*, Beiner, R (ed), 1982, Chicago: Chicago UP

Arendt, Hannah, *On Revolution*, 1990, New York: Penguin

Baecker, D, Krieg, P and Simon, FB (eds), *Terror im System: Der 11. September und die Folgen*, 2002, Heidelberg: Carl-Auer-Systeme Verlag

Balke, F, *Der Staat nach seinem Ende: Die Versuchung Carl Schmitts*, 1996, Munich: Fink

Beardsworth, R, *Derrida and the Political*, 1996, London: Routledge

Benda, J, *La trahison des clercs*, 1927, Paris: B Grasset

Bendersky, JW, *Carl Schmitt: Theorist for the Reich*, 1983, Princeton: Princeton UP

Bendersky, JW, 'Carl Schmitt and the Conservative Revolution' (1987) 72 *Telos*, pp 27–42

Benjamin, W, *Selected Writings*, Vol 1, Bullock, M and Jennings, MW (eds), 1996, Cambridge, MA: Harvard UP

Bohman, J and Lutz-Bachmann, M (eds), *Perpetual Peace: Essays on Kant's Cosmopolitan Ideal*, 1997, Cambridge, MA: MIT Press

Bolz, N, 'Die Furie des Zerstörens: Wie Terroristen die Kritik der liberalen Vernunft schreiben', in Baeker, Krieg and Simon, 2002, pp 84–99

Brecht, B, *The Measures Taken and Other Lehrstücke*, Willett, J and Manheim, R (eds), 2001, New York: Arcade

Brzezinski, Z, *The Grand Chessboard: American Primacy and its Geostrategic Imperatives*, 1997, New York: Basic

Burnham, J, *The Managerial Revolution*, 1960, Bloomington: Indiana UP

Colas, D, *Civil Society and Fanaticism: Conjoined Histories*, Jacobs, A (trans), 1997, Stanford: Stanford UP

Colliot-Thélène, C, 'Carl Schmitt versus Max Weber: Juridical Rationality and Economic Rationality', in Mouffe, 1999, pp 138–54

Davidson, E, *The Trial of the Germans: An Account of the Twenty-two Defendants before the International Military Tribunal at Nuremberg*, 1997, Columbia: Missouri UP

Davidson, E, *The Nuremberg Fallacy*, 1998, Columbia: Missouri UP

Deleuze, G and Guattari, F, *What Is Philosophy?*, Tomlinson, H and Burchell, G (trans), 1994, New York: Columbia UP

Derrida, J, *Writing and Difference*, Bass, A (trans), 1978, Chicago: Chicago UP

Derrida, J, 'Force of Law: The "Mystical Foundations of Authority"', in Cornell, D *et al* (eds), *Deconstruction and the Possibility of Justice*, 1992, New York: Routledge, pp 3–67

Derrida, J, *The Politics of Friendship*, Collins, G (trans), 1997, London: Verso

Fichte, JG, *Addresses to the German Nation*, Kelly, GA (ed), Jones, RF and Turnbull, GH (trans), 1968, New York: Harper & Row

Fuller, Maj Gen JFC, *The Conduct of War, 1789–1961: A Study of the Impact of the French, Industrial, and Russian Revolutions on War and Its Conduct*, 1968, London: Minerva

Gauchet, M, *The Disenchantment of the World: A Political History of Religion*, Burge, O (trans), 1997, Princeton: Princeton UP

Geuss, R, *Morality, Culture, and History: Essays on German Philosophy*, 1999, Cambridge: CUP

Geuss, R, *History and Illusion in Politics*, 2001, Cambridge: CUP

Goux, JJ and Wood, PR (eds), *Terror and Consensus: Vicissitudes of French Thought*, 1998, Stanford: Stanford UP

Habermas, J, 'Modernity vs Postmodernity' (1981) 22 *New German Critique*, pp 3–14

Habermas, J, *The New Conservatism: Cultural Criticism and the Historians' Debate*, Nicholsen, SW (ed and trans), 1989, Cambridge, MA: MIT Press

Habermas, J, *Between Facts and Norms: Contributions to a Discourse Theory of Law and Democracy*, Rehg, W (trans), 1996a, Cambridge, MA: MIT Press

Habermas, J, *Die Einbeziehung des Anderen: Studien zur politischen Theorie*, 1996b, Frankfurt: Suhrkamp

Habermas, J, *A Berlin Republic: Writings in Germany*, Rendall, S (trans), 1997a, Lincoln: Nebraska UP

Habermas, J, 'Kant's Idea of Perpetual Peace, with the Benefit of Two Hundred Years' Hindsight', 1997b, in Bohman and Lutz-Bachmann, 1997, pp 113–53

Habermas, J, *The Inclusion of the Other: Studies in Political Theory*, Cronin, C and Greiff, PD (eds), 1998, Cambridge, MA: MIT Press

Habermas, J, *The Postnational Constellation: Political Essays*, Pensky, M (ed and trans), 2001, Cambridge, MA: MIT Press

Hardt, M, *Gilles Deleuze: An Apprenticeship in Philosophy*, 1993, Minneapolis: Minnesota UP

Hardt, M and Negri, A, *Empire*, 2000, Cambridge, MA: Harvard UP

Hegel, GWF, *Early Theological Writings*, Knox, TM (trans), 1971, Philadelphia: Pennsylvania UP

Heine, H, *Deutschland. Ein Wintermärchen*, in Briegleb, K (ed), *Sämtliche Schriften*, Vol 4, 1997, Munich: DTV, pp 571–644

Hirst, P, 'Carl Schmitt's Decisionism' (1987) 72 *Telos*, pp 15–26

Holub, Renate, 'Between Europe and the USA: The Rise and Decline of the Journal Telos', *Bad Subjects* 31 (March 1997), http://english-www.hss.cmu.edu/bs/31/holub.html

Horkheimer, M, 'Materialism and Morality', in *Between Philosophy and Social Science: Selected Early Writings*, Hunter GF *et al* (trans), 1993, Cambridge, MA: MIT Press, pp 15–47

Husserl, E, *The Crisis of European Sciences and Transcendental Phenomenology*, Carr, D (trans), 1970, Evanston: Northwestern UP

Kant, I, *Kant's Political Writings*, Reiss, H (ed), Nisbet, HB (trans), 1970, Cambridge: CUP

Kant, I, *Kritik der Urteilskraft, Werkausgabe*, Weischedel, W (ed), Vol 10, 1974, Frankfurt: Suhrkamp

Kant, I, *Critique of Judgment*, Pluhar, WS (trans), 1987, Indianapolis: Hackett

Keane, J, 'The Modern Democratic Revolution: Reflections on Lyotard's *The Postmodern Condition*', in Benjamin, A (ed), *Judging Lyotard*, 1992, London: Routledge, pp 81–98

Kervégen, J-F, 'Carl Schmitt and "World Unity"', in Mouffe, 1999, pp 54–74

Kline, M, *Mathematics: The Loss of Certainty*, 1980, Oxford: OUP

Koselleck, R, 'The Historical-Political Semantics of Asymmetric Counterconcepts', in his *Futures Past: On the Semantics of Historical Time*, Tribe, K (trans), 1985, Cambridge, MA: MIT Press, pp 159–97

Krabiel, K-D, *Brechts Lehrstücke: Entstehung und Entwicklung eines Spieltyps*, 1993, Stuttgart: Metzler

Larmore, C, *The Morals of Modernity*, 1996, New York: CUP

Las Casas, B de, *Apologia*, 1975, Madrid: Nacional

Lask, E, 'Rechtsphilosophie', in Windelband, W (ed), *Die Philosophie im Beginn des 20. Jahrhunderts: Festschrift für Kuno Fischer*, 1905, Heidelberg: Winter, pp 269–320 [Reprinted in Ollig, H-L (ed), *Neukantianismus: Texte der Marburger und der Südwestdeutschen Schule, ihrer Vorläufer und Kritiker*, 1982, Stuttgart: Reclam, pp 182–226]

Leibniz, GW, 'On the Ultimate Origination of Things', in his *Philosophical Essays*, Ariew, R and Garber, D (ed and trans), 1989, Indianapolis: Hackett

Lessing, GE, *Lessing's Theological Writings*, Chadwick, H (trans), 1957, Stanford: Stanford UP

Lewis, W, *Rude Assignment: An Intellectual Autobiography*, 1984, Santa Barbara, CA: Black Sparrow

Liddell Hart, BH, *The Revolution in Warfare*, 1946, London: Faber and Faber

Linebaugh, P and Rediker, M, *The Many-Headed Hydra: Sailors, Slaves, Commoners, and the Hidden History of the Revolutionary Atlantic*, 2000, Boston, MA: Beacon

Löwith, K, 'The Occasional Decisionism of Carl Schmitt', in his *Martin Heidegger and European Nihilism*, Wolin, R (ed), Steiner, G (trans), 1995, New York: Columbia UP, pp 137–69

Luhmann, N, 'Organisation und Entscheidung', in his *Soziologische Aufklärung 3*, 1981, Opladen: Westdeutscher Verlag, pp 335–89

Luhmann, N, 'Staat und Staatsräson im Übergang von traditionaler Heerschaft zu moderner Politik', in his *Gesellschaftsstruktur und Semantik: Studien zur Wissenssoziologie der modernen Gesellschaft*, Vol 3, 1989, Frankfurt: Suhrkamp, pp 65–148

Luhmann, N, *Political Theory in the Welfare State*, Bednarz Jr, J (trans), 1990a, Berlin: Walter de Gruyter

Luhmann, N, 'The "State" of the Political System', in his *Essays in Self-Reference*, 1990b, New York: Columbia UP, pp 165–74

Luhmann, N, *Gibt es in unserer Gesellschaft noch unverzichtbare Normen?*, Heidelberger Universitätsreden 4, 1993, Heidelberg: CF Müller Juristischer Verlag

Luhmann, N, *Social Systems*, Bednarz Jr, J with Baecker, D (trans), 1995, Stanford: Stanford UP

Luhmann, N, *Die Gesellschaft der Gesellschaft*, 1997, Frankfurt: Suhrkamp

Luhmann, N, *Die Religion der Gesellschaft*, Kieserling, A (ed), 2000, Frankfurt: Suhrkamp

Lukács, G, 'Tactics and Ethics', in his *Tactics and Ethics: Political Essays, 1919–1929*, Livingstone, R (ed), McColgan, M (trans), 1972, New York: Harper & Row, pp 3–11

Lukács, G, 'Bolsehvism as a Moral Problem', Tar, JM (trans) (1977) 44.3 *Social Research*, pp 416–24

Lyotard, J-F, *The Differend: Phrases in Dispute*, Van Den Abeele, G (trans), 1988, Minneapolis: Minnesota UP

Lyotard, J-F, *The Postmodern Explained: Correspondence 1982–1985*, Pefanis, J (ed and trans), 1993, Minneapolis: Minnesota UP

Lyotard, J-F and Thébaud, J-L, *Just Gaming*, Wlad Godzich, W (trans), 1985, Minneapolis: Minnesota UP

McCormick, JP, 'Transcending Weber's Categories of Modernity? The Early Lukács and Schmitt on the Rationalization Thesis' (1988) 75 *New German Critique*, pp 133–77

Marquard, O, *Aesthetica und Anaesthetica: Philosophische Überlegungen*, 1989, Paderborn: Schöningh

Maschke, G, *Der Tod des Carl Schmitts*, 1987, Vienna: Karolinger

Meier, H, *Carl Schmitt and Leo Strauss: The Hidden Dialogue*, Lomax, JH (trans), 1995, Chicago: Chicago UP

Milbank, J, *Theology and Social Theory: Beyond Secular Reason*, 1990, Oxford: Blackwell

Mouffe, C, *The Return of the Political*, 1993, London: Verso

Mouffe, C (ed), *The Challenge of Carl Schmitt*, 1999, London: Verso

Mouffe, C, *The Democratic Paradox*, 2000, London: Verso

Müller, J, 'Preparing for the Political: German Intellectuals Confront the "Berlin Republic"' (1997) 72 *New German Critique*, pp 151–760

Nickerson, H, *Can We Limit War?*, 1934, New York: Stokes

Noack, P, *Carl Schmitt: Eine Biographie*, 1996, Frankfurt: Ullstein

Nolte, E, *Der europäische Bürgerkrieg 1917–1945: Nationalsozialismus und Bolschewismus*, 1997, Munich: Herbig

Pagden, A, *The Fall of Natural Man: The American Indian and the Origins of Comparative Ethnology*, 1986, Cambridge: CUP

Pagels, E, *The Origin of Satan*, 1995, New York: Random House

Rancière, J, *Disagreement: Politics and Philosophy*, Rose, J (trans), 1999, Minneapolis: Minnesota UP

Rasch, W, 'Emergenz und Entscheidung, Oder: Carl Schmitt und das Rechtssystem', in Wägenbaur, T (ed), *Blinde Emergenz? Interdisziplinäre Beiträge zu Fragen kultureller Evolution*, 2000a, Heidelberg: Synchron

Rasch, W, *Niklas Luhmann's Modernity: The Paradoxes of Differentiation*, 2000b, Stanford: Stanford UP

Rasch, W, 'Introduction: The Self-Positing Society', in Luhmann, N, *Theories of Distinction: Redescribing the Descriptions of Modernity*, Rasch, W (ed), 2002, Stanford: Stanford UP, pp 1–30

Rawls, J, *The Law of Peoples: with, The Idea of Public Reason Revisited*, 2001, Cambridge, MA: Harvard UP

Rose, G, *Hegel Contra Sociology*, 1981, London: Athlone

Russell, B, 'Mathematical Logic as Based on the Theory of Types' (1908) 30 *American Journal of Mathematics*, pp 222–62

Sainsbury, RM, *Paradoxes*, 2nd edn, 1995, Cambridge: CUP

Scheuerman, WE, *Between the Norm and the Exception: The Frankfurt School and the Rule of Law*, 1994, Cambridge, MA: MIT Press

Schmitt, C, *Gesetz und Urteil: Eine Untersuchung zum Problem der Rechtspraxis*, 1912, Berlin: Verlag von Otto Liebmann

Schmitt, C, *Theorie des Partisanen: Zwischenbetrachtung zum Begriff des Politischen*, 1963, Berlin: Duncker & Humblot

Schmitt, C, *The Concept of the Political*, Schwab, G (trans), 1976, New Brunswick, NJ: Rutgers UP

Schmitt, C, *The Crisis of Parliamentary Democracy*, Kennedy, E (trans), 1985a, Cambridge, MA: MIT Press

Schmitt, C, *Political Theology: Four Chapters on the Concept of Sovereignty*, Schwab, G (trans), 1985b, Cambridge, MA: MIT Press

Schmitt, C, 'The Legal World Revolution' (1987) 72 *Telos*, pp 73–89

Schmitt, C, *Der Nomos der Erde im Völkerrecht des Jus Publicum Europaeum*, 1988a, Berlin: Duncker & Humblot

Schmitt, C, *Positionen und Begriffe im Kampf mit Weimar – Genf – Versailles, 1923–1939*, 1988b, Berlin: Duncker & Humblot

Schmitt, C, *Die Wendung zum diskriminierenden Kriegsbegriff*, 2nd edn, 1988c, Berlin: Duncker & Humblot

Schmitt, C, *Legalität und Legitimität*, 1993a, Berlin: Duncker & Humblot

Schmitt, C, *Land und Meer: Eine weltgeschichtliche Betrachtung*, 1993b, Stuttgart: Klett-Cotta

Schmitt, C, *Die Diktatur: Von den Anfängen des modernen Souveränitätsgedankens bis zum proletarischen Klassenkampf*, 6th edn, 1994a, Berlin: Duncker & Humblot

Schmitt, C, *Das internationalrechtliche Verbrechen des Angriffskrieges und der Grundsatz 'Nullum crimen, nulla poena sine lege'*, Quaritsch, H (ed), 1994b, Berlin: Duncker & Humblot

Schmitt, C, *Staat, Grossraum, Nomos: Arbeiten aus den Jahren 1916–1969*, Maschke, G (ed), 1995, Berlin: Duncker & Humblot

Schmitt, C, *Der Hüter der Verfassung*, 1996, Berlin: Duncker & Humblot

Schmitt, C, *The nomos of the Earth in the International Law of the Jus Publicum Europaeum*, Ulmen, GL (trans), 2003, New York: Telos

Schneewind, JB, *The Invention of Autonomy: A History of Modern Moral Philosophy*, 1998, Cambridge: CUP

Scott, JB, *The Spanish Conception of International Law and of Sanctions*, Carnegie Endowment for International Peace, Division of International Law, Pamphlet No 54, 1934a, Washington, DC: Carnegie Endowment for International Peace

Scott, JB, *The Spanish Origin of International Law: Francisco de Vitoria and His Law of Nations*, Publications of the Carnegie Endowment for International Peace, Division of International Law, 1934b, Oxford: OUP

Sorel, G, *Reflections on Violence*, Jennings, J (ed), Hulme, TE (trans), 1999, Cambridge: CUP

Spencer Brown, G, *Laws of Form*, 2nd edn, 1979, New York: EP Dutton

Spinoza, B de, *A Theologico-Political Treatise and Political Treatise*, Elwes, RHM (trans), 1955, New York: Dover

Steinweg, R, *Das Lehrstück: Brechts Theorie einer politisch-ästhetischen Erziehung*, 1972, Stuttgart: Metzler

Steinweg, R (ed), *Brechts Modell der Lehrstücke: Zeugnisse, Diskussion, Erfahrungen*, 1976, Frankfurt: Suhrkamp

Stevenson Jr, WR, *Christian Love and Just War: Moral Paradox and Pol'tical Life in St Augustine and His Modern Interpreters*, 1987, Macon, Georgia: Mercer UP

Strauss, L, 'Comments on Carl Schmitt's *Der Begriff des Politischen*', in Schmitt, 1976, pp 81–105

Taubes, J, *Die politische Theologie des Paulus*, Assmann, A and Assmann, J (eds), 2nd edn, 1995, Munich: Fink

Todorov, T, *The Conquest of America*, Howard, R (trans), 1984, New York: Harper

Tuck, R, *Natural Rights Theories: Their Origin and Development*, 1979, Cambridge: CUP

Ulmen, GL, *Politischer Mehrwert: Eine Studie über Max Weber und Carl Schmitt*, 1991, Weinheim: VCH Acta Humaniora

Vitoria, F de, *Political Writings*, Pagden, A and Lawrance, J (eds), 1991, Cambridge: CUP

Walzer, M, *Just and Unjust Wars: A Moral Argument with Historical Illustrations*, 2nd edn, 1992, New York: Basic

Weber, M, *From Max Weber: Essays in Sociology*, 1946, Oxford: OUP

Weber, M, *The Protestant Ethic and the Spirit of Capitalism*, Parsons, T (trans), 1958, New York: Scribner's Sons

Weber, M, *Economy and Society: An Outline of Interpretive Sociology*, Roth, R and Wittich, C (eds), 1978, Berkeley: California UP

Weber, M, *Die protestantische Ethik I: Eine Aufsatzsammlung*, Winckelmann, J (ed), 1991, Gütersloh: Gütersloher Verlagshaus Gerd Mohn

Wellmer, A, *The Persistence of Modernity: Essays on Aesthetics, Ethics, and Postmodernism*, 1991, Cambridge, MA: MIT Press

Whitehead, AN and Russell, B, *Principia Mathematica*, Vol 1, 1910, Cambridge: CUP

Wolin, R, *The Terms of Cultural Criticism: The Frankfurt School, Existentialism, Poststructuralism*, 1992, New York: Columbia UP

Wolin, R, *Labyrinths: Explorations in the Critical History of Ideas*, 1995, Amherst: Massachusetts UP

Index of names